From Monkey Sapiens to Homo Intentional

The phenomenology of the non-violent revolution

Published by
Adonis & Abbey Publishers Ltd
P.O. Box 43418
London
SE11 4XZ
http://www.adonis-abbey.com
Email: editor@adonis-abbey.com

First Edition, October 2006

Copyright 2006 © Sylvia Swinden

British Library Cataloguing-in-Publication Data
A catalogue record for this book is available from the British Library

ISBN 1-905068-40-9

The picture on the cover is courtesy of Rafael Edwards

Printed and bound in Great Britain

From Monkey Sapiens to Homo Intentional

The phenomenology of the non-violent revolution

Sylvia Swinden

Adonis & Abbey
Publishers Ltd

Table of Contents

PROLOGUE

Four blind men are asked to describe an elephant. One touches the side of the animal and says that an elephant is like a wall. Another touches the leg and says it is like a column. A third one touches the trunk and says an elephant is like a water hose, and the fourth one touches the tail and says it is like a piece of rope. And here ends the story designed as a teaching metaphor for Eastern Philosophy students about the subjective limitations of the mind and perceptions.

Life however does not end when the point is made, but continues beyond the punch line. So our four blind friends have a variety of options to choose from.

They may sit down to muse about what is this object that appears so dissimilar to each of them and the need for co-operation to approach a more accurate view of things as they are. In this case they may start to get an approximation of what an elephant looks like.

They may, however, engage into a heated discussion about who has the true vision (notwithstanding the fact that they are blind), they may even start a fight between them until the strongest manages to kill one or two of the other blind men, suppressing in this way some of their points of view. And if the third one submits the victor will proclaim that his is the only vision to be accepted and will run the view of the other man left alive underground; that man may leave a few secret notes for others to find at a later stage. With time some people may doubt the veracity of the official version that has come down to them and they may try to resurrect the suppressed visions. Legends may be heard about The Sighted, beings that can actually see the elephant, and as they spring forth they will confirm that elephants are walls, columns, hoses and ropes, depending on who is telling the story. Others may even suggest that there is no such a thing as an elephant and that they are all children's stories to scare people into behaving this or that way. The elephant in the meantime would go about its business of looking exactly like an elephant. In time others could dedicate their lives to study the shapes, the textures, the smells and the sounds, carefully and systematically, but the history of the violence and the power struggle unleashed by the different perspectives will forever cloud their judgement. Unless...

This book has no pretensions of teaching anybody what an elephant looks like. It is rather about the way it appears to the writer, to share and add to other visions so that the whole picture comes a little closer. It is based on the ideas and concepts of the Argentinean thinker Mario Rodriguez Cobos (penname Silo) whose phenomenological studies and commitment to finding and treating the roots of violence have inspired so many to seek the road of non-violence and co-operation, essential for seeing elephants properly and, hopefully, other more interesting things. A truly invaluable contribution of New Humanism, the current of thought that arises from this author's and other people's writings is the vision of not only conscious, aware and sentient human beings, but also of intentional ones, builders of their own future.

Chapter 1

THE GREAT METAPHYSICAL QUESTION RESOLVED?

Determinism vs. Free Will: the old metaphysical question. Far from being an academic irrelevance better left to the "specialists" to worry about, assumptions about how free we are to decide the direction of our existence rule the social world. At a time when the "developed" world (Europe, North America and other OECD countries) dominate not only the political and economic landscape but also dictate existential trends, Africa, Latin America and some Asian countries struggle to find their place in a world shaped by those who disregard their culture and their needs. A sense of inevitability poisons many incipient efforts to effect change. Understanding the process of increasingly free decision making power is essential to make the 21st century the time when the entire population of the planet, without any kind of discrimination, achieves truly human existence.

Traditionally Determinism has been described as the situation in which everything we do and everything that happens has already been decided, by God, by Nature (including human nature), by Fate or Destiny or simply by cause and effect in Newtonian physics. The concept of karma would also fit into it. New forms of determinism have been added to the classical ones by recent currents of thought and (pseudo?) scientific contributions: market forces in Capitalism, productive forces in Communism, the stars and planets in the revival of Astrology, the unconscious in psychoanalysis and social conditioning in the Behavioural Sciences. They can be grouped within the argument in favour of determinism in spite of not referring necessarily to an absolute form, but rather to a subjective perception of lack of freedom and of living in a world beyond our voluntary control.

Free will is seen as the power of human beings to extricate themselves from any previous conditioning and to know the absolute truth, the absolute good, and to be able to act with complete freedom in the world. It has fewer arguments in its favour, but not less powerful ones: if God had not provided the human being with at least some degree of Free Will, the whole issue of original sin and the offer of salvation would have been just a puppet show. And for those who deny the very existence of a God it is even simpler, it is just up to us.

As we can see, God lives up to His/Her ubiquitous quality by playing for both sides of the argument. Remorse is seen as another evidence of free will because if we could not choose we could not repent. In the same line of thinking, punishment follows the assumption that we possess free will to decide whether we are going to offend or not.

In physics, quantum mechanics came to destabilise Newton's carefully determined universe. Amongst other rarities of the quantum world Heinsenberg's Uncertainty Principle refers to a subatomic set of probabilities where knowing one characteristic of a particle precludes the observer from knowing another, something like not being able to tell if a snooker ball is coming or going once we have determined its colour. The observer is furthermore included as one of the factors that may affect the direction of a phenomenon. Chaos theory studies non-linear systems which are those where every step of the process may result in a number of different outcomes, like the weather, or the rabbit population in Surrey. Researchers have concluded that in some situations the outcome cannot be predicted, which calls into question the very concept of determinism. Not surprisingly, Illya Prigogin, the Chemistry Nobel laureate, called his book about the peculiarities of the quantum world and chaotic systems *The End of Certainty*. The most difficult argument against determinism to sustain theoretically, but also the most difficult to refute because of its empirical (and shared) quality, is the personal experience of responsibility and choice.

In spite of these recent contributions from science to the philosophical argument, the fact that an outcome may not be calculated or that it is probabilistic adds nothing to the determinism vs. freedom controversy. The problem resides, in my view, in the fact that the natural world and human consciousness are grouped together as if they were the same type of phenomenon. It could be argued that there exist not two but three elements in this controversy. The first one, determinism, exists at some levels. A stone falling will continue to fall until something interrupts its fall, in the same way that a person born today in London will have access to computers whereas somebody born two centuries ago did not. The second one, probability, is what we get from the statistical method to ascertain how likely we are to die of a heart attack considering the ways we eat, smoke and worry. Probability is also used to make calculations at the quantum level and for the study of Chaotic Systems (like the weather). The third one is Freedom, or Free Will.

What is will? It is the inclusion of an intentional act into the equation. The former two are mechanical. It does not matter whether we can predict the outcome or not, the outcome is the result of mechanical forces pushing from the past towards the future. Not being able to calculate the factors going in one or other direction for lack of powerful enough computers does not mean that the forces are not computable, only that they will take longer and more advanced technology to sort out, or that they will behave in a random, unpredictable manner, but a manner still dependent on previous conditions. Intentional forces, instead, belong exclusively to the world of consciousness, which forms an image of what is to be achieved and influences the outcome from a projected future. Let us see the Statement of Seville, the conclusion of a UNESCO sponsored conference in 1986.

> We conclude that biology does not condemn humanity to war, and that humanity can be freed from the bondage of biological pessimism and empowered with confidence to undertake the transformative tasks needed in this International Year of Peace and in the years to come. Although these tasks are mainly institutional and collective, they also rest upon the consciousness of individual participants for whom pessimism and optimism are crucial factors. Just as 'wars begin in the minds of men', peace also begins in our minds. The same species who invented war is capable of inventing peace. The responsibility lies with each of us.
> *Seville, 16 May 1986*

That is, a belief in a peaceful future is essential to start working for peace. The question of absolute determinism vs. absolute free will is, as we can see, not about whether we may or may not calculate all possible variables in a computer but rather whether we comprehend the way human consciousness functions on the bases of intentional acts which provide some, but not complete, freedom. This happens because they act upon a world that combines huge mechanical forces with other, not always friendly or clear, intentions. Edmund Husserl developed the concept of Intentionality to describe the way our consciousness (this word is used here to denote an ambit of the psyche that coordinates all its functions) structures the perceived world. For Husserl and other phenomenologists there could not be consciousness in isolation, but rather the consciousness of something. That something was to be "constructed" by the ways and the state of that consciousness. Silo stressed that Intentionality is an active process that carries an underlying intention, and that determinism and freedom are not two static mutually exclusive states; rather, for humans, they are part of a process that moves *from* determinism *towards* freedom, mediated by Intentionality. Understanding the mechanical deterministic forces into which we are born and bred (Nature, History, the already existing Society) enables us to start to make progressively more intentional choices.

How can we perceive our own Intentionality in action? The structuring power of our consciousness can be seen in processes of progressive complexity. This increase in complexity is accompanied by an increase in subjectivity, as our consciousness needs to "recruit" more elements from memory, personal concepts and beliefs to make sense of the perceived object or situation. The final result of this process is that consciousness bestows a particular meaning upon the object considered.

Figure 1: Here we see four lines that do not touch. Our consciousness "completes" the square.

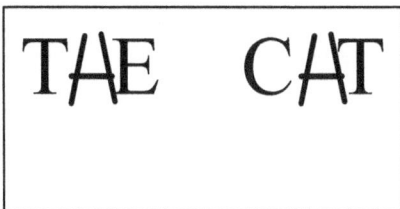

Figure 2: Here the mind gives a different meaning to the same symbol according to the context in order to make sense of the words

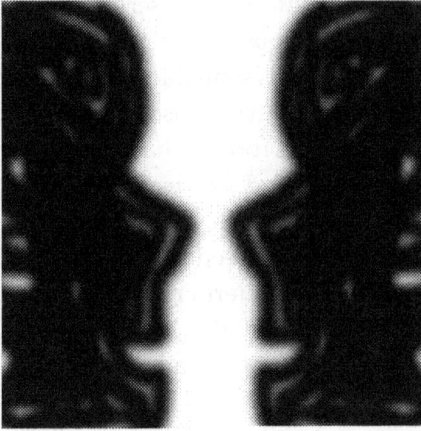

Figure 3: In this classical figure we may see either two faces or the background of the two faces as a candlestick, that is, our consciousness may structure this perception in two different ways. We can start to see the 'choice' we make to alternate between them.

Figure 4: The same applies to this more complex figure where we can see either six or seven cubes.

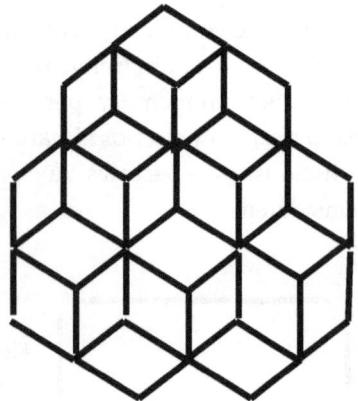

> "HE WAS TAP DANCING AND FELL OFF THE SINK"
>
> "SEX APPEAL, GIVE GENEROUSLY"

Figure 5: In these two examples of contextual meaning there is a very rapid shift in the meaning given to the words "tap" and "appeal". It is this type of shared experience that enables different people to understand each other's jokes.

> "HOW MANY FREUDIAN ANALYSTS DO YOU NEED TO CHANGE A PENIS, WHOOPS! I MEAN, A LIGHT BULB"
>
> "WHY IS THERE ONLY ONE MONOPOLIES COMMISSION?"

Figure 6: Equally, if two different people were not capable of attributing meaning by placing these terms within a shared contextual background these two jokes would be completely incomprehensible.

Figure 7: The Rorschach test used in Psychology (the figure is a mock ink block) as a projective test, works in a similar way to simply looking at the clouds. After a while we begin to notice that "forms" begin to appear. This shows us evidence of the structuring power of our consciousness. The psychologist administering the test interprets it in order to know something about the subject. Our consciousness bestows a meaning on these perceptions according to the way it sees the world. However, when we add an external "look" to the process (the examiner) we must also consider how this consciousness under observation may be affected by a desire to impress the observer one way or another, and the observer may also add his/her own contents to the final interpretation.

Another example of the shared process by which we delve into our cultural background in search for the piece of knowledge that can help us understand a joke can be found in the following examples of *The Simpsons'* humour:

> HOMER (ABOUT TO DO A HOMER SIMPSON): OH, WHAT THE HELL, YOU ONLY LIVE ONCE
>
> APU (FROM INDIA): SPEAK FOR YOURSELF!

> HOMER SIMPSON: IF JESUS SAW WHAT PEOPLE ARE MAKING TODAY OF CHRISTMAS HE WOULD BE TURNING IN HIS GRAVE!

Another important piece of evidence that we can have access to other people's constructions carried out by their intentionality can be found in famous quotes. Quotes are pearls of wisdom, the synthesis of many concepts that come together to explain a complex issue and which later get repeated by others who have been helped to understand the issue by the phrase they are quoting. Gandhi's "Be the change you want to see in the world" leaves us all a little wiser about what is to be done.

Viktor Frankl, initiator of the third school of psychotherapy also known as Logotherapy, describes an anecdote that also allows us to see intentionality in action. After a conference he receives a written question from a member of the audience that reads: "What is the meaning of 600 in your theory?" Puzzled by this, he asks for clarification. The man asking the question (a theologian) had actually scribbled "God" in such a way that a number of people read God and others 600 (presumably according to differences in past experiences, beliefs systems and their own handwriting). We notice that Frankl thought it important to point out that the man was a theologian, opening the issue to many interpretations of why this should be relevant. Did he think it was familiarity with the theme that produced the confusing handwriting? Or was it a simple note about the man's interest in God?

This capacity of our consciousness to construct the meaning of its perceptions is clearly stated by the Reader Response Theory that emphasises that a book does not have an "objective" content but rather depends on what the reader makes of it in a meaning-conferring act.

The process of structuring carried out by our consciousness is too fast for us to perceive step by step. Computer generated stereoscopic pictures (Magic Eye books for instance) can give us a glimpse of this process by slowing it down. Confronted with a picture that does not make sense and aware of the correct technique, the eyes seek unusual positions in a random way. As soon as the smallest recognisable shape (fast comparisons with previous experience from memory) appears the eyes lock into position and continue to scan the picture until the rest of the shape develops, until the perception "makes sense" and we see something to which we can attribute meaning.

We can imagine the variety of meanings that can be read in a same social situation, for instance, "I see two friends of mine talking (or rather whispering) in a corner of the room. From time to time they quickly glance in my direction and giggle. Then they continue to whisper." One attribution of meaning could be "they are laughing at me", but a less paranoid one could be "they are sharing an embarrassing secret and they fear I may hear what they are saying". Whatever my interpretation it does not remain as a completely private act in my head, but rather it will colour my actions in that situation, my future relationships with those people and my future attributions of meaning in similar situations.

These interpretations carried out by our consciousness are also given a value judgement by different currents of thought. Transcendental Idealists (Kant *et al.*) enjoyed the enthusiasm of discovery. After centuries of God and the "real world' occupying the focus of study they discovered The Mind, and embarked on the great adventure of seeing itself reflected in the objects under observation with obvious zeal and appreciation. Once we reach in our studies the divers into the Unconscious such as Freud, Adler, Klayne, etc., the subjectivity of the perception takes a turn for the worse. The structuring power of consciousness becomes in many ways an objectionable monster sabotaging our capacity to see reality with objectivity, something like looking at the real world through a dirty piece of glass. Jung somehow defects from this sort of negative value judgement by including in the unconscious a large portion of mystical landscape. Frankl attempts even higher heights by reaching for the divine, as he finds the unconscious inhabited by a connection to God. The phenomenologists in general behave towards this area of the mind in a more descriptive manner, presenting it as the power of human consciousness to structure the world and itself in a glorious creative quest (although they would probably indicate that all value judgements in this respect should be carefully "bracketed"). Continuing this line of thinking, but more unashamedly humanist, Silo places intentionality firmly at the centre of the power of transformation that our consciousness exerts upon the world to make it more fit for human existence.

The scientific method is, in a way, an acknowledgement of the intentionality of the observer. It tries to neutralise his/her point of view to make it "objective" (here we can see again subjectivity likened to seeing reality through a dirty piece of glass, but in this case there are obvious advantages in not getting caught in one's own beliefs). To this effect science has developed a variety of strategies that try to bypass the subjectivity of the researcher as well as his/her desire for positive results. The statistical method also tries to eliminate chance results and non-specific effects (placebo). Intentionality, however, may not be defeated so easily. One does not often see in advertising claims that reflect accurately what the statistical method can actually say, e.g.: "It is only probable that this toothpaste may be just marginally better than the one you have been using". Furthermore, even for scientists, who are very aware that results of statistical analysis are only speaking of probabilities and that the next study may refute their present findings, it is difficult not to fall a little bit in love with their own discoveries and wish to defend them as if they were somehow more definitive than they really are.

Intentionality is, for our consciousness, a way of being in the world, never as a passive reflection of that world but always as consciousness of something which is structured, interpreted, and felt according to previous experiences, future expectations and the actual sensations (physical and emotional) of that consciousness that perceives "the object in itself". This is all enveloped in a more general "trend" or intention of what that consciousness wants to achieve - generically, less suffering and more happiness - as well as its perception of how close it is to such an objective that particular day. All this appears as an "internal state" or "mode" under which our consciousness is functioning, that will bestow different meanings according to what mode prevails.

We can see in this example how the same event may be interpreted in ways that produce different reactions:

Event: A group of trees is to be felled by the Council to make room for a motorway.

Mode 1 - Rational attribution of meaning: trees produce oxygen and help reduce CO_2, which contributes to the greenhouse effect. Therefore I oppose the move.

Mode 2 - Magical thinking (which generally corresponds to animistic beliefs like the ones we all have in childhood): The spirits of the trees are going to feel the pain, therefore I oppose the move.

Mode 3 - Intuitive (great scientific leaps have been the consequence of intuition but it is also notoriously unreliable when choosing the queue for paying at the supermarket!): I am not sure but I feel that felling trees may bring bad consequences; therefore I oppose the move until more information is collected.

Mode 4 - Pragmatic: My journey to work will be shortened by the construction of the motorway, therefore I support the move. And please do not make me think about the long-term consequences. I am too busy just surviving today.

We can see here that even if the final decision is the same in three of the cases (it could have been different), the motivation for the action will be based on a diversity of interpretations of the situation. The mode of action fuelled by them will probably be different too.

Intentionality is much more than a simple subjectivity, it is a permanent attribution of meaning to every event that interacts with our consciousness and it tends to modify those events according to the meaning it constructs.

A very particular act of bestowing meaning is that which our consciousness attempts to give to itself. The complexity of this perception of consciousness looking at itself from outside as an object at the same time that it remains internal to itself, and the variety of states that accompany these looks, explain the diversity and variability of this "meaning of one's own life" that we find in society throughout history. And yet there is a commonality in most human beings, not only about the search in itself, but also about some registers obtained in the process. There is a particular "tone", an easily recognisable contemplative state of being that makes words suffused with identification with the experience of others, such as "fellow traveller".

Intentionality, this actively structured vision of the world, guides every action in which our consciousness happens to be involved, and in this way it tends to modify the world in its own particular direction. A part of that world is registered by our consciousness as the internal world. It is felt at times as a simple addition of sensations coming from the internal senses such as kinaesthesia (position of limbs and the body in space) and coenaesthesia (the diffuse register of one's body in general), but more significantly registered as a psychological space where consciousness of something is consciousness of oneself. In this context intentionality becomes the capacity of our consciousness to structure its own function and give meaning to itself, therefore opening the door to the possibility of intentional self-modification. The combined capacity of human consciousness to modify the surrounding world and itself places intentionality as the strongest force in the known universe to oppose entropy (understood as the mechanical forces pushing everything to a state of disorganisation from where no further change is possible), which is a highly deterministic tendency in physical terms. It does so by creating ever-increasing complexity and unstable systems. It is also fair to say that intentional life is undoubtedly its highest expression in our physical world.

Intentionality has been shaping human society by the predominance of one or other view within the same generation and by the cumulative effect of interpretations and reinterpretations of history, depending on the preferences of historians or the intended proposals for the future of politicians and opinion formers in general. A poignant example has come about with Hollywood, the Mecca of the film industry and the manufacturer of products that appear to the public more real than life itself without even attempting the smallest pretence of historical accuracy and taking "poetic licence" to its most ruthless expression. So we have seen through the making and (endless) re-making of the Robin Hood legend the creation of idealised heroes (Richard the Lion Heart, a King who actually only spent about six weeks in England as ruler) and evil villains (his brother John who dealt with tumultuous changing times with cruelty but not too differently from other rulers of the epoch). A cursory survey of what the public (outside the UK, hopefully) knows about these two people would probably show that history books come a distant second to films as a source of information.

Intentionality in itself has no morals and may shape human society towards the most ideal or towards the basest, towards the most peaceful or the most violent, but it is always human intentionality that does it. The attribution of intentionality to superior forces that allegedly control, regulate and organise social life (God, Nature, the stars, Market Forces, the Productive Forces, etc.) often corresponds to the combined intentionality of a human group which attempts to control or manipulate others by the use of the authority allegedly lent to them by those superior (but usually rather silent) forces. This says nothing about the existence and/or real influence of intentions outside the human ones. Nor is this an attempt to deny the remarkable inspiration and strength of action that derives from the religious experience or political ideas. It is important, however, to observe the way in which many abuses have been committed in History by those who feel attracted to the hierarchies of political, religious, social and economic institutions only by the power they confer over others. Can anybody sincerely say that they are able to exercise their position without even the smallest influence from their past history, their previous frustrations, and their little, or not so little, compulsions?

The spiritual search is as old as humanity and inevitably there will be some who are ahead of others in experience and knowledge but it is important also to recognise that sometimes those who erect themselves into interpreters and representatives of forces we struggle to understand impose on others their own intentionality. And we know full well that their intentionality will be guided by their own sensations, ideas and attributions of meaning. We are given, then, many models of behaviour delivered as if coming from supra-human powers and this is registered as deterministic, since we have no control over them, dampening down our potential for freedom. Such lack of freedom is, however, not necessarily felt to be oppressive by everybody when it is traded in for the certainty that a Supreme Being guarantees a pleasant afterlife for the believer as well as order and justice in the universe.

Intentionality shapes the natural world. The growth of science and technology is the tool developed by human intentionality in its defence against the elements, illnesses, dangerous animals, hunger and death. Ah, and other human beings. The excesses committed against the natural environment are now becoming recognised and the potential danger from pollution, the depletion of the high ozone layer in the atmosphere and the greenhouse effect add themselves now to the cohort of environmental phenomena humans have been defending themselves against. The awareness that intentionality may be destructive as well as constructive, and that its destructive action in the social and physical environments eventually returns as destruction for oneself and those we care about, is at the basis of the development of any ethical conscience. This may happen even in the absence of yet another "superior force" that we must obey, and it is this heightened intentionality, now aware of its own potential destructiveness, that can orient human activity towards the overcoming of pain and suffering.

Apart from manufacturing social trends intentionality has its expression in the human body. It has developed prosthesis such as false teeth or artificial limbs, because it cannot accept the deterministic loss of an existing function. It has also enhanced the scope of our senses with microscopes and telescopes and it has increased the power of our muscles with machines. It has tried to defeat the deterministic limitations of space by developing actions at a distance. From telephones to missiles, from voodoo to multinationals, our intentions reach out to others who are not in close contact with us to make them instruments or co-participants of our own projects.

Now we are meddling with our own genes, the ultimate deterministic barrier regarding the possibilities of the human body with the mind it sustains and affects, and therefore influencing the intentionality giving direction to it. Nothing can dispel the sense of dread at the chance that by so doing, things may go Horribly Wrong. At the same time, nothing can diminish the sense of hope and expectation about pushing back the boundaries of determinism, which appears to us in the shape of illnesses, ageing and death, an unimaginable distance.

Chapter 2

SOCIAL DARWINISM GOT IT WRONG

One of the most important debates of these times is the relationship between human beings and nature. For some the human being is one more animal. For others, human beings are somehow alien to nature and destructive to nature. For yet others the human being is a hybrid between a natural body and a spiritual soul.

These visions of the human being are not neutral or dispassionate opinions expressed in friendly discussions or academic interchanges. These differences support and sustain the power structure that allows some human beings to control and access more resources leading to longer life expectancy in better physical conditions. In this world of "money as the measure of all things" it is also tacitly understood that those who monopolise more resources than others also live happier lives. This is the message that pervades literature and the media alike. Happiness is, however, a complex aspiration that emerges from a diversity of situations, and it is not clear that wealth or the control of resources necessarily leads to happiness. However, on the basis of the belief (or rather, the myth) that wealth equals happiness a social order has been created that tries to extrapolate the rules that govern relationships between animals in the world of nature to the rules that govern human beings in society. There are very good reasons to think that this is nonsense.

Intentionality shapes the human body by setting its own rules in the "survival of the fittest" contest. An example of simple biological natural selection, what we call "survival of the fittest", would be the relationship between Malaria and Sickle Cell Anaemia. The latter makes it more difficult for the Plasmodium (the malaria agent) to thrive in the host's red blood cells. For this reason it confers some protection against the infection. This means that more babies with sickle cells will survive into adulthood in malaria infested areas and as they reproduce they will pass the sickle cells genes to their children. Are the sufferers of sickle cell anaemia the "fittest"? Well, yes, but only for that environment. In absolute terms years of pain and organ failure mean that they would prefer not to have the honour. Here we can see that the word "fittest" is misleading as it only means more adequate for a particular environment. In the same way we could say that giraffes are the most successful (the fittest) in an environment where there is little grass but tall trees with succulent leaves are abundant. Giraffes, however, do not look very happy at the waterhole. Fittest does not mean "the best" in any given situation. Hearing a superlative, however, may be irresistible for the human species which is so painfully aware of its own limitations. The possibility of finding an advantageous position tends to stimulate competition amongst those who live in fear, under some degree of oppression or with a poor self-image induced by comparing oneself with impossible ideal social stereotypes of desirability. Survival of the fittest applied to the social world rather than the natural one was a concept and a term first coined by Herbert Spencer (chronologically before Darwin), but once it was appropriated by the neoliberal dogma it led to a whole system of abuse and oppression justified in the name of biological superiority.

There are strong elements of determinism in a living being's adaptability to a particular natural environment, but society is not a natural environment, it is a human-made historical/cultural environment and it can be made, intentionally, more (or less) conducive to the development and survival of a particular type of individual. If we take for example skin colour we can see that the colonial Eurocentric vision of an inverse relationship between pigmentation and superiority has pervaded into the post-colonial (or, rather, neo-colonial) era. Thus not only do people with dark skin suffer discrimination in the "developed" world, but also in Africa skin products that lighten the colour are advertised as ways to increase a person's beauty and attractiveness. It is well known that the most attractive people also get an advantage over their counterparts in terms of getting jobs and promotions, which is known as the "halo effect". In other words what is being advertised is "Race-Change Soap makes you the fittest". Intentionality, working from the worst human instincts, is in this case adapting the environment for the most powerful to stay in power (whilst proclaiming "we can do this because we are the fittest, we have a God given right to it") instead of allowing those who are more able to thrive in a particular environment just to do so.

In the same way those who possess great amounts of money are making the social environment behave as if money made a person the fittest. Mechanisms of accumulation of wealth via multinationals, monopolies and the concentration in banks and financial institutions in the so-called developed countries are creating a culture where individuals born into their privileged strata are regarded and regard themselves as a product of natural selection and monopolise power "naturally".

The thought that tall and muscular bank managers may have their chances of reproduction maximised by the present political and economic climate might be felt as something somehow ominous. However, intentionality is permanently acting to defeat any kind of determinism and it is possible to observe a lot of "cheating" in relation to the desirable stereotypes, e.g., children who appear to be short may receive growth hormones so that they do not develop into vertically challenged adults, many men use anabolic steroids to look stronger, often with horrific consequences, and make up, fashion and possessions complete the mimicry with the ideals of the hour.

Natural selection, whilst not being completely absent from human evolution, must interact with much more human-made forces. The state of a society and the perception of the future, as well as religious beliefs, change completely the pattern of reproduction away from the law of survival of the fittest, assumed to be the regulatory force in nature. In very poor countries the poorest families (least fit according to economic markers) will have the largest number of children because only a few of them will survive into adulthood to be able to look after their ageing parents. Richer societies that look after their old through pension schemes tend to have fewer children per family. These are also the most likely people to have free access to, and education about, contraception. Some religions prohibit contraception, allowing only day counting (mockingly known as "Vatican Roulette"), whilst a few countries have promoted policies of fewer births (China) or increased number of births (Romania) for political/economic reasons. Visitors arriving from abroad to Franco's Spain, dominated at the time by an unholy alliance of extremely conservative Church and State, pointed out that sex was not really a sin but rather a miracle. The fact that most religions have something to say about sexual activity (teachings about when, how, with whom, etc., also known as "morality") makes any claim to human natural selection a complete nonsense. The mechanisms of wealth inheritance, access to nourishment and education dependent on social class and country of birth also create completely different conditions during the formative years for different human groups, but many insist on the view that those differences are "natural". The most at the mercy (or ruthlessness) of "natural selection" in its biological sense are those who live without access to health care, education, good housing, drinking water, appropriate nourishment and peace. If the social world was anything to compare with the natural one there would be a stampede to marry these owners of outstanding chromosomes and a clearly superior gene pool that allow them to survive in such circumstances. They are, however, the most discriminated against, the most excluded from human society.

In spite of great protestations of trying to do things more naturally the fact is that the most "developed" societies are using progressively more elements derived from science and technology to reproduce, moving in this way further and further away from the concept of natural selection. The little instinctive impulses that still turn up in the choice of partner pale in comparison to the number of social cues that participate in the final act of pairing for procreation. Social status, media-driven ideals of beauty, acceptability to family and friends, sharing interests and even ideologies, all socially determined characteristics rather removed from genetic determinism, further contribute to detach the human being from the tyranny of natural selection. In the future we will see an increase in the role of genetic counselling and awareness about inborn illnesses and the inevitable progression towards using genetics to breed progressively more perfect babies, that is, perfect in the eyes of heavily biased parents convinced that certain temporary fashions in terms of skin colour, eye colour, height, hair texture, etc. will make their offspring the fittest to succeed in a particular society.

There is no point (or hope) in trying to stop the advance of science or the use of technology to satisfy the craving for superiority, or rather, the fear of inferiority that an unfair society instils in its members. We can only work towards creating social justice so that no child gets neglected, bullied or abused to grow into a monster with such degree of low self-esteem that only conquering the world can compensate for it. Very wisely somebody once said that if Hitler had been praised for his artistic talent in childhood humanity might have saved itself the pain of the Second World War with its 61 million dead people. If it is difficult to imagine 61 million dead people think about the death of every adult and child in the UK, it is close enough. Perhaps it is a little farfetched to think seriously that a war might have been avoided if somebody had told little Adolf that his paintings were very good and encouraged him to spend more time with his brushes. The historical conditions were ripe for somebody like him. Nevertheless, next time we find ourselves with a child who suffers from very low self-esteem and we are too tired or distracted to notice what the child is doing, let us remember that a few words of praise today may save in the future, if not 61 million lives, a lot of grief both for the child and for others.

Unfortunately a competition geared society in which all parents want their own children rather than other people's children to be the "fittest" of the future is likely to continue producing people for whom the compulsion towards more and more power, more and more money, more and more control of resources is the only antidote for the humiliation they have felt and continue to feel for not being the biggest fish in their pond.

Whose responsibility is it to change this mad rush towards dominance? It is the model and the values of the society we choose to live in and prepare the new generations for. Here we have some possible models of the relationship between the state and the population.

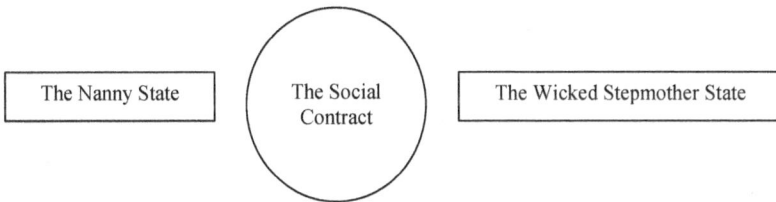

The Nanny State	The Social Contract	The Wicked Stepmother State

At one end of the spectrum we find the Nanny State phobia. Once people have their basic needs resolved, sometimes they lose sight of the process by which their nourishment, housing, education and healthcare, not to mention electricity and drinking water, are actually delivered to them. So they begin to feel that paying taxes and accepting rules that allow human groups to live together are unbearable intrusions on their liberty. Being told when one can smoke or inhale other people's smoke, when one can drink or be run over by a drunk, when we can work, sleep, make money, have our rubbish collected or go to war is felt to be infantilising, interfering and over controlling. The Nanny State becomes identified with a large state, expensive and self-perpetuating. Nanny looks after everyone but keeps a watchful eye over her charges.

At the other end of the spectrum the system behaves like a Wicked Stepmother State that reduces its concern to include only its own favourite children to the detriment of others'. This is the neoliberal state, the model and the values of the globalised economy headed by financial institutions and multinationals. The perfect situation in this conception is a tiny state, plenty of deregulation to allow unbridled development of private enterprise. Profit can be made out of anything including basic needs without any sense of duty or responsibility other than keeping the privileged in luxury. When the state retreats there is nobody to take care of the less able or the less fortunate. No one to respond to natural disasters, even less man made ones. Today, help for those whose lives have been dramatically affected by earthquakes, hurricanes, tsunamis and stolen pension funds depend more and more on sympathy and charity (inevitably selective and easily discouraged when some story about misuse or corruption emerges) and nobody can really rely on being rescued by the state. As it shrinks as a provider, abdicating also its power in favour of faceless management structures and shareholders, it also leaves a void for those who wish to express serious grievances. Unsurprisingly their violence is now directed towards "soft targets", that is, the general population. If this sounds farfetched just remember the last time you tried to reach a Government agency to ask an important question and spent ages being passed on from automated response to automated response ("If your house is flooding press 1...") without being able to hear the voice of a human being to tell them that none of the options fits your query.

Neither Nanny nor the Wicked Stepmother have anything to do with a mature society. Adults can look after themselves and when they cannot they seek to make agreements with other adults for mutual protection and benefit. In exchange they accept a proportional reduction of their freedom. In other words, to access certain rights, we accept certain responsibilities. I shall call this The Social Contract, aware that this is not exactly the way Rousseau meant it.

For Rousseau "Man is born free; and everywhere he is in chains" and "The strongest is never strong enough to be always the master, unless *he*[1] transforms strength into right, and obedience into duty". Apart from questioning that we are born free (we are all born already with a baggage of family background, cultural do's and don'ts, the

---

[1] My italics

consequences of accidents, nourishment and stress in our mothers' pregnancy and for many children in poor countries, a portion of the Foreign Debt over their heads), these statements are still applicable to our modern society.

The role of the state in the social contract is to create the right balance between rights and duties in such a way that all citizens feel that it is *their* state, an agreement amongst equals to ensure that basic needs are covered, including protection from and after disasters, for everyone. It is the role of the citizens to remain engaged in the process of negotiation between rights and duties. They cannot abdicate it in favour of a group of "managers" of the state because this is how a power structure takes on a life of its own. Many parliamentary democracies see in election after election a reduction in the percentage of the voting population, a clear sign that the electorate does not feel represented by their politicians. Real, rather than purely formal, democracy requires that a certain percentage of time and energy is dedicated by all citizens to making proposals and following them up both in their communities and in the wider world. In this age of migrations, newcomers to a community should be offered the chance to participate in the social contract of that community rather than being excluded from the beginning or having only obligations without any rights.

Change will not come easily to the cultures of the Old World, very much set in their ways, but the countries and continents coming now into their "modern" state have all the choices open to them. Africa and Latin America are the best examples of regions where turmoil and instability should not be seen as reasons to adopt the model of their old colonial masters. It is essential that this wonderful opportunity to do something different is seized and developed, for they can be the vanguard of a new state of the world, a human race working in unison for the benefit of all.

Chapter 3

THE UNCONSCIOUS: WRONG NAME, BAD PRESS

Those who cannot see the connection between the workings of the mind and the biochemistry of the brain have never been drunk.

Dr Gerry Silverman

Let us deal now with another concept believed to be a stumbling block in the development of *Homo Intentional*.

The list of factors tending in favour of determinism presented in Chapter I included the unconscious. This concept has been developing over the centuries. It began when thinkers, mainly the Transcendental Idealists such as Friedrich Schelling[2], started to notice that a part of our lives is directed by impulses apparently outside our voluntary control, and culminated with the works of Freud and Jung. Rebellion against determinism has moved humanity to try to understand and direct those impulses, but in this process belief systems have been created that jeopardise the development of truly intentional possibilities. Since we live in a social world created by human intentions, the implications of what we are/are not free to decide is central to the whole organisation.

It may appear inappropriate to develop a critique of a system of thought and psychological understanding that has developed in professional circles in a book that is not specifically addressed to the specialists in these matters. And yet, the psychological comprehension of human consciousness has already developed as a *culture* that permeates every aspect of our society and in particular the power structure. To illustrate this point I shall mention that Tony Benn, the UK Labour politician, once said that "racism is the *id* of society", and most people in the audience, sadly, understood what he meant. It is therefore licit to open a debate about how we utilise the knowledge that arises from the observation of human consciousness, and whether

---

[2] *System of Transcendental Idealism* (1800)

the way we regard the mind in our present culture moves us in an intentional direction or back into mechanical obscure tendencies.

From a developmental point of view we spend a large proportion of the first months of our life in simple trial and error exercises. Babies produce all kind of random movements when they are trying to grab objects for the first time until they achieve a "hit", a positive result. Several hits will reinforce a particular sort of behaviour, one that has now been "learnt". This is basic science performed by babies. We may not yet be aware of it but when we repeat an event many times and choose the one that elicits the most positive results we are of course creating (or re-inventing) the statistical method.

Generally we do not remember how we learned to handle utensils and objects of common use, which is very useful as we can perform these actions mechanically, not having to think every time how we did it the previous time, and that leaves our focus of attention free to concern itself with higher tasks.

Not all patterns of behaviour need to be found through a process of trial and error, since in childhood we have a great capacity for imitation. However, an imitated pattern is not learned until it is tried out and it scores a hit, that is, there is no learning without experience. We learn by doing, not by watching. Interestingly new technologies bring about changes also in the pattern of learning. The process of imitating violence from TV, or from family and society, used to happen in two steps. Step 1, witness the violence; Step 2, action, which could lead to several outcomes, some positive (power) some negative (punishment, isolation). With the advent of video games, children learn these forms of behaviour in just one step since they are already in action, and the consequence of violence is always generally positive, unless someone writes a programme where violence is useless and reproved, which however would not be expected to be a commercial success in the present social climate.

What is not easily available through imitation is tested by children more randomly and, for the parents, more alarmingly in what has been called "pushing the boundaries", a more advanced form of trial and error, until a clear stop is found: e.g., children try to put their hands near fire until they burn themselves or until adults consistently block their access.

If the successes and limits found by a child in the exploration of the world are more or less consistent (similar responses follow similar behaviour), many forms of learned behaviour become mechanical, that is, there is no longer a need to remember alternative forms tested and failed, nor the precise moments when the behaviour succeeded.

It is becoming more understood from empirical data that learned behaviour may correspond to particular neural paths in the brain that are reinforced by the success of an action. The model developed by Gerald Edelman, creator of the theory of "Neural Darwinism", has suggested a putative correlation between learning behaviour and the reinforcement or disappearance of neuronal connections in response to stimuli. Although there has been some controversy about this model it correlates quite well with Learning Theory and images in some advanced scanning methods. Other researchers prefer to speak more of Brain Plasticity, also alluding to this self-rewiring of the brain in response to different experiences. However it works, we are now aware that the brain is not a fixed structure and this aids us in the understanding of our intentional choices.

During adolescence a large number of neuronal connections disappear in a process referred to by some scientists as "pruning". About 40% of the brain synapses appear to be lost. Most probably those connections reinforced by the positive feedback from successful behaviour will remain and many of the non-reinforced ones will become extinct. A great many alternative unused connections (and recent studies suggest that new ones will may also appear) must remain because humans are capable of continuing to learn new forms of behaviour throughout their lives, but it becomes more difficult with time. Old age has been characterised by a certain "rigidity", people are "set in their ways". This suggests that the progressive decay of unused connections continues throughout life and tends to limit the capacity for trying and learning alternative forms of behaviour in the declining years. This process is less deterministic than could be assumed, as demonstrated by the many people who decide to learn new skills or have a career change in their middle or old age.

If during our early years, instead of finding more or less uniform responses in front of similar situations, we encounter grossly inconsistent feedback from our attempts to find the appropriate behaviour, i.e. occasional success and occasional failure, no clear pathways may develop. In such cases we must continue to try random and imitated actions, that is, we behave like much younger children. This view seems to be supported by evidence that serious inconsistencies in the environment in which a child is growing up tends to produce more immature children. In other words, when adults in charge of forming children deliver anger/love following their own moods rather than responding to the behaviour of the child those infants often tend to test the boundaries more persistently than their peers and are more inclined to imitate TV models in search of "successful" behaviour. Consistency and affection are closely related since they are both linked to the attention youngsters will receive from their carers in their formative years. John Bowlby's[3] Attachment Theory describes this consistency as the basis for secure attachments essential for the development of self-confident individuals.

Perhaps one of the problems in these observations is that they have been carried out almost exclusively in relation to the family and the effects of inconsistencies in the wider social environment have not been well researched. Education systems persistently attempt to give the young the idea that honesty, goodness and ethical positions will make their life better. However, children are immediately confronted not just by TV's fictional violence promoted as the main way to succeed in whatever endeavour, but most poignantly by real life violence in the form of wars, discrimination and oppression where the survival of the richest or the one with the biggest weapon is clearly visible. This social influence also reaches into the youngsters' homes, and they cannot help but observe their parents (the good people) being bullied, dismissed from their jobs and treated in the most unfair ways by faceless "baddies" (the system) in total contradiction with what they are being taught by the same parents as well as by teachers and religion: that goodness is rewarded and evil never goes unpunished. Today not many people take home the message that they feel rewarded with respect and security in their jobs for their commitment and responsibility. This is an inconsistency that cannot be easily balanced by parents and teachers for the sake of the young.

When no consistency happens over long periods of time in the formative years, a young adult continues to present more patterns of behaviour which are appropriate for children: self-centredness, impulsiveness, inability to recognise and accept social boundaries, etc.

---

[3] Bowlby, J. (1973) *Attachment and Loss*. London: Hogarth Press; New York: Basic Books; Harmondsworth: Penguin (1975).

These adults often run into trouble with the law, with interpersonal relationships, and with their sense of self-worth because they are still "trying and erring". Society tends to be divided about this delinquent group of individuals, between those who feel they should be given extra consistency and the opportunity to catch up with their peers on the one hand, and those who simply want them locked up on the other. Joel Bakan[4] in *The Corporation*[5] has already referred to the behaviour of multinationals and financial institutions as "psychopathic", borrowing from psychiatry a description that fits such attitudes. But what for psychiatry is part of the abnormal world is for society developing into the norm rather than the exception. If our society continues to increase its contradictions it is likely to produce whole generations which are immature, impulsive, childish, self-centred, demanding immediate gratification, lacking in internal ethical reference and keen to follow strong charismatic leaders who appear at least to give firm, consistent, guidance. Epochs of strong social injustice and disorientation are often followed by fascism. There is an intense relationship between the psychological makeup of the population and the leaders they choose or follow.

Learned behaviour, the "hits", is stored in our memory and classified in an organised way for future reference (to be used in similar situations) without the need to remember how it was acquired. This is the main substratum of the so-called "unconscious", which is by and large the mechanical use of previous experience with a clear corollary. One of its roles is to give instant responses to future events without the need to engage the focus of attention, that narrow beam able to illuminate only a small part of the structure world/consciousness at a given time. If I think: "What am I doing right now?" surely the answer is about the task that occupies the focus of my attention; but how many other things am I doing without realising? In fact most of our activity happens under the regulation of this mechanical fast processing, ever-present and yet seemingly invisible unconscious. The way previous experience is organised to carry out this fast information processing task seems to be guided by a general tendency to avoid pain and suffering and move towards pleasure and

---

[4] Professor of law at the University of British Columbia

[5] The Corporation : The Pathological Pursuit of Profit and Power, (Constable, London)

happiness. We start to glimpse here an "intention" that is difficult to grasp because of its pervasive quality. I will refer to this later.

Should most childhood experiences, in an ideal world, lead to consistent learning? The answer to this is probably based on the usual common sense, that all extremes are questionable. The obvious advantage of retaining a capacity for random trial and error is original creativity, the discovery of new ways of doing things, but in a society that demands that people conform to certain accepted patterns too much of this is generally problematic. Moreover, having to try and err in most situations in life is very anxiety provoking, and it does not allow free energy to do more complex things, since the focus of attention is permanently engaged in trivial matters. On the other hand too rigid an upbringing most likely reduces the capacity for experimentation and the ability to adapt to new and unforeseen situations. There is probably a wide range of situations in the formative landscape that lead to the "right balance" between sufficient numbers of reinforced and potential neural pathways. We require the former to produce appropriate automatic behaviour, which, in dealing with simple things, serves as a base for more complex operations. It is not necessary to "learn" what is a computer, a mouse, a program, a finger, a letter, etc, every time I want to create a new document. In addition we need enough instances that are left open to the possibility of newly discovered behaviour, which in turn, opens the way to creativity and flexibility.

What happens then with experiences that fail to reach a positive corollary, a satisfactory conclusion with predictive value? Our consciousness cannot classify and store them in conjunction with other similar ones for future reference, so it tries to do something with them, some process, to extract a conclusion and then fit them somewhere. So it goes through them again and again until some resolution happens. Most people have experienced repetitive dreams that sometimes stop suddenly after a modification in the plot. Most people experience repetitive daydreaming, finding that their thoughts often wander to the same point that, apparently by coincidence, is the ideal compensation of what they see as their unhappy reality. Most people have also the experience of engaging in the same type of behaviour, such as a string of very similar relationships, again and again, even when they recognise them as a source of suffering.

This re-enactment of unclassifiable experiences (because they were painful, had contradictory consequences or failed to reach a successful outcome) was noticed by Freud and others who concluded that these experiences were repressed into the unconscious beyond the focus of attention (which they largely identified with the "*ego*"), bringing from this darkness their burden of pain and suffering. Their unavailability created the need for the presence of another person, the therapist, to help bring them into the light. This understanding of how certain undesirable behaviour was under the control of repressed impulses and experiences, coupled with the interpretation of the re-enactment of those situations with the therapist who fulfilled the role of a difficult figure from the past (transference), was part of the curative process in what was called "psychoanalysis".

This is an obvious oversimplification of the theory attempting only to give some context to its critique. It is possible, in my view, that many experiences follow an alternative pattern: some conflictive experiences may not be repressed into the unconscious but may rather become the ones pushing to receive attention, so that they can become classifiable and storable for future (automated) reference, whilst the others, the great mass of things we do not remember, go about quietly fulfilling their task of making the necessary mechanical connections to give rapid responses to new situations. The fact that very often we do not remember the painful event that created the conflictive search may be seen either as a general protection against that pain (memories stored as little "islands" of difficult access) or simply as what memory does best, that is, allowing a general sense of self from the overall recall of one's existence rather than from precise details of every moment of our lives, which would indeed clog the focus of attention with unnecessary junk.

The supporters of Phenomenology had already pointed out that our consciousness is always consciousness of something, structuring perceptions, events etc., in a particular way, connected to previous experiences, our emotional tone and expectations, all with a certain direction, but not necessarily within the focus of attention, and they named this process Intentionality. The advantage of this way of conceptualising this process, rather than seeing it as "the unconscious", is that there is no attribution of specific qualities (selfish, libidinal or sexually charged, aggressive) to the mechanical processes that produce the final structuring of a perception or event: its meaning. Furthermore, it is easy to see that the general direction of the consciousness of a person also has a strong influence in the process of Intentionality. This helps avoid the sense of *"not-I"* that can be created by the belief that one's unconscious has its own murky agenda. This, in turn, has implications in terms of responsibility. In this way we can also avoid the problem of considering the unconscious as outside consciousness instead of an integral part of it. Observed experience shows that every conscious act can be so because there are a multitude of operations happening at a mechanical level and delivering the context within which it is possible to make sense of the object in the focus of attention. For instance, if I am reading a book and trying to understand some concept I do not need to pay attention to making sense of "book", "words", "page", "study", "chair in which I am sitting", "light from the window", "English language", "hands holding the book" or "interest in the theme", as all these issues are delivered to me ready structured and with a clear meaning by this fast information processing part of my consciousness.

As the process of learning is guided by feedback of pain and pleasure derived from the successes and failures of the tried forms of behaviour over our neural connections, at a very basic level we can say that the general direction or intention of the structuring process of the consciousness (intentionality) is towards pleasure and away from pain. There are additional rewards for getting something right: a small squirt of Endorphins in the brain and approving looks from those whose opinion we care about. However there is nothing stronger that the personal sense of advancement and meaning.

So even if a person misinterprets a situation as negative when in fact it is neutral or positive - e.g., two friends giggling in the corner of the room and glancing in the direction of a Speaker (see Chapter I) - the basic intention of that person's structuring is towards self-protection. In order to perform consistently self-protective structuring actions the consciousness needs to function on an intact brain. If the biochemistry of the brain has been affected by genetic, traumatic or chemical events leading to malfunction then the whole structuring process is contaminated by this malfunction, as we can see in mental illness, hallucinogenic drugs and brain damage.

There are also situations in which, although the brain is intact, events surpass the capacity of the consciousness to structure and make sense of them. We may include here situations such as wars, catastrophes and the collapse of the frame of reference that a person has learned to live in. Many people behave under these extreme conditions as if they were suffering from mental disorder. This has been seen in refugees displaced by war and famine who end up in environments completely alien to their previous experience, and is a form of what has been called "culture shock". It has also been predicted as the effect of the acceleration of change in the social and technological world, and called in this context "future shock" by Alvin Toffler. Silo has warned about the consequences of the acceleration of the historical tempo, also predicting a variety of disturbances including an increase in suicide (already significantly happening among young men in many parts of the world) and in the sense of alienation and dehumanisation.

Depression also appears to be on the increase and it has been predicted that it is likely to continue to do so, in parallel with social fragmentation and uncertainty about the future. The World Health Organisation has already warned that depression, in its evolution from reaction to adverse situations to full blown mental illness, is advancing as it is likely to overtake many other causes of disease burden[6] by 2010. Curiously enough most proposals about defeating depression have to do with an increase in production of antidepressant medication or access to cognitive therapy, both well recognised forms of treatment. But what are we saying, and doing, about prevention when all other branches of medicine are concentrating on vaccines, healthy diets and the right composition of air and water? Should we not be addressing as a matter of urgency the social trends that increase depression? Should we not attend to the progressive fragmentation of the family, of the community and of society in general that lead to the psychological destruction of the human being as a valuable marker that shows this is not the right direction? The answer is: it depends on how cruel we want to be.

The limited, immediate structuring that takes place in specific situations may seem to work like a pragmatic simple pain and pleasure switch, and for most of the time it is relatively neutral. As the eye scans a room the consciousness recognises objects (table, chair, door, and window) in an almost instantaneous perception-data-from-memory-recognition that helps us have a sense of familiarity about the environment in which we act. When the place is unfamiliar attempts to

---

[6] The personal and socio-economic consequences of illnesses.

identify some contents with known objects also help us feel safer (e.g., infuriating holidaymakers who find that everything reminds them of something "back home"). This instant structuring of events happens within the global structure, our consciousness, which is also trying to make sense of itself, to structure its own meaning. In this context a bigger, more permanent consideration about purpose and direction may supersede many simple, almost reflex perceptions. This process is no longer neutral. This is our consciousness' intention towards the pleasure of making sense of itself, understanding it as a cohesive whole with an open future (which we shall call happiness, acknowledging that it is different from immediate short term pleasure) and the pain of not making sense that submerges us in a vortex of fragmentation leading to nihilism, cynicism and Sartre's "nothingness". Post-modern thinking tries to find a kind of pleasure in this deconstructing magma, not completely unlike enjoying a drug that makes us feel dizzy or in a trance-like state.

As for the sensation that many people have of being at war with their own unconscious, which seems to play tricks on them and move in a direction opposed to the one chosen "consciously", we must take into account that if we send contradictory intentions to this fast processing mass of inter-connective network which is sorting out neurological impulses at truly fantastic speeds, we will have unpredictable results as the outcome of the process.

If a contradiction is defined as thinking in one direction and feeling in the opposite one in such a way that every action is registered as self-betrayal (because it will necessarily go against one or the other), we must understand that being at war with oneself is never a purely individual problem as it always affects others. We can see the following example:

A is very angry with a friend, B, following B's failure to fulfil a commitment. At the same time A understands the reasons why B failed, but this does not help minimise the anger. A decides to continue his/her friendship in spite of such anger on the basis of an intellectual understanding of B's problems. At a party A accidentally pours red wine on B's expensive designer outfit. Although A is clear that there was no intention to do this, in the back of A's mind there lingers a doubt about how "accidental" this has been. A does not extract this from an idea but rather from a register in which the anger suppressed and pushed aside has made a comeback managing to deliver its own agenda outside of A's conscious control. Not altogether unconscious, though: A knows something is wrong but is unable to deal with it as it may spoil a friendship that A is keen on keeping. A feels not completely in control of his/her own mind. A seeks therapy.

In the same way that we do not forgive ourselves for the actions we cannot control or the parts we dislike about ourselves, we also fail to forgive small imperfections and compulsions in those we regard as our models. In many ways, the more we idealise them, the angrier we become with them when we discover their flaws. We would like our models to be completely coherent and almost perfect. But the ideals expressed by those we admire are aspirations, perhaps even more so because they recognise in themselves, and strongly disapprove of, a quality, a compulsion or a belief.

Much has been said about Mahatma Gandhi hitting his wife for not wanting to clean a toilet, as that was an Untouchable task. Many have stated that this invalidates his Non-violent teachings. But who are in a better position to propose the need for non-violence than those who recognise it, acknowledge it and are committed to overcoming it in themselves?

When we glimpse something in ourselves that we dislike we can do one of several things. First, we can push it so far into the background that we can no longer see it (denial). In this way we do not just deny the uncomfortable truth to others, but also to ourselves. This is the case of some homophobic bigots (but not all, let us hurriedly point out) who possess repressed homosexual feelings. Another example can be found in many fanatics of this or that morality who hide unmentionable immoral compulsions. If they are found out giving way in anyway to these compulsions then they are called hypocrites, and so they are. We can punish ourselves and live solely for the purpose of cleansing our sins, feeling completely unable to build anything good because we feel we are worthless and evil. There is a warped logic in this position that actually absolves us from the responsibility of going out to change the forces that led us into such contradictions, both for our own sake and for the benefit of others.

If, instead, we take a good, long look at our compulsions and internal violence, and without punishing ourselves or others we explain that we want to change, we begin the road to an open future. We include in this process not just ourselves but also society because we are aware that these compulsions grow with us in our formative years in an environment that promotes them. If it is our desire to eliminate them not only outside but also in our interior, then our quest becomes coherent and honest. The risk of "accidents" can be reduced in this way by acknowledging that parts of our own minds may try to sabotage our actions, and we prepare for this through attention. We gather help from our environment to be a mirror, to give us warning signals, to limit the effects of our mechanical actions and to be present with indicators of progress in the path we have taken.

If we can be compassionate towards our own imperfections we can be more comfortable about finding out that people held up by history as "models" also had their own weaknesses. So Bertrand Russell was a womaniser and had bad breath? We can still admire his clear thinking and commitment to peace. So Leonardo da Vinci's sexuality may have contained a darkness that is not yet wholly understood? His paintings and engineering projects remain pretty amazing. So Mikhail Gorbachev advertised for Pizza Hut? Yet he ended the Cold War, after humanity lived for 40 years teetering on the edge of Total Nuclear Annihilation. Our heroes have clay feet but their contributions should remind us that we can also attempt to make our small contributions, even if we do not yet feel liberated from our own compulsions and imperfections. Moreover, our actions in the world can be an important factor in overcoming them. Social actions carried out for the benefit of others may often contain elements of integration and transformation of the self that can be the envy of any self-respecting therapy.

Let us have a look now at this very interesting phenomenon called "transference", which in psychoanalysis is seen as the re-enactment of a conflict in the relationship with the therapist and one of the basic curative factors. It is possible to detect, however, this re-enactment happening in most areas of our lives when guided by attempts of our consciousness to reach a corollary and be able to store safely conflictive experiences. It could be postulated that if part of our education were dedicated to learning to observe and to reflect upon our repetitive behaviour, we would gain a much deeper understanding of our underlying conflicts. Furthermore, if after recognising their toxic effect on the human mind we were capable of creating an environment with less social contradictions for children to be brought up in, we would end up with a society where individuals would suffer much fewer personal ones.

Whether aware or not of our repetitive behaviour, our consciousness usually tries to perform a "transference" to integrate an offending theme. That means that it will try to associate it with a new object that is similar but not identical to the one encountered at the time the conflict situation developed. It could be, for example, a new relationship, a punishing teacher, an accident, etc. In this new incarnation the mind will try to give it a different outcome that allows it to be stored "for future reference". Thus, spontaneous transferences happen during dreams, daydreaming, planning for the future, different activities, and in certain types of narratives that allow the subject to identify with a character who is undergoing transformations as he/she goes along a path. This takes place in myths, children's stories, legends, soap operas, etc. The role of the "hero" in Greek theatre has already been analysed by Nietzsche with reference to this identification and transformation in the viewer. Hollywood endlessly compensates the register of powerlessness of modern people with its stories of individual heroes that take on the system, and win!

There is no doubt that when a person's life breaks down completely he/she may need the aid of a professional to help them set it back on course, but the expansion of the "therapy" culture has become a form of "medicalization" (or "therapization") of all kinds of social conflicts as people have become convinced that they have "personal problems", even when they see so many of others in the same situation. There is very little in the education system geared towards understanding and communicating with others about one's own mental processes. In the same way there is little understanding about how these "personal problems" arise from social relationships that are becoming more dehumanised and more objectifying. Instead of tackling them at their point of origin, for instance, by dealing with injustice, the fragmentation of society and the lack of communication, we are encouraged to seek refuge in individual therapies. This, in turn, leads, at least in form, to a reinforcement of individualism and loss of solidarity, notwithstanding that the "patients" may adopt a different direction in their mental contents.

Since our consciousness is always storing experiences for future reference and launching perfected images of what is to be achieved, without which nothing could evolve, the future is outstandingly important for the functioning of the whole structure. During the 1960's hybridisation of local Western thinking with Eastern philosophies gave rise to a search for a "living in the present" that degenerated into hedonistic pragmatism. This could be understood as the immediate satisfaction of all wishes and a search for pleasure without reference to future consequences, which is probably partly responsible for the sense of emptiness and anomie[7] experienced by many people today. Aldous Huxley's somehow paternalistic book *Island* (in which the natives achieve a higher sophistication of consciousness when they learn to speak English) introduces a bird that reminds the inhabitants to exist in the "here and now, boys". This type of pseudo-Eastern import suggests that there may have been a huge misinterpretation of the "timeless" feeling of being at peace with oneself and with the world, a desirable state proposed by most forms of Eastern meditative practices. The search for such states led to behaviour that treated these philosophies as yet another product to be consumed, together with harmful mind altering drugs, at a time when the threat of a world-wide nuclear catastrophe and the prospect of being drafted into a meaningless war (Vietnam) transformed the future into a monster better to be forgotten about. Many would state here that the future does not look much better now that the "war on terror" has been unleashed amongst us. In the end it will depend on how much we have learned from previous experiences and how much we are prepared to work to make every human being feel at home on this planet.

Returning now to the theme of the mind, it is interesting to observe that the exploration of lost memories gave much material for strange interpretations of the contents of the unconscious. What most observers of these mechanisms found out was that we have memories that do not fit exactly what we think has happened. From the False Memory Syndrome to past life regression, the proliferation of interpretations of these strange memories has created lawsuits and new religions, all consequences of assuming that the role of memory is to remember things literally as they happened and to remember everything. It is a now well documented fact that experiences are stored after a process of elaboration so that they can be used to make sense of future perceptions, and that the way we remember is affected by what is

---

[7] Emile Durkheim (French sociologist), in his book "*The Division of Labour in Society*" (1893). The term refers to the breakdown of social norms that leaves the individual disoriented.

happening in the present and what we believe about the future. There seems to be also a process of reorganisation of memory as time goes by and other experiences join and qualify previous ones. In other words, the role of memory is not necessarily to "remember" but perhaps to learn from past experience and be able to structure a perceived situation in the best possible and fastest way, that is, to aid the process of intentionality. Remembering is of course important to have a sense of self with continuity in time, but this does not require memories to be accurate. Nor should we assume from now onwards that all memories are inaccurate and therefore nothing we remember can be trusted. The general framework and description of remembered situations tend to be reasonably accurate, in particular for the most meaningful and highly emotional times. But we have to learn to live with the understanding that we do not remember everything as it happened, that our memories change over time and that our vision of the past may be as plastic and changeable as our vision of the future.

An interesting test of the way memory works that anybody can perform at home is to watch films seen in the past, from very recent ones to others further away in time. What percentage of those films do we remember seeing? For some films quite a lot, in particular if the theme was related to emotionally charged events we were experiencing at the time we watched them. In other films we hardly recognise anything. Some scenes are vaguely familiar whilst others are strangely different from the way we remember them.

It is not difficult to imagine that our social memory, also known as "History", is also plagued with numerous re-elaborations and re-interpretations according to the intentions of those who made records at the time and write today about it. In other words, the "lessons we learn from history" are taught in a rather distorted and biased classroom. This does not invalidate the search for information in our past, but imposes the need to apply to the study of History a point of view that understands intentionality in it as much as in the comprehension of our own minds.

Chapter 4

THE INTENTIONAL MIND:
WHO IS HIDING IN MY UNCONSCIOUS?

Freedom is not just an aspiration; it is a need for human beings struggling to break the chains that enslave them. But when the chains are internal, of our own making and regarded with some affection as they have the flavour of "oneself", we may choose to paint them in pretty colours rather than letting go of them. Advertising helps the process by selling us extra chains, more attractive, more subtle and more "unconscious". South American indigenous peoples used to catch monkeys with a hollowed pumpkin and a peanut inside. The opening in the pumpkin just about allows the monkey's hand in. In order to grab the peanut the monkey makes a fist, which no longer goes through the opening. If the animal lets go of the peanut it is free. But...

Modern Man feels trapped. We are told we are free. There has never been so much choice. It must be our "unconscious" then.

By now this word has been used to refer to the most diverse regions and experiences of human consciousness. We have already mentioned that for Freud the unconscious was inhabited by libidinal and unmentionable desires, whilst for Jung it contained universal archetypes and some form of mystical connections. For Victor Frankl it was the seat of the very personal meaning of anyone's life and from there a line to God; for Reincarnation enthusiasts it contains memories of past lives (and presumably the karma) and for Adler the Will to Power. For the physicist Roger Penrose the processes of consciousness cannot be reproduced by an algorithm (a sort of flow chart in maths speak), which is his argument against Artificial Intelligence. However, the unconscious just might be. This view suggests that whilst consciousness is a totality, a synergic complex whole, the unconscious functions like a series of successive steps, a sequential search for a specific piece of information.

Perhaps this is the right time to review this cultural assumption that humanity is fighting a losing battle against this unknown, deterministic, sometimes dark and sometimes shiny, but always controlling, alter ego and begin to see both it and consciousness as an intentional totality. The unconscious cannot be the enemy within - this vision reveals an irate allegorisation of our own mechanisms of consciousness, not surprisingly, since wars and repressive regimes and cultures formed the background against which these theories were created. At times human beings have been very angry with their contemporaries and with themselves - no doubt with very good reasons I would dare say. But going around punishing everybody is not the answer as it leaves us in the same vicious circle. Opening the future is more interesting.

Many things can be said about the profound motivations for our actions, and so many fit the situation well, even if they contradict one another. Determining which one is the real reason for doing anything can be a daunting task. Consciousness escapes William of Ockham's razor. That is a principle attributed to this 14th century friar, as an effort to streamline causation - later reported as the principle that we should not multiply entities beyond what is needed. This meant that if the reason for the occurrence of a natural phenomenon is clear there is no need to assume also the presence of other forces and/or a divine cause. This proposal made at the dawn of scientific thinking continues to show validity today... except when we analyse the way intentionality structures a myriad of reasons for and against, encouraging and inhibiting feelings to lead to the final product, an action in the world.

Why do I write this book? Well, because I have been thinking and I have things to say, and because I want to share with my contemporaries some thoughts from other people I admire and criticise others I do not admire so much, and because I'd like some recognition from those around me, and because I would like something of me to transcend my physical death, and because I see the world in a mess and would like to make some proposals that can fix some of it, and because I do not like to see others suffer, and because the process of writing clarifies my own thoughts and because others do not very often understand what I am trying to say and so putting it in writing may be a better way, and because I wonder if I could become a professional writer, etc., etc., etc. There are of course reasons for not writing this book: perhaps my ideas are not so hot after all and even if some of them are right perhaps I am a boring writer, and there is so much written about these themes that one more book is unlikely to make any difference, and maybe some of my conclusions are so wrong that they could be misleading, and getting published these days is so difficult that this may well be a complete waste of time, etc., etc., etc. Whether I sit down to write or not depends on the balance of the day.

If an agent external to me were to interpret the reasons why I write this book he/she would probably get it right. There are so many that it would be practically impossible not to hit a number of them. This external agent, however, might organise the weight of those reasons in an order different to the one preferred by me. Most probably he/she will see that order in a rather fixed way, whereas I observe that my reasons reorganise themselves with great plasticity in response to internal and external situations. Others will see the more static me because of the way we "classify" people. We pick up a few characteristics we detect on a particular day and pigeon-hole the person there. We want our environment to be predictable. That reduces our stress. We want to know where we can find things, who we can count on. Therefore very few will relish the awareness that many things keep changing in my consciousness; that some of my reasons come and go in response to inner and outer cues. Moreover, my reasons may become unavailable to me some days to resurface later, moving quite comfortably across the dotted line we are supposed to draw between conscious and unconscious.

I apologise for this phenomenological indulgence; this critique is simply an attempt to point out that the concept of the unconscious as it is formulated today, may serve purposes alien to its original description. Image-makers (or "spin doctors") sell politicians and policies to our unconscious. Advertising sells products to our unconscious. Society's establishment sells a model of organisation and a morality to our unconscious. And they are able to do so because we do not know our unconscious, as we have accepted the culturally-driven premise that it is unknowable and inaccessible by our own efforts. A wide debate about changing its name in order to change its conceptualisation (i.e. Fast Mechanical Processing Experiential Data System or, if this sounds too computerese, Co-presence as described in the Psychology of New Humanism[8], to indicate phenomena outside the

---

[8] More information about the concept of Co-presence can be found in *Contributions to Thought and Psychology I, II and III, Collected Works* by Silo, Latitude Press

focus of attention) may induce a deeper understanding of consciousness as a whole.

It will not suffice to start referring to this area as "the so-called unconscious" or "the unconscious" (with finger movements to indicate "quotes") as the force of habit will soon impose the most effortless form of communication and the name will stick, together with the concept and the belief that a little monster is lurking in the dark areas of one's mind impervious to voluntary control. *Homo Intentional* must not be so lazy.

The Eureka! Experience

If we agree then that the "so-called Unconscious" is not the enemy within but a great friend to help us make sense of the world, let us see one of its talents. We have to solve a complex problem. We think hard, nothing happens. We stop thinking about it. We start doing other things for minutes, hours, days, and suddenly in a flash, we know the answer. Something we are doing which is apparently unrelated guides us back to the problem, this time resolved. Roger Penrose has beautifully described this in the TV introduction to Steven Hawkings' book *A Brief History of Time*. He is walking on the street and suddenly he gets restless, he wonders why and suddenly he realises he has found the solution to a problem he has been musing about for some time. He nearly misses it, makes an effort and brings it to full awareness. Where is all this happening? In the unconscious, of course! Is this then the unconscious that stocks up repressed painful memories and manipulates us from the darkness with shameful desires? Or are we not observing the wonderful capacity of our consciousness to make automated connections between already experienced and properly classified knowledge, reaching at the end conclusions without the need to occupy the focus of attention, which is left in this way free to continue accumulating experience? This ability to continue processing complex as well as trivial information in the background whilst maintaining the general direction of the structure of consciousness appears to have amazing evolutionary value.

There are of course many processes of search that are carried out from the focus of attention, but many people also use the automatic pilot deliberately when they cannot find something like a name, an object, a memory, ("it will come to me later") etc.

Whether we are searching automatically using "auto-pilot" or with our attention, the moment of finding the answer is generally met with a feeling of elation. In particular, difficult problems that find their solutions seem to bring a quality of pleasure that makes us breathe deeper, our heart beat faster, and we are filled with meaning as if finding this answer means there is no reason why we should not find all other answers. Our consciousness expands into the future with its unlimited possibilities. The Eureka! experience is a very interesting form of expansion of the intentionality as it guides consciousness towards better knowledge and better understanding. These hidden capacities of the mind have been giving signals all along; if people have remained blind to them it would be very useful to study the reasons and how to unblock our awareness. There may be a lot more that is giving signals to blind spots. Moreover, the recognition in others of this moment of realisation consolidates the inter-human link, the awareness of "the other" as "one just like me", one who has these weird little moments, just like mine.

Here something perfectly normal and experienced by most people may be given mystical status. This was very common in the past but it has not disappeared completely. Many thought that these answers were brought into their dreams or daydreaming by gods, dead relatives or angels, raising the unconscious to wondrous heights and assuming it also had the capacity to communicate with external entities. It is not difficult to imagine that the process of asking ourselves when awake: "What would so and so (somebody respected or revered by me) do in this situation?" could be reproduced in allegorically and symbolically charged dreams, where I could see myself actually asking the question in person to someone appearing to me in the form of a mythical or mystical figure. When solutions to problems or a piece of advice arrive in this dramatic packaging, we tend to remember them. When they just emerge as awareness but without any special fireworks, we often forget them.

How much wisdom do we let go unrecorded by forgetting these moments of awareness! The problem is solved for our consciousness and there is no longer the search for a solution that will eventually sprout another moment of clarity. Here is another thought for *Homo Intentional*: always carry a little notebook and never let these gifts of your own consciousness go unrecognised.

Pragmatism v Idealism

Let us see now forms of thinking that may contribute to our intentional mind. Our consciousness builds up its first and basic structure on the basis of simple and immediate pleasure (scoring a hit) and pain (failure to do so). This has contributed to developing a whole system of social organisation based on pragmatism. Although the immediacy of success (or failure) was not the essence of the original proposal,[9] only the short term success or failure of people's actions became the parameter to be considered in order to decide on the rightness or wrongness of those actions. This transformation was promoted by its application to a consumerist society that was already becoming infantilised by its advertising-driven compulsion towards immediate gratification.

Since the trial and error on/off switch seems to work well in the formative years it might appear at first sight, logical to think that it will continue to work later. However, already in our childhood people start to ask us: "What would you like to be when you grow up?" Later we begin to ask ourselves this question and proceed to form an ideal of how we would like to spend the rest of our lives and the things we would like to achieve. Many will continue to live with simple pleasure or pain short-term objectives but most people develop ideals, or models of how the world, and themselves, should be in order to attain happiness.

In other words, pragmatic forms of thinking are immature, child-like and immediate (or "short-termist", as some newspapers have started to call policies based on this philosophy). Ideologies are the result of the next evolutionary step, one in which the intention of a human being or human group shapes their future relationships. Intentions are not necessarily good, but it is mature to accept responsibility for them, whereas in pragmatism the forces that seem to shape behaviour are seen as coming from outside, from others in a purely behaviourist conception and even from outside humanity. The latter is clear in the economic expression of pragmatism, the Free

---

[9] Based on the thought and works of Charles Peirce, William James, John Dewey, in the late 1800s.

Market Economy, in which it is supposed that Market Forces will regulate people's behaviour as long as we do not try to interfere with them by planning. The effect of applying this ideology in its most ruthless form has already led to extreme poverty and collapse of whole economies in many parts of the world in a sort of global postcode euthanasia.

In Silo's definition "Human beings are historical beings whose form of social action changes their own nature", we can see the basis for intentional existence. By proposing ideals of how we would like to live we can launch actions into the world that ultimately will transform it and us. What is interesting to note is that nothing guarantees that such ideals will ever be reached, and it is likely that ideals will change over time, given that the formative landscapes of those launching the ideals will also be different. In this way the Hegelian Absolute that inspired Marx's Ideal Socialism can be seen as a static view of the process of evolution in need of a "final" point, a state to be achieved from where change is no longer necessary (or possible? a sort of social entropy?). More recently Francis Fukuyama repeated this conceptualisation by characterising Liberal Democracy as "the end of history". We should not confuse "ideals" with an inability to imagine processes that continue to produce change and development indefinitely. Similarly it would be an act of violence to attempt to chain future generations to our own idea of perfection. Intentional life is our escape from determinism and our search for freedom as long as we acknowledge the same right to intentional life for others. The acknowledgement that we are capable of changing our own "human nature" may be felt as something that puts a lot of responsibility on our shoulders. However it also opens a tremendous amount of freedom towards the future for each person that accepts that no matter how complete and monumental the oppression felt in a particular situation, there is always a possibility to apply one's own intentions to modify it. Even if our body is chained, even if we are about to die, we are still able to change our attitude and our point of view in that situation.

If we give up our ideals, if we accept that pragmatism is the correct way to plan (by not really planning beyond the first step, or rather, by believing that we are not planning but choosing to ignore that others are), in the future we will continue to repeat the mistake of giving financial and military support to those seen as today's allies on the grounds that it is tactically convenient without regard for the long-term consequences. Both Osama bin Laden and Saddam Hussein were given that kind of support by Western countries in their fight against communism and Islamic fundamentalism respectively. What new fiends are being created today? Who is being fed money and weapons to help fight today's Most Hated Enemy? Like boomerang Frankenstein's Monsters these creations will continue to come back to haunt the next generation, our children, our children's children. Under attack, our descendants will also ask themselves "Why do they hate us so much?" Well, ask Grandad.

Is it not time to end this pragmatic and vicious circle of support to violence that ensures that more violence will continue to taint everybody's lives later on?

Not only we are pragmatically choosing our bedfellows very badly, we are also pragmatically burning all our fuel, filling our planet with rubbish, making our air unbreathable and selling to private companies the services such as healthcare, water supply, electricity etc. that should be available to all who enter into the unwritten social contract. The only way to guarantee that services will continue to be available to all is to administer them from democratically elected bodies that represent the would-be users of those services. We have pragmatically allowed the concentration of wealth and resources in fewer and fewer hands, waiting for the famous free market dogma that wealth shall trickle down, eventually, if we allow it to accumulate in the first place. This model does not take into account the need to reinvest the accumulated wealth in maintaining the system so that it continues to allow for the accumulation of wealth. Wealth does not trickle down because money is busily bribing (or as it is euphemistically called "lobbying ") politicians to produce more tax cuts for the rich and paying for the electoral campaigns of those who shamelessly represent the interests of the ones who do not need any more money, but for whom making money has become their meaning in life. Britain has woken up to the awareness that Royal Honours are bestowed in exchange for making large contributions to political parties. The only surprising thing was the pretence of surprise about this murky business.

More worryingly, the accumulated wealth is also paying for the electoral campaigns of corrupt politicians in other much poorer countries who will ensure that more money goes to the very rich in developed countries than to the very deprived in their own ones.

Many people, many rich people, feel bad about this state of affairs. Most poor people feel bad about this state of affairs. Why does it continue then? Why do we continue to vote for the same candidates that keep the same system going? We do so because we are being "pragmatic". We are following the line of least resistance. That is the way that requires the least energy. It is easy to accept the view, coming from our colourful plasma screen TV that "there is no alternative". Not having faith in the possibility of change is closely linked to not having the energy to engage in creating such a possibility. It is a chicken and egg situation: "I do not trust any politician, therefore I do not vote", "I do not really know any of the new faces, therefore I vote for the usual ones even if they have already betrayed me and my hopes", or I give my vote to them again because there is another candidate that feels even worse, also known as tactical voting, etc. The politicians are only too happy to play the game. "Don't you worry your pretty little head about how to create social justice, peace and affluence. Just leave it to us".

Having ideals is hard work; living by one's own ideals close to impossible. The pressure to comply with the status quo is massive. And yet, if we want to feel well there is no alternative but to live by a positive set of ideals. Michael Moore, in his book *Dude, Where is my Country?*, reports that the actor Tim Robbins asked this question: "If the neo-Conservatives are winning, if they have all the power and all the money and all the security, why do they still look so angry?" The answer is because they are being pragmatic. They are living for the immediate future, for their immediate family and friends circle, for the immediate satisfaction of their pleasure. Someone should tell them that pragmatism is not the road to feeling happy. They have plenty of ideas but no ideals. Their view of the world is that if they only had more money and more power (including the power to invade more countries with impunity) they would be happy. They are angry because they do not realise that the climate of paranoia they are helping to create boomerangs back into their own lives to increase their fear. Acting pragmatically in the face of fear, not caring about the deep roots of aggression but just shooting back, is not the way to achieve happiness.

The intentional mind rejoices in the ideal world that might exist one day. The work done in this direction already makes it real for those who share the dream. It does not detach them from the suffering of the poor and the victims of discrimination, but as long as there is action for change there is joy and there is hope. Here is by way of example a quote from Martin Luther King's speech the day before he was assassinated: "...And I've looked over, and I've seen the Promised Land. I may not get there with you, but I want you to know tonight that we as a people will get to the Promised Land. So I'm happy tonight. I'm not worried about anything. I'm not fearing any man."

Ideals should not be confused with simple desires. Wanting a new house, a new car, more sex or even a better self-image are objectives that move us in the world towards things that are basically temporary and unable to give real meaning and direction to a whole life. Ideals refer to new ways of being, for us and for others, that leave this world in a better state than we found it. They may even be unreachable in our lifetime, and yet they make us feel profoundly connected to them, as if they were already around us. They link us also to whichever generation may actually see them become a reality. In the image of an ideal not only does the world become perfect, but our own self, submerged in it, also achieves the glow of such perfection. Idealists are often dismissed as hopeless dreamers. The difference between the two is action. Dreamers who fail to pursue their dreams fear to wake up. But dreamers who are Idealists, are activists who feed themselves with energy from their image of a better world and utilise that energy to work tirelessly to achieve it. They are, indeed, more awake than anybody in the world.

These are not mechanical positions, things that just "happen" to us, differences in our "nature". These are choices. There is much in the world we have not chosen. There is a culture and a body we have not chosen. We can choose to change them, to improve them, to humanise them and to become intentional beings.

The Future

A better and open future is very much connected to making sense of one's consciousness, as death imposes a limit to that future and to that meaning. Therefore our view of death is central to human existence. Some currents of thought, generally religious, have projected an after-life similar to life. No problem there. If one is capable of believing it feels quite nice. The identification of the mind with the brain creates more problems, the brain dies, and the mind disappears. The solution: cryogenics. Not to everybody's taste, and very expensive.

Philosophers have spent a lot of time debating about the Brain/Mind relationship. Why is this so if there is no similar problem with the Stomach and Digestion? Probably because we do not identify the meaning of our lives with the continuing existence of our digestion but we do identify our transcendental existence with the persistence of our minds and in particular to the register of personal identity.

Strategies for not dying: we fuse, we merge, with something that will stay around for ever, or at least for a long time. We can do it by falling in love, idealising the other person to the point of believing the sentiments that unite us to them eternal, and then becoming so involved that we "disappear" as an independent being. We fuse, we merge, with them. This is Chemistry masquerading as Eternity. It does not last very long. The auto-hypnotic idealisation of another human being soon clashes with unexpected behaviour, little imperfections and their own mortality. So we blame the other for failing us, because they failed our dream of the forevermore.

We fuse and merge with God in religions, with Nature in the green culture, with the Cause in politics and with King and Country to go to war. As long as fusing with an idealised eternal entity can stun our individual finality we can forget our fear of death.

Reincarnation is gaining sympathisers in the West. It is of great interest to see how much the plot of going through successive incarnations until we get it right reminds us of the normal process of transference that our consciousness carries out in order to elaborate conflicts by re-enacting them in dreams   (often allegorically), daydreaming and behaviour until we find a more positive outcome to those experiences. This creates the suspicion that the semi-awareness of what is going on in our minds may acquire the status of a whole belief system by extrapolation under appropriate circumstances. Once more we are reminded of the old Sufi adage "Angels are the hidden powers of men". Conversely, of course, we may be resonating in life with much higher processes. There are compelling artistic expressions of this theme in literature (*Jonathan Livingston Seagull* by Richard Bach) and in cinema (*Groundhog Day*).

Phenomenology and its Eastern cousins quieten the rational mind and go fishing for experiences. Gnostics and agnostics claim possession of the truth.

The most important issue escapes us in the midst of so many diverse answers: we are all asking the same question and we are also capable of having the same experiences. We differ in the cultural interpretations, in the narratives, in the forms. Perhaps this is the time to remember our friend in the Prologue, the elephant.

Chapter 5

VIOLENCE (*is*) FOR DUMMIES

Intentionality lies at the point of intersection between two complementary qualities of the human being: individuality and sociability. The recognition that each consciousness must structure the world and itself in its own particular way, for the simple reason that there are no two people with identical experiences, is the base for the sense of uniqueness and the right of every individual to his/her own subjective point of view. On the other hand we also recognise in others a commonality of mechanisms of consciousness such as a direction away from pain and suffering and towards happiness, a capacity to learn and discover as well as to believe and to wonder whether our choices are pre-determined or free, a craving for, and fear of, freedom and so many other things. By acknowledging this we also realise that intentionality itself is the most important common characteristic shared by all people and therefore the basic building block for solidarity between human beings, seen in this way as a joint struggle for the right to diversity in our vision of the world.

It is possible to design a simple cognitive exercise to shift one's intentionality either towards individualism or towards solidarity "modes" of operation.

Mode 1 - Individualism: thinking about one's personal death and the fact that the world as we know it will disappear when our brain based mind functions cease to exist creates a sense of separation from all other human beings. Likewise concentrating only on the times when we were let down or attacked by others strengthens a sense of alienation from other people. Giving way to fears about the future that are usually presented to stimulate competition such as: "unemployment is increasing", "only the rich will survive an environmental catastrophe" and "violent crime will get us unless we live in a fortress" can also close the door of our hearts and minds to all, save for a few relatives and friends.

Mode 2 - Solidarity: If we start to look at things around us we may notice that the chair/sofa/stool on which we are sitting has been made by someone else The same is true for most other objects in our rooms/houses and the technology we use every day (TV, car, washing machine, sliced bread, non-drip oil bottle top, mobile phone), as they have been developed by other people. Similarly the thoughts in our minds are the result of thousands of years of human evolution and our language, gestures and beliefs have all been strongly influenced by interaction with other people and by our education. In this way we begin to see that if any of us were the only or the first human being on Earth his or her life would be completely different. The contents of one's minds would be completely different; in fact we would be entirely somebody else. If we think about the future we may also perceive that problems or illnesses that we might suffer from later in life are probably going to be resolved by others who are still to develop those solutions. This should make us review our contribution to those people, i.e., are we making it possible for them to get there? Or are we contributing to putting stumbling blocks in their way? Could that child dying in this or that war (which apparently bears no connection with me) be the one with the potential to save my life or the life of one of my loved ones in the future? And from a wider perspective, are we helping children from all social strata and all geographical areas receive a reasonable education and a healthy diet so that they develop their full potential for everybody's (including our own) benefit?

As we can see, solidarity with other human beings can be triggered even by the most selfish reasons, also known as enlightened self-interest. If in addition we remember the way we felt in the past when we were able to help someone else, when we managed to communicate at a deeper level than our "normal" social interactions, when we were able to open the future for another person or when we felt compassion for others, a whole new chapter can open in our interaction with the social world. If we imagine then the number of people who we may be able to help and to whose future development we may be able to contribute, our expansion and connection with the rest of the human species may have no limits. It is not possible to feel solidarity when the future is threatened if we only realise the future is threatened for ourselves.

When Edmund Husserl, seen in general as the father of phenomenology, described intentionality he saw a social world of granted inter-subjectivities, as if nothing could deprive human beings of their own personal point of view. Perhaps his intense concentration on the study of consciousness made him less sensitive to the power of social interaction, even after seeing his own brilliant disciple Heidegger who, having dedicated to his teacher, a Jew, his most important book *Being and Time*, was to be, if only temporarily, so completely swallowed by Hitler's huge propaganda machine as to actually become a member of the Nazi Party.

J-P Sartre introduces the influence of "the look" from another human being upon the way we construe or structure a situation. His example presents to us a person looking through a keyhole into another room. Suddenly he hears footsteps and immediately he feels "shame", he sees his own actions as reprehensible. But if he discovers that the steps belong to an animal rather than to a person this external "look" disappears and he can engage again in his Peeping Tom activities. Other phenomenologists (e.g. Silo) have studied more in depth the way "looks" modulate the effects of intentionality in the interaction with the social world. He concluded that intentionality is not such a guaranteed right. There exists a massive influence allowed to politicians, opinion formers and public figures in general, who have their views carried by ever-present and intrusive mass media. In general terms these media are owned by the same social layer they report on and respond to, and they subject the intentionality of the individual to reality testing external pressures, and even the struggle for survival. These are strong influences, which added to education and a good dose of TV and cinema throughout our formative years put a lot of pressure on our consciousness to structure the world in one direction or another.

> *The denial of the intentionality of another human being is the common denominator to all forms of violence.*

A person's consciousness structures the world in a particular way. It is not, as we have seen, just a passive subjective interpretation (a dirty piece of glass through which we look at the things that surround us), but rather it is an active process that guides all the activities developed by that person. At each step he/she is going to receive a feedback from the world, inanimate but more particularly social, which will corroborate or contradict the original interpretation made by his/her consciousness. Corroboration is received as proof of being right. It produces a sense of pleasure, of agreement and of expansion. The opposite is less pleasant and leads to a reappraisal of the original structuring which may be ratified (moving to confrontation with the source of negative feedback) or changed (leading to agreement with it). The person may also choose to suppress his/her own point of view for self-preservation (leading to a sort of "shrinkage" of the intentionality, a sense of reduced freedom and of oppression).

Let us see an example: A person walks into an interview for a job thinking: "I am the best candidate". He/she answers the questions asked by the interviewers and leaves convinced that they were satisfied with the responses. The following day this person receives one of two possible phone-calls:

(1) "Yes, you got the job". Here our subject experiences a sense of expansion, agreement, pleasure and open future. The Universe has order. It makes sense. "There is a God after all", thinks our friend.

(2) "No, you did not get the job". Here the flow chart splits. Three reactions are possible:

Reaction A: "Maybe I was not the best candidate. The person who got the job may have had more experience, or did better in the interview. I must prepare myself better for next time"; here there is still agreement with the environment, the future is still open, but postponed.

Reaction B: "I was the best candidate but they did not give me the job because the panel was racist/sexist/classist/friends with the person who got the job/deceived by the successful candidate". Here there is a strong sense of confrontation with the way the environment has structured the situation, but intentionality keeps the future open, even if a degree of struggle and defiance will be needed to progress.

Reaction C: "It's OK; I know I didn't deserve a promotion". Here intentionality shrinks, accepts defeat, lets the future become closed.

We have grown used to the commonly held belief that the way our minds react to a situation is fixed; we are this way or that way. Seeing a glass as half full or half empty has been used to describe whether a person is optimistic or pessimistic. Much more interesting is to note the capacity of consciousness to intentionally shift the view between those two perceptions. We can choose to see the glass half full or half empty. We can choose to see the crisis we are living in the world today as a disaster or as an opportunity for change. We can choose to see our history of violence as proof that the human being is incapable of peaceful co-existence or as evidence that if we do not change fundamentally the way we organise ourselves, eliminating social injustice for all, the future will indeed be rather unpleasant. We can choose to see all scientific advances as a threat or as a hope that has to be well directed by ethical principles.

We tend to justify not making choices on the basis that one of several possibilities is more "true" than the others or in a sense of inevitability. This is correct in certain situations. If a person jumps from a 15th floor he/she will die on reaching the pavement. There is a real world in which determinism applies. A child in the middle of a famine in Africa who goes without food for a long time will also die or be dramatically damaged in terms of brain development. There are other situations that admit a variety of interpretations that will lead to different outcomes. In these cases, very often it is our actions that make one possibility truer or more likely. We must learn to pay attention in order to detect which situations that admit several possible futures are presented to us as if they were deterministic. These are common examples from politicians: "Free Market Capitalism may not be perfect, but it is the only possible system", or, "A vote for a small party is a wasted vote" even if that party represents the voter's exact aspirations.

When a person's ideas or beliefs do not coincide with those of the majority (or rather, with those of the dominant sectors of society with exclusive access to the dissemination of their point of view), the intentionality of this person suffers a process of successive clashes with "reality". Initially he or she may try confrontation but after a while they may feel overwhelmed and forced to retreat into a progressively shrinking intentionality. This is registered by consciousness as oppression/suffering and several reactions may develop:

Option 1: To continue shrinking until disappearing into nihilistic oblivion, as we can see in suicide and cynicism. A partial form of this option can be seen in single issue politics, where those involved may become compulsively active in changing a minute part of a whole system they perceive as wrong but too big and too strong to change in a more general and meaningful way. In spite of knowing that their efforts are akin to attempting to straighten the pictures on the walls of one's house in the middle of an earthquake, the register of having some control over their environment gives nevertheless an outlet for the shrinking intentionality. In some cases, this may even lead to a widening of the effort to tackle deeper and more general issues.

Option 2: To expand into an unreal world where no more "reality" testing is possible, such as hallucinogenic or mood destabilising drugs. Many "Ecstasy" users have described a sense of togetherness and closeness with other people given by its use in "raves", suggesting that it is taken in an attempt to compensate for a sense of isolation in the real world. Deaths produced by this drug do not seem to deter its users who are generally adolescents enjoying the most universal right of passage: that for the first time they are at liberty to risk their lives. Video games have also been used in this way, often leading to addictive behaviour. Virtual Reality has been heralded as the ultimate form of escape from reality testing.

During the decade of the 1960's and in the midst of a widespread rebellion against the established order, psychosis was seen by some as another form of flight from reality. Whilst it is clear now that stress may precipitate psychosis in predisposed individuals (and the more severe the stress the less predisposition is needed) psychosis itself is rarely a pleasant experience, and more often than not it leads to a much higher level of stress and suffering. Most films reflecting psychosis from an experiential point of view are in fact horror films. The blurring of boundaries between psychosis and rebellion against the establishment not only led countries like the USSR and to a lesser degree the USA to treat dissidents and rebels as being mentally ill; it also resulted in many ordinary (and very disoriented) people following profoundly psychotic individuals as if they were social and religious leaders, with lethal consequences in some well publicised cases. Moreover, many saw psychosis as a "right" or a "choice", not accepting that biochemical and/or structural brain changes, as well as environmental factors, may cause a breakdown in the capacity for intentionality to structure the world in the most adequate way. Whilst this extreme vision of mental illness may have been misguided it drew nevertheless attention to the important role of social stress in the genesis and recurrence of mental illness. It also led to a more holistic approach to its treatment, although sadly not yet to its prevention. In spite of a wealth of research related to the increase in mental disorder brought about by social trends such as unemployment and the breakdown in social cohesion, very little is being done to reverse these tendencies. Rather we witness an exacerbation of policies that fragment neighbourhoods, families and workplaces. The attitude towards psychological damage is a preference for relying more and more on finding the next "happy pill" that can both compensate for the effects of social distress on the unfortunate individuals who happen to be sensitive to it, and absolve the rest of us from the responsibility of creating a more human-friendly environment. Let us not forget in this equation the profits of a few pharmaceutical companies. There have been, of course, great advances in the pharmacology of treating mental illness, but as more and more of the people who fifty years ago would have spent the rest of their lives in an institution are rehabilitated back into society, we discover that society is not such a wonderful place after all. In fact it has a tendency to send people back into the institutions by discriminating against them and by being more uncaring and stress-inducing as time goes by.

Option 3: To expand in solidarity by finding others who feel equally oppressed in their points of view in order to attempt to modify the prevailing order or ideology. This is the principle operating in the formation of some political parties, trade unions, self-help organisations, social movements, community associations and pressure groups. This is the most creative channel for putting frustration, anger and aggressive feelings at the service of making improvements in oppressive conditions. It must be differentiated from the suppression of such feelings, which, for instance in the face of a potential war, may give rise to a limp pacifism akin to acquiescence and resignation, different from active non-violence that transforms frustration into an proactive and joyful changing force. Activation of people who share their sense of oppression puts intentionality at the centre of human evolution.

Option 4: To expand in revenge by joining an extremist or terrorist group where the ideology is mainly an excuse for cathartic violence. The ensuing persecution both confirms the initial structuring made of the oppressive situation, in a sort of self-fulfilling prophesy, and promotes an even stronger oppression that reinforces the vicious circle of violence and destruction. At a very primitive level we see that the bullied become bullies whenever they have the opportunity to do so, unless they have managed to transform their negative experiences into a creative force. Felicity de Zulueta in her book *From Pain to Violence* gives a sound psychological understanding of these mechanical tendencies. There is no possible resolution to the violence of individuals or whole peoples until we understand and help relieve the pain at its root.

Option 5: To adapt to the ways of expansion actually promoted by the same system that is registered as oppressive. Or, in other words, "If you cannot beat them, join them". This process can be seen in many people who make money compulsively as a way to ensure acceptance by others from whom they feel isolated or experience discrimination. The immense success of the "rags to riches" novels speaks of the massive identification with these stories by ordinary people feeling the shrinkage of their intentionality in an uneven economic system. However, given that in this case money is not used to satisfy needs but as a "universal expander" or self-esteem builder, a compensation for an inner sense of inadequacy and insignificance, those who succeed can hardly find how much is enough. This becomes therefore another factor in the process of concentration of wealth, since what is felt as meaningful is not "having" money but "becoming" richer.

On the other hand, in systems where power is concentrated in only one political party such as Communism, the expansion of the individual's intentionality is achieved by rising through the ranks of that party, as it happened, for instance, in the ex-Soviet Union. For a hierarchical structure to exercise the strongest pull towards its highest echelons it has to provide true privilege to its most successful members. Communism recreated in this way the forces found in societies based on a monarchical and aristocratic system of privilege, rather than eliminating it as stated in its intentions. These mechanisms perpetuate and increase the oppression they attempt to compensate.

No consciousness is completely free from external influence. This in itself is not a form of violence because a historical accumulation of ideas is essential for new ones to appear (otherwise each new person being born would have to discover anew the use of fire and invent the wheel), but this historical accumulation provides a cultural and personal substratum that is not neutral. It rather depends on what information about historical events has been made available to a particular generation or human group. This is of course also under the control of those in power at the time. We do not remember all this information, or how it got in. During our formative years we were told about people who did things in the past and they were presented to us as models that deserved to be imitated. Others were depicted as the bad guys, but still the message was that they managed to do something that was important enough for us to remember them. Some of them were people whom today we would have no problem recognising as being full of unspeakable hatred or profoundly disturbed. People whose compulsions, whose deviant behaviour, whose violence secured them a place in history simply because they viciously wiped out the opposition and lived to write the History books, were presented to our innocence as "our human history". What amount of alternative reading must one do to neutralise the influence of so much bias in favour of violence, when we are not even capable of remembering most of the generals and kings who, famous only for their conquest of other lands and total disregard for the lives of those who inhabited them, lie at the bottom of our consciousness, influencing our judgements and pretending to be part of our "human nature"?

Many see utilitarian value in our history of war and violence. It is easy to see that during wars records of events are kept feverishly and obsessively in all their gory details. Wars are factories of heroic deeds to be used at a later stage as models. Therefore, none must be lost. The memory of those who die for their country, for others, must be kept alive, being the only saving grace of an otherwise completely meaningless act. War is glamorised, sensationalised, advertised. Peace, in contrast, can be taken for granted and therefore it does not produce the same motivation to make records of events or describe individual remarkable acts. Therefore, if it had not been for the moments of conflict we would not have had so much information about our past. This argument, however, fails to recognise that the most important revolutions, the great creative moments of humanity, have been linked to attempts to overcome this history of mindless violence. The Renaissance followed the Dark Ages and something akin to the League of Nations was Kant's brainchild to end wars in Europe. Similarly those who see positive spin-offs coming from research into weapons of mass destruction should remember that Germany and Japan achieved their highest level of technological development during the post-Second World War years, when they were not allowed to have their own armies or develop their own weapons. Human beings have learned to create positive outcomes out of tragic situations. We could say that we have vaccines thanks to smallpox and more international co-operation on nuclear safety thanks to Chernobyl. These positive spin-offs do not, however, render the original tragedies any less destructive, and this also applies to technology that emerges from military research.

Not everything we learned during our formative years was, of course, about war and violence. We must also acknowledge the influences that opened our eyes to more constructive visions. How many of us would have realised by ourselves, after spending about 20 years of education repeating in parrot fashion the history lesson about the Discovery of America, that the American Continent was not "discovered", that this is a Eurocentric vision of history since this "New World" had its own inhabitants (who were later decimated by the process of colonisation) and that a more appropriate way of looking at it would be that Europe "became aware" of the existence of the Americas? How many other insights came to us after reading or hearing about other people's ideas? And how are we to differentiate, then, those influences that lead to increasing our freedom of choice, empathy and an open future from those other ones, the subtle (or not so subtle) manipulation of those intent on using us as instruments of their own machinations, the power mad, the tyrants, the dictators?

Perhaps a good start in this selection process would be the use of our attention to our own feelings and sensations as the most powerful filter, because the register of suffering and oppression of one's own intentionality bullied by a bigger one is unmistakable. It may express itself as a register of being subjected to physical, economic, racial, religious or sexual violence, or as less easily visible forms such as psychological violence. Attention to the consequences of the ideas we hear about and comparing them with our own experience is the key to individual freedom in a context of active communication. When we become aware of an idea that opens the future without excluding anyone, promoting solidarity and social justice, it is worth listening to it very carefully, even if it does not come to us packaged in the glitzy kudos that makes political and commercial advertising so attractive to the senses.

Chapter 6

(SELF) HELP!

The register of oppression at both psychological and bodily levels expresses itself as stress. Stress has been defined as "loss of control over one's own environment". There is a particular form of stress that appears after catastrophic events that are outside the remit of usual human experience, such as serious accidents, plane hijacks, wars or earthquakes. It can lead to a clinical condition that has been called Post Traumatic Stress Disorder[10], and it is characterised by painful re-living flashes of the catastrophe, avoidance of situations that are similar or remind the person of the original event, numbness, and feeling startled by normal everyday occurrences such as somebody knocking at the door. An important feature of the syndrome that contributes to a better understanding of the relationship between intentionality and violence is that some research has found that this condition is most severe when the traumatic situation is manufactured intentionally (wars, terrorist attacks, torture, etc.), as opposed to accidents and natural phenomena, and in the former cases not only the victims but also the perpetrators are likely to develop it. This has been seen, for instance, after the Latin American military dictatorships of the 1970's that consistently used torture as an instrument of social control (torture is *always* an instrument of social control, albeit "justified" by the need to obtain information). Today not only the victims but also many of the torturers are emerging with this syndrome. It appears that the most profound violations of other people's intentionality leave the deepest scars, and that in the realm of violence there are no winners.

More usually people live in situations less dramatic, where stress could also be described as "a sensation of not being able to express freely one's own intentionality in an environment where there exists a situation of power". In this case stress is the symptom that arises from a

---

[10] Previously known as Shell Shock and Soldier's Heart. The first description appears to have been in Shakespeare's Henry V

scenario of social violence. However, this kind of stress has often been medicalised and individualised as if the sufferer had a "personal problem" or, in other words, he or she had "something wrong with him/her", something that required "treatment". There may be also a sense of being weird, maladapted or inadequate.

For this reason many people tend not to express their stress. They suppress it, trying at the same time to appear (except for extreme cases) more or less at ease with their situations. When stressed up individuals look around and find that other people appear to be fine they follow their example and also (at least try to) appear to be fine. This collective deception helps perpetuate the situation of oppression acting upon each individual's intentionality. People need to overcome their fear of being rejected by others for being "the odd one out"; "sticking one's head out" or in the more poetic Indian phrase "being a tall poppy" has its risks, and many situations of oppression continue for long periods of time before someone dares to challenge them.

In spite of this (or perhaps because of it) solidarity is seen as a weakness in any highly competitive system. Individualism is reinforced in so many subtle ways not only as a form of strength (Hollywood repeats endlessly the myth of the individual who defeats the system all by himself, the lone hero) but also as a form of freedom.

The old axiom of social manipulation "Divide and Rule" is rooted in these mechanisms. Re-establishing the capacity for communication in a human community not only leads to an increase in empathy and a decrease in interpersonal violence, it also empowers its members to recover their intentionality and their right to choose in which way they want to live.

Words like dehumanisation and objectification attempt to describe social processes whose core is the emptying of the intentionality of an individual or of a group of people who are then seen as simple instruments of the intentionality of others, mainly of those in power. These are subtle forms of violence (no blood and/or guts) but they can destroy the spirit of a society because even those who dehumanise others end up surrounded by "things" and follow the same process for lack of human contact and empathy. Dehumanisation is a boomerang. In order to stop feeling for others one must harden oneself, put one's own emotions on ice. This has been expressed by those who promote and justify this order of things in the phrase "it is lonely at the top", but there is nobody left to feel compassion...

The 'Other'

One of the problems in the search for the meaning of consciousness is that when the mind investigates itself it goes into a kind of solipsistic or insular mode in which "the other" seems to recede into the background. If we take into account that everybody's consciousness would have been be completely different if we had been discussing this a few centuries ago, we can start to put the study of consciousness into a different perspective.

Consciousness is the product of social and historical evolution and the very fact that many researchers and philosophers are asking themselves now if it possible for a computer to develop consciousness, and whether we are surrounded by consciousness-less zombies who just appear to act like humans, is the product of the social environment in which we find ourselves today. There is nothing more epochal than the way we interact with the objects presented to our consciousness.

The simple relationship we have with animals has changed historically beyond recognition. Take the example of the Human and The Lion:

Stage 1: Man is part of lion's staple diet.

Stage 2: Man builds protection against lion and learns to use fire to keep it away.

Stage 3: Man builds weapon that kills lion, first as self-defence, later as rite of passage.

Stage 4: Man finds lion's head aesthetically pleasing in his living room.

Stage 5: Man learns to catch lion alive and displays it in zoos both for information and for affirmation of his power over lion.

Stage 6: Man feels sorry for caged lion and its possible extermination. Man develops a protective role towards lion.

Stage 7: Lion presented to the public in nature films as a regular family guy, Man as the bloodthirsty beast.

Stage 8: Man holds long international conferences to debate the relative rights of Man and Lion. Lion yawns and flips a fly with its tail.

Stage 9: Lion gains the right to inhabit a reserved piece of land. Man (some people, poor ones) evicted from it so that Man (other people, more affluent) may visit Lion in its natural environment.[11]

---

[11] *Barred from animal's kingdom*: by Lucy Johnston, The Observer 3 April 1997

Not only the relationship has changed but basically the concept of lion: from danger to endangered passing through entertainment, ornament, object of study, proof of power and sitting tenant, what we think about lions is largely an epochal, cultural, economic and even geographical matter.

You may have noticed in this example a departure from the use of non-sexist language that is pervasive in other parts of this book, but the symbolic role that lions have played in human history, in particular our need to assert our power over them, has been largely a masculine pursuit.

Our relationship with our own consciousness and that of others is a more complex but equally epochal process. The conceptual bricks accumulate vertically in such a way that new constructs are only possible because the old ones have been laid down. In Sir Isaac Newton's assertion (in a rare moment of humility, if we are to believe the gossip about his relationship with colleagues) "If I have seen further it is by standing on the shoulders of giants", he acknowledges the role of the necessary accumulation of knowledge throughout history.

Returning to the substratum of beliefs we acquire uncritically during our formative years, it is interesting to see that not all the bricks are equally solid and amongst the foundations of our ideas and belief systems we count not only on the genius of the Galileos, the Socrates and the Einsteins but also on a long tradition of famous mass murderers who found a place in history precisely because they imposed their power upon others by force, such as Alexander the "Great" and other "Conquistadors". And again we should remember that it is quite possible that a few ideas arising from people who were profoundly disturbed also got into this pile of bricks. And this building we call "human nature" in the absence of awareness of the way our consciousness is formed throughout our lives (but more precisely over our formative years) by the social learning of historically developed human attributes. However, this learning is not mechanical and, depending on the development of a critical sense and feedback from our environment, we start to pick and choose and to decide on our direction. A critical sense can also be learnt, encouraged or discouraged by our formative process. These choices are strongly related to the shape that the social environment takes around us. A sense of generalised injustice and isolation creates different choices than a loving, caring environment ruled by solidarity and empathy. We must also point out here that no matter how homogeneous or monolithic one's social environment may be, it is never completely deterministic. Dissidents, critics of the established order and rebels have appeared in every situation where there is pain and suffering to be overcome.

Most currents that uphold the existence of a fixed and unchangeable "human nature" sin on the side of laziness or bad faith by discouraging and curtailing the efforts of those who see opportunities for the development of a different human being, free from violence and fear.

The process of dehumanisation has become a social climate within which discussions about artificial intelligence and whether "the other" is felt as a person, a mindless zombie or an object are generated. It also has a long history but its tempo has been accelerating since the beginning of the Industrial Revolution. At the time many noticed that as production became divorced from those who manufactured it in the production line, it felt as if people were becoming part of the machine. Films such as Fritz Lang's *Metropolis* (1926) in Germany and Charles Chaplin's *Modern Times* (1936) in the USA communicated this awareness and much was discussed and proposed by different currents of thought, but the needs created by two world wars somehow moved the concerns to the problem of security where "the other" existed mainly as a hostile intention and, as in all wars, had to be completely dehumanised so that perfectly normal and usually non-violent people could kill one another.

It is precisely this sense of threat from "the other", and the consequent lack of control over his/her intentions, that lead to a sense of frustration at not being able to gain direct access to the other's consciousness. This is at the basis of the alienation or anomie[12] of a society in a state of fragmentation, where most information reaches us through the one-way system of the mass media. Whilst common sense and experience show that communication with "the other" can be easily re-established in local communities or places of study and work, the search for access to and control of "the other's" mind does not cease.

---

[12] Emile Durkheim, a French sociologist, introduced the concept of anomie in his book *The Division of Labour in Society*, (1893) to describe the breakdown of rules so that people no longer knew what to expect from one another.

There have been rebellions against the apparent separateness of minds from each other and from their environment, sometimes expressed as a craving in many to demonstrate the non-locality of mind (a concept stemming from quantum theory in its questioning the concept of space as it appears to our ordinary experience) such as mind reading, telekinesis, etc. Perhaps the enforced indirectness of contact with other people's consciousness should not be seen as a barrier but as a safeguard for intentional connectivity and for the development of an evolving consciousness seeking its own coherence and capable of developing solidarity. In this context "the other" can be seen as an equal, a pal, a companion for such quest, someone who can share discoveries and a source of verification of phenomena by comparison of experience.

Trying to possess or manipulate another's mind is violence. Objectifying others by denying they have a subjective mind is violence. Expecting the other to conform to our rules, our beliefs, our lifestyle and morality is violence.

Making agreements for the common task liberates us from this violence. Listening to others and communicating our ideas, beliefs and principles openly and without expecting to impose them on others releases us from violence.

Non-violence is an intentional process that needs to be learned anew because we cannot trust our historical background to lead us to it mechanically. We are not completely free to make a choice between violence and non-violence since such a background has left a heavy mark on our capacity to make future choices, but knowing that those choices exist is the first step towards our own liberation. Those who choose violence in their quest for political power should be aware that in doing so they also condone violence perpetrated against themselves, their families and their friends, most probably for many generations to come. Although Gandhi's fasts may not translate well into hunger strikes in a Western world where feeling hungry means that the diet is working, non-violence must remain creative to continue to reach out to the heart of "the other" to make them aware of our shared human quality.

There are vested interests that obstruct the efforts of those struggling to end violence, such as the people who benefit financially from the Arms Trade and others who depend on violence to win elections. Dr James Gilligan and his team started an education programme for the inmates of a Massachusetts prison. There was some evidence that six months after release those who had completed the programme were at reduced risk of offending. When the new (Republican) governor of Massachusetts heard about this, he stopped the programme "in case it encouraged people to commit crimes to get an education." [13]

The end of violence cannot come easily to humanity in pain. It cannot come easily to those who live in fear or with the memory of atrocities perpetrated against themselves and their loved ones. Compassion, not just for one's fellow oppressed but also for one's oppressors, may appear ridiculous and absurd in situations of such obscene injustice that our whole being clamours for revenge. And yet, when we become aware that oppressors are also suffering the pain of previous experiences of violence, that they also live in fear, when we realise that the only way to stop the endless cycle of violence is to stop today's injustice without creating *a new set of victims* who will later come back to claim their "rightful" vengeance, and when we see that a great deal of pressure from their environment has been at the root of their own role as oppressors, only then we can emerge from mechanical life towards becoming *Homo Intentional*.

---

[13] BMJ 2001;323:289 (4 August) Book Review: *Preventing Violence* by James Gilligan

Chapter 7

NEW PHYSICS, NEW WORLD ORDER, NEW AGE, OLD HAT

In the struggle to understand the world around us many points of view have been developed to study what we experience. Those points of view became later objects of study in themselves and the struggle widened to include antagonising perspectives.

In the early stages of human development primitive societies were characterised by supernatural explanations of natural phenomena, animism and magical thinking. More recently, thinkers and researchers seem to be aligning into two large tendencies: Reductionism vs. Holism. Reductionists try to understand the parts in order to understand the whole. Holists look at the general processes on the basis that "the whole is more than the sum of its parts"[14].

Polarisation into different (often opposing) positions is a positive process by which humanity becomes enriched by diversity. For Hegel this was the basic mechanism for the evolution of human thinking towards the Absolute, via successive stages of Thesis, Antithesis and Synthesis. However, the power struggles that develop between factions are often destructive and may lead to the suppression of one of the points of view, depriving the future of humanity from interesting lines of thinking.

Structural Thinking, developed by Silo during the 1960's and 70's, may offer a methodology to study systems that can help overcome the dichotomy between Reductionism and Holism opening the door for increasing comprehension. In a structural way a system can be studied in its different aspects:

a) *Composition*: Observing the parts that integrate the system.

b) *Relationships*: Observing how different elements within the structure are connected and how they influence one another.

c) *Process*: Following the structure from its origins, observing its direction, meaning and possible future.

---

[14] Aristotle

There are symptoms of the development of present thinking towards a structural view of the world. Structuralism, developed by Claude Lévi-Strauss, sees language as a structure that forms the cultural background from which the individual cannot be seen in isolation. However, it leaves the intentionality of consciousness somehow relegated to a rather passive role. It appears as a receptacle for the structuring power of society which is seen in this vision as the active element that conditions each individual consciousness. This process is carried out through the acquisition of language containing the social codes. Consciousness is therefore a passive reaction rather than being the ultimate motor for such structuring. Gestalt Theory also studies structures of behaviour, also pointing out that the whole has different qualities than the simple addition of the parts. System theories unite electronics and psychology in a more structural view of their subjects.

Other currents of thought have attempted to see the connections that exist between the most diverse elements. Arthur Koestler saw in Relativity Theory points in common with Astrology. Mystics are embracing enthusiastically concepts from Quantum Theory as explanations for the supernatural. Traditional and alternative medicines are beginning to mingle in practice. The statistical method is being applied to the study of the paranormal, and Chaos Theory is introducing precise mathematics to the unpredictability of natural phenomena.

After the discovery that the Earth was not the centre of the Universe but rather a smallish planet in a solar system located towards the periphery of one amongst a myriad of galaxies, came those who thought that our world of ideas was in anyway insignificant in the context of the macrocosms. The return to a more human centred vision of science has been partly the work of the Anthropic Principle (which points out that this is the only possible universe since if it were any different we would not be here to observe it) and partly of the quantum mechanics' view that the observer is part of the observation - which recalls Cézanne's statement that in art "the viewer is part of the view". These attempts to comprehend the interconnection between human beings and their environment, as well as trying to make sense in a structural way of what we understand from consciousness, not surprisingly appear coincidentally with the de-structuring and fragmenting context that became the hallmark of post-modern thinking. It was possible then to promote the destruction of the social fabric as a desirable state of being, an idea represented famously by Margaret Thatcher in her statement that "there is no such thing as society".

A structural vision of time lets us see that within the human consciousness time is not linear but rather a permanent interaction between past, present and future. Memory accumulated in our formative years creates the need to project into the future ways to reinforce the joys and compensate for the frustrations. This process affects our present-day planning, feelings and actions. An example of this would be: I produce in my mind an image of what I want to achieve, e.g., a University degree. This image pulls me from the future and helps me go through unpleasantly stressful exams. If I finally obtain the degree the future opens and all the suffering of the previous years (and even that of the more distant ones) becomes meaningful and necessary. If I fail the future becomes (momentarily) closed, my efforts meaningless, a review of my past takes place, in which events I had thought forgotten or overcome reopen and somehow become responsible for my failure. All this continues bringing suffering to the present until I manage to create another image of something I want to achieve in the future that sets me again into action. A more dramatic example is the one seen in soldiers and civilians who suffer from painful memories and the re-living of their experiences after witnessing the horrors of war. The symptoms that follow these past events may apparently disappear but often they just lie dormant until a threat to the person's future (job loss, loss of partner, health problem) brings them back to the fore with renewed intensity.

Processes that take place in the individual consciousness also happen in large human groups. The acceleration of the pace of change experienced by people in the second half of the twentieth century, as anticipated by Alvin Toffler in *The Future Shock* and by Silo in his concept of "acceleration of the historical tempo", and the consolidation of political and economic trends that increase human suffering have created an unclear and somehow threatening image of the future. This fear has become reinforced by the dangers of nuclear war, ecological catastrophe and massive unemployment as well as "The war on terror". Large numbers of people are trying to find in the past a measure of safety, in a way similar to what is known in psychology as "regression" (e.g., a child who goes back to thumb-sucking or bed wetting after the birth of a little brother or sister). This return to the past, to imaginary "safer" times, is expressed in the form of fundamentalist positions, whether Islamic, Christian, Jewish or belonging to any other religion or ideology. During the 1980's there was an attempt in the UK to turn back the clock and return to "Victorian values", a sort of moral fundamentalism.

We have also seen a return to magical thinking such as beliefs in witches and supernatural forces in what are generally known as "New Age" ideas. This is a return to very old traditions and a "holistic" view of the environment and people, many following an intuitive belief that we once "knew" and modern life has made us "forget". A particular case of magical thinking is animism, which was mentioned earlier. In childhood we may normally attribute intentions to inanimate objects and invisible friends. Early cultures have in the past attributed intentions to the sun, the moon, the winds and all types of natural phenomena that were in their eyes inexplicable and therefore believed to be under the influence of gods' intentions. Recently the Gaia theory acquired different interpretations according to various currents of thought. Some saw it as a simple description of homeostatic (self-regulatory) mechanisms in the Earth's atmosphere, but others attributed to our ecosystem the character of a living organism with intentionality, believing even that the Earth has the capacity to return to take revenge on the eco-offenders. Apart from its animistic character, this view may be counterproductive, as it creates the false impression that it is not necessary to look after the environment because it can look after itself.

Science Fiction, which in the 1940's and 1950's incorporated the incipiently spreading concepts arising from quantum and relativity theories in the form of time travel, hyper-space jumps and cybernetic minds, showed us also the preoccupation with the uncontrollable energy being released, and so many stories ended in catastrophe and destruction. The 80's and 90's Sci-fi shows us an interesting phenomenon: a predominance of post-nuclear holocaust societies and a return to Roman Empire and Mediaeval style times full of magic and irrationality. It is as if the consciousness, tired of waiting for the final catastrophe, pretended it had already happened and took refuge in the "safety" of the past (carefully ignoring the Plague, etc.).

The Structural Revolutions

A revolution is a party of the uninvited (from a sticker on a lamppost).

There are times in the history of humanity where the direction of many years to come is strongly influenced by events taking place at a particular juncture. Those moments are characterised by an acceleration of changes, which tend to happen in all fields, and a profound dislocation of the concept of right and wrong and of values, as new ones appear. An example of this was the Renaissance.

Around AD1500 and in a relatively short period of time, all the "objective reality" surrounding the European world fell apart. The belief in a flat (although many already adhered to the spherical model), small, central and fixed Earth, supported by a monolithic Christian Church, seemed to have the conditions to last forever. There was safety in ignorance, since books were only available to a selected elite as they were copied by hand, generally in monasteries. In a relatively short period of time all this seemed to change. Columbus opened the way for the exploration of the seas. Europe became aware that the Earth possessed an unknown massive continent, as pointed out by Americo Vespucci. It went round the Sun, as proposed by Copernicus (although he did not publicise his view in order not to oppose the Church) and reaffirmed by Galileo Galilei and Giordano Bruno, with the Reformation giving alternatives forms of worship and with books suddenly made available to ordinary people by the invention of the printing press by Guttenberg.[15]

The Renaissance was much more than an artistic phenomenon. It was a profound revolution and it showed how changes in the perception of "reality" (size, shape and location of the Earth in the universe) happened simultaneously with a profound internal change in people, in their beliefs, in their relationship with the establishment, in their view of nature, in their search for the truth. Not surprisingly, the word Humanism, which concentrated the most important ideological aspects of that moment of change, not only implies a return to the Greek perception of "Man as the measure of all things" but also allegorises a revolution that touched on every aspect of human activity.

---

[15] This authorship is debated. The Printing Press may well be one of those inventions that took place simultaneously in different parts of the world.

The recent acceleration of the rate of change also seems to point to a new moment in which the direction of humanity is considered and defined for another period, another structural revolution. Science has provided this moment with new paradigms that are shaking the foundations of the beliefs of our times in the shape of what has been called "New Physics" and in particular Relativity and Quantum Mechanics. Relativity questioned our assumption of a linear and uniform passage of time and provided Einstein's own structural view for the interaction between matter and energy in his famous equation $E=mc^2$. Quantum Mechanics dislocated the accepted views of space and determinism. These two concepts arising from science are now penetrating culture, albeit in an allegorised and simplified manner, and opening a new chapter in our vision of the world. The indivisible atom was split again and again with reductionist zeal searching for the smallest component of matter, but in opening the last (?) box ... matter became energy, the particle could also behave like a wave.

The behaviour of particles in certain experiments (e.g. the Einstein, Podolsky and Rosen[16] paradox), lent some rationale to otherwise unexplainable or paranormal phenomena. Mystical and irrational beliefs felt proven by science and shouted an "I told you so" that not only embraced the small areas opened up by matter's strange behaviour but also gave blanket approval for all things metaphysical.

This may well be just another example of "phenomenological logic", a manifestation of intentionality at the level of logical processes. Classical logic tells us that we first set the premises in order to reach a conclusion, e.g.: "All men are mortal. Socrates is a man, therefore, Socrates is mortal". If we take intentionality into account we see that what happens is something like this: I believe that Socrates is mortal, in the first place, therefore I arrange the premises to reach that conclusion.

What New Physics is showing is difficult to understand even for physicists. The complex mathematics that accompanies the development of these curious concepts is only comprehensible to the

---

[16] "...experimental results, carried out when the technology became available, do demonstrate the non-local effect, effectively refuting the EPR trio's original purpose. The "spooky action at a distance" that so disturbed EPR consistently occurs in numerous and widely replicated experiments". Wikipedia

specialists. For the mathematically challenged these concepts are described in the form of allegories, e.g. Schrödinger's cat, in which a cat inside a box can be killed by a poison if the container of the poison is hit by a particle. Since at this weird quantum level the particle can be in two places at any given point, the cat can be dead and alive at the same time, that is, until we open the box and look at it. This is a way to describe the uncertainty that exists in quantum experiments until a measurement is carried out. From a magical perspective grounded in irrational beliefs and wishful thinking probabilities may be seen as incontrovertible truths, theories as "reality" and allegories as the word of God.

With the advent of quantum theory the Universe became a great big whole with all the points interconnected and influencing one another. Only the human brain seemed to be excluded from this (in theory) Oneness. The mind boggles just to imagine how a wise campfire storyteller would have allegorised for his/her listeners such insight about our banishment from the bliss of knowing everything, even if we would not have had the awareness of such knowledge.

So, some speculative possibilities: Did banishment from the quantum universe became allegorised as expulsion from Eden? Did the matter/anti-matter particles clash in the first milliseconds of the existence of the Universe, with its tremendous release of energy, now thought to have played an important role in its creation, appear in mythology as the very widespread stories about brothers with opposing qualities who fight until one of them (Mr Matter in this case) prevails? Are dragons, giants and Godzilla the myths that arise from finding dinosaur bones in so many parts of the planet? Allegories have been used to explain complex issues to simple minds, quantum theory being one of the worst offenders or, seen from another viewpoint, one of the most prolific. The reverse process is also possible: that scientists may be constructing and shaping theories under the influence of existing allegories and past myths.

Humanity has endlessly allegorised our fear of knowledge. Biting Eden's forbidden fruit, turning around to have a look and becoming a salt statue in Sodom and Gomorrah, or Icarus flying too close to the sun and losing his feathers, are joined by their more modern equivalents such as Frankenstein and the mad scientist that blows up the world. They all point to our suspicion that others will use Knowledge at best stupidly and at worst with evil intention rather than for the common good. The stories and myths are there as warning signs. And in truth, knowledge without a strong ethical conscience is indeed a double edged sword, as those who unleashed the powers of the atom soon realised. But ethical and responsible minds come and go, whilst once the genie is let out of the bottle it refuses to get back in. Attempts to keep Knowledge locked away and only accessible to a "responsible" minority have been made under the justification of safety, but these strategies have created new problems. They infantilise everybody who is not among the chosen few. They are paternalistic and discriminating. They create a craving towards power that attracts not only those "responsible" but also those who feel oppressed and carry a compulsive desire for revenge, or simply imagine (or see) all kinds of privileges associated with Knowledge.

How do we guarantee ethical use of knowledge for the future? One of the problems in the past has been that the guiding ethical light has been located outside human consciousness, in God(s)' words, but the expressions of religious experience are very much cultural and epochal. Therefore, the precepts followed by one particular culture may no longer be valid for the next civilisation or even for a coetaneous neighbouring one. An attempt to move ethics to the realm of human-based decision-making brought the argument to a long and fruitless debate about the very existence or non-existence of God, which is not the issue. The most important point for an intentional society is how it is going to develop Ethics based on human experience: A phenomenological kind of ethics that can apply to both believers and non-believers, independently of culture and time. The indicator of the development of such ethics would be a real and generalised register that we are moving at a steady pace towards social justice, for there cannot be an ethical attitude towards knowledge without an ethical attitude towards our fellow human beings and the environment that sustains them. Whilst pragmatism and money-as-the-only-reward rule the world, knowledge will continue to feel like a threat. Knowledge may well be the engine that leads to responsibility and a mature humanity, but it must be inclusive.

Knowledge used to be kept hidden from the masses both for power and for security; now it is kept hidden mainly for profit, so that when it finally falls into the hands of the poor and the disenfranchised (and those craving for celebrity status) it has sometimes a tendency to be used with resentment and in a destructive way. Our fear may lead us to join some fundamentalist safety-in-the-past-and-in-ignorance type ideology, or to buy the latest Fort Knox security system, but thanks to computers and the information revolution, we no longer have a choice. Humanity is a child playing with fire. Growing up or burning down the house (with all inside) are two distinct possibilities. Going in one or another direction is everyone's responsibility. This is felt by many to be a little too heavy a burden on their shoulders, and for that reason they try to resort again to magical ways to get rid of such burden and to transfer it to stronger, omnipotent shoulders.

Sadly, a wholly rationalist view also risks some losses. The placebo effect, for instance, may be greatest when a person's faith in the particular benefits of the treatment they are taking is strongest, but information about the limitations of modern medicine may conspire to reduce the faith in the doctor and in the treatment that may contribute to improvement in a non-specific way. The public's growing interest in alternative medicines, which preserve an air of magic about them, may reflect also the more powerful placebo effect they are capable of (leaving aside any judgements about other more specific effects). Rationalism also leaves us bereft of the spiritual experiences that have been so important in marking a direction for humanity, that have given so much comfort to those in pain, that have moved people to build cathedrals and travel to faraway places to take their inspiration to others.

Science may appear scary today, as apart from a new paradigm in our understanding of reality, it has also given us a glimpse of choices through genetic engineering, maternal surrogacy, organ transplants, In Vitro Fertilisation, cloning, transgenic animals and so many other procedures which are touching on the very core of what we understand to be natural determinism. What these options have in common is that they create ethical and legal conundrums that nobody can solve with any certainty. Furthermore, the awareness in people that money has become the only valid reason for doing or not doing something (i.e. research) in the pragmatic era (also known as New World Order) opens the door for the imagination to consider the disastrous consequences of these new technological advances falling into "the wrong hands". They create instability for our consciousness. Magical thinking becomes not only a return to the past, to imagined "safer" times, but also an attempt to invoke supra-human protection against these not altogether improbable risks.

The evolution of the political and economic structures in the twentieth century towards the "Free" Market Economy accelerated the sense of uncertainty about the future suffered by the majority of people. The promises from politicians about the fairness of Market Forces and their assumption that they could be understood and accurate predictions could be made about them have all failed. New developments in the world of mathematics were invoked to purport to understand how it all works. Chaos Theory was recruited to "explain" the vagaries of the Stock Market.

Chaos is a relatively new concept derived from the study of the so-called "non-linear systems". For instance, the way a tree develops its branches is non-linear. Differences in temperature, light, water and parasites as well as the genetic code, have an influence upon the points of bifurcation of the branches. Early points of bifurcation have an influence upon later points of bifurcation, the thickness of the branches, their length, the point from where other branches emerge, the size of the leaves, etc. The result of this is that nobody can predict the exact shape of a tree at the time of sowing the seed. Similarly, other systems like the weather seem to respond to this format. Allegorically this is explained by what has been called "the butterfly effect", that is, a butterfly flapping its wings in one point of the planet may unleash a cyclone in another if it happens at a certain critical moment and place, where the probabilities of different direction and strength of winds "branch out". This is what makes weather forecasting so difficult, and probably nobody can predict the weather, in spite of new technology such as satellite pictures and weather balloons, for more than four or five days ahead.

In applying Chaos Theory to the world economy, attempting to make sense of rock solid predictions that vanished into thin air, we can see that it has been done excluding the human being from the equation.

The system operates on the assumption that if market forces are left to their own devices there is going to be first a concentration of wealth in the hands of the ("naturally") more capable and then this wealth will start to "trickle down" towards the less well endowed. Since this does not take into account all possible factors at the point where the probability of what will happen next is due to "branch out", what we have seen in reality keeps taking the economists by surprise (or at least they manage to look so).

The main unpredictable factor in this process is human Intentionality. If unlimited accumulation is allowed in the hands of a few people there is nothing to stop those people using their wealth to buy status symbols such as gold and precious stones, paintings, the company of the rich and famous and even nobility titles or Royal Honours for services to political parties.[17] These articles will have no impact on the expansion of production. This ensures that very little indeed will "trickle down". Alternatively, they may simple use their money to speculate. Since this trickle down is the way economists claim the system will redress social justice and the needs of the less fortunate, we can understand that if we accept uncritically this form of organisation the future of the majority of the world population is completely unpredictable. Economists of the neoliberal dogma justify the actions of the Market Forces as a god, favouring covert protectionism by the powerful and imposing "free" trade on the weak.

During the crisis that forced the British pound out of the European Exchange Rate Mechanism in 1992, one individual, a Mr George Soros, made about US$1.1 billion in one day by betting against the pound, that is, out of pure speculation. A butterfly flapping its wings is much more romantic an image than a businessman flapping his dollars, but the effect is the same. Mr Soros went on to warn the world about the dangers of speculative capitalism, whilst he continues to play at the International Stock Market Casino, pretending he has not become in himself a self-fulfilling prophecy, since when he bets against a currency everybody runs.

What is then the model represented by this New World Order, this Francis Fukuyama's End of History, this neo-liberal society of individualism (every man for himself, not to mention women and children), Social Darwinism and market deregulation (grab as much as you can as quickly as possible)? We have come full circle back to the Amoeba Society, the realm of the lowest common denominator where human intentional planning and solidarity have been abolished *de facto* on the grounds that they represent "ideology", and that is so-o-o-o last season!

---

[17] http://www.guardian.co.uk/guardianpolitics/story/0,,1759821,00.html and
http://www.guardian.co.uk/guardianpolitics/story/0,,1763201,00.html

Chapter 8

THE MARKET DRIVEN WARS

War has accompanied humanity from its beginnings but in this era of communications, techniques for negotiation and the possibility of establishing international dialogue in the forum created by the United Nations, the continuing existence of war is at best incomprehensible, at worst heinous. Ethnic friction may be responsible for local skirmishes and tribal wars, but the massive destruction of human life and resources and its consequent displacement of millions of refugees to unwelcoming lands, point to a more ominous process.

The way older generations in power have manipulated the young to risk their lives at war has varied. Some such as the Romans offered money, land and honours. Other societies promised benefits in the after-life for dying in defence of a particular religion or culture, as it is mentioned in the invitation to Odin's banquet in the Valhalla for Viking warriors, in the Christian Crusades in spite of Jesus' non-violent teachings, and in the Muslim *jihad* or Holy War. George Bush (senior) during the 1991 Gulf War pre-empted the unavoidable sniggering that would have followed the usual claim to having "God on our side" by stating that "we are on the side of God". The generational revolution of the 1960's was precisely a rebellion, in a country just recovering from the Korea war whilst sinking more and more deeply into Vietnam, against governments seeing the life of the young as disposable instruments of war.

The post-Soviet Union-collapse international wars, Gulf I, Bosnia, Kosovo, Afghanistan and Iraq (perhaps Iran next?), no longer purport to be in any way a struggle between ideologies. In the New World Order where Big Capital is King, all kinds of justifications are brought in to invade and to kill - protection of Human Rights, Weapons of Mass Destruction, finding Osama Bin Laden, public enemy No1 - but it is clear to most people that the only reason is Money, or its equivalent in resources such as Oil.

In the Gulf War we saw a tin pot dictator (largely created and fed by Western powers) suddenly become a gigantic threat to the whole world. Many well informed strategists have expressed the opinion that the invasion of Kuwait could have been stopped since the movement of troops previous to it was clearly visible in satellite pictures, but it was in the interest of the USA to:

(a) participate in a war and win it, as a way to recover national pride, badly affected by losing in Vietnam;

(b) have a say in the control of the oil that Kuwait produces in order to boost the US economy, seriously challenged at the time by Europe and Japan. After liberating Kuwait the US did not proceed to defeat Saddam Hussein inside Iraq, as the presence of a continuing threat to Kuwait was in fact desirable and it justified the US role of protector and its presence in the oil-producing region. Another reason for not toppling him was that Saddam Hussein kept Iraq fairly secular, preventing Islamists from taking power. This was also seen as interesting by the US. Only when Iraq became a threat to the dollar in the post-Twin Towers Really Really New World Order did Bush junior see a reason to go after Saddam;

(c) organise a marketing exercise in which new weapons could be displayed (in action) in order to support the lagging arms trade, affected by the end of the Cold War. The way images of the accuracy and precision with which a plane could destroy a bridge were shown, again and again, as well as minute details of the qualities of missiles, etc, strongly recalled TV shopping. We heard much later that they were not that precise and there had been plenty of civilian casualties (called "collateral damage", to dehumanise them), but business is business.

The war in Bosnia presented certain peculiarities that in my view demand some further analysis of the political undercurrents that led (and will continue to lead in the future) to the state of war.

It was clear that Yugoslavia was fertile ground for a war, with a 400-year history of ethnic conflict. However, there may have been some help at the beginning of the hostilities. For instance, there was a five-year media campaign inside Yugoslavia suggesting that Bosnia's Muslim government was intent on the creation of an Islamic state modelled on Iran. This was patently not true as the Bosnian Muslims saw themselves as very moderate and there were no great fundamentalist tendencies. But the rumour grew until it became a "fact" and the conflict began. The Serbians had kept most of the weapons of the Yugoslavian army and they started to feed them to the Bosnian Serbs. An international arms embargo was claimed to be in place but Serbia continued to give help to its friends. Only one year after the beginning of the war were economic sanctions imposed on Serbia for giving weapons to one of the factions, and only immediately after Boris Yeltsin's election as Russian president. It is difficult not to see a connection between these two events, which suggests there existed a fear that sanctions against Serbia by the West could have hampered Yeltsin's electoral chances (his rule was necessary for the opening of the emerging Russian markets to the Western powers), given the close relationship between Russia and Serbia. Not surprisingly the economic interests of those countries looking to boost their profits in the Russian markets took precedence over the life of those trapped in the war. As things developed it became clear that this war had a *script*.

The UN moved in with the most inadequate equipment and strategy. The UN peace mission *had* to fail, and it did. It had to fail because if the UN were capable of protecting small countries against invaders then many small countries would choose to give up their armies and their weapons, use those savings to produce much needed improvement in their health and education, and put themselves under the protection of the UN, in the way Costa Rica has. This would be bad for business indeed, in particular for countries like USA, Britain Russia and France whose economies are still substantially dependent on the arms trade. Only NATO with its powerful weapons could save the day and bring "peace". The old warfare-promoting adage "if you want peace you must prepare for war" had to be proven correct.

The rest of the script was the script of so many formula Hollywood films. The goody and the baddy begin a fight. The goody starts by losing, so that when he recovers and fights back the audience does not question his use of violence as it feels wholly justified and everybody applauds. Since there were no goodies and baddies in Bosnia they had to be created. The Serbs were allowed to see themselves as invincible for a while, so they became bolder and more demanding. There were atrocities committed by all sides but perhaps those who had the upper hand for a longer period of time had better opportunities and the media reported almost exclusively on the Serbian atrocities. In the meantime the Croats were being armed by "Germany, their old ally", and the US only provided "strategic support", but as there was supposed to be an embargo they could show their weapons only if there was international support for it. The imminent fall to the Serbs of the two enclaves (Srebrenica and Zepa) was announced with enough anticipation for someone to do something about it. But nothing was done. Immediately after they fell (more atrocities, etc.), the Croats showed their newly acquired military power. The audience applauded. Nobody mentioned the embargo. NATO moved in, its existence justified once more. Even some European pacifists had been calling for NATO to intervene. The script was played to the last comma and all the market demands were satisfied, including a promise to expand the markets for weapons to the ex-Soviet Union through the inclusion in NATO of countries previously in the Warsaw Pact. The entry of those countries later into the European Union was also used to commit the whole of Europe to participating in any war started by NATO, through an attempt to include in the European Constitution the principle of automatic mutual defence. The rejection of the Constitution by some countries has not eliminated this principle, since most articles are being introduced piecemeal via the Parliament.

Sure enough, 1997 saw an increase in revenue from the arms industry for the USA and the UK, which jumped from 4th to 2nd in the league table of arms exporters.

In 2002 there were mass resignations from the Dutch Government, as suddenly the Dutch, whose forces had been in charge of defending Srebrenica in 1995, decided to do the gentlemanly thing and fell on their swords, taking responsibility for the massacres. The bigger picture appears to remain blurred, even to the players themselves.

What can be said about Iraq that was not vociferously predicted by the anti-war lobby? There can only be a resounding "I told you so". Of course there were no Weapons of Mass Destruction or immediate threat of attack in 45 minutes, and this made the war, in fact, illegal under international law. Of course Bush, Blair, Berlusconi, etc. lied to their people. Of course the "reconstruction" money was spent on contracts awarded to US companies and never more than a pitiful 2% was ever invested in Iraq, the security problem being given as the justification. This problem would have been easily solved by giving the contracts to more neutral countries.

Of course the Iraqi oil was exploited by the invaders, making huge profits for the private companies that pay for their politicians' election campaigns. Of course the destruction of the country's infrastructure, including water and health services, will continue to cause death and grief to the civilian population for many years to come. Of course the terrorist threat has increased, not decreased as a consequence of this war. Of course both soldiers and the civilian population involved in the war will suffer more psychological problems, more Post Traumatic Stress Disorder, more alcohol and drug addiction and antisocial behaviour that accompany this syndrome. Of course there is a whole generation of children without access to a good education. Of course there has been a massive exit of professionals from Iraq, their skills now being used by the rich countries that supported this war.

The catalogue of "I told you so's" could be endless. Let it be a check list for the next time politicians ask us for an act of faith that their "inside knowledge" of the danger a country presents to all of us justifies our trust in their decision to go to war.

The most extraordinary thing about the war in Iraq is the success in keeping a number of events that may have contributed to a great extent to the decision to go to war almost completely outside public awareness. Since they continue to operate at present and will no doubt influence other possible wars they deserve some attention.

Chronicle of a war foretold:

In 1992 Martin Feldstein, wrote in the Economist hinting at a scenario of international conflict between the EU and the US as a result of the introduction of the Euro.

In October 2000, the United Nations approved Iraq's plan to receive oil-export payments in Euros in the Oil-for-Food programme. The UN issued a report saying it could cost Iraq up to £270 million as at the time the Euro was in rapid descent; but soon it increased by 17%, and the dollar began to decline, making a tidy profit for Saddam.

"On January 31 2001, seven months before the World Trade Centre massacre, former senators Gary Hart and Warren Rudman, co-chairs of the bipartisan US commission on national security, produced a document of 150 pages, *Road Map for National Security: Imperative for Change,*.... The conclusions were startling. "States, terrorists and other disaffected groups will acquire weapons of mass destruction, and some will use them. Americans will likely die on American soil, possibly in large numbers." Hart told Harold Evans, author of the article[18]: "We got a terrific sense of the resentment building against the US as a bully which alarmed us." The report was a devastating indictment of the

---

[18] *The Guardian* October 2, 2001: Harold Evans in New York: *We can't say they didn't warn us*

"fragmented and inadequate" structures and strategies to prevent and then respond to the attacks the commissioners predicted on US cities. Hart specifically mentioned the lack of readiness to respond to "a weapon of mass destruction (WMD) in a high-rise building".

One wonders, if there was awareness that such a degree of resentment was likely to lead to an attack, why a change in the foreign policy was not considered.

In April 2002, Javad Yarjani, Head of the OPEC Petroleum Market Analysis Dept put forward several compelling reasons why its members might one day start selling their produce in euros.

According to the analyst William Clark the invasion and installation of a U.S. dominated government in Iraq was to force the country back to the dollar and to dissuade further OPEC momentum toward the Euro, especially from Iran, the second largest OPEC producer, who was discussing a switch to Euros for its oil exports. Clark considered that as the dollar slipped, central banks would start to move their reserves into safer currencies such as the Euro, precipitating the collapse of the US economy. This was reported in *The Guardian* by George Monbiot[19] but was otherwise largely absent from the Media. So, there *was* a WMD after all, and it has not gone away.

We appear to have entered into a new era in which the old Cold War paradigm, that is, the struggle between two empires, the American and the Russian, is being reproduced in the struggle between the Euro and the dollar. It is a more polite struggle, with the two sides actually remaining reasonably friendly. But in the same way that the old Cold War avoided real death and real desolation in the territories at the centre of the empires by taking their armed battles to places like Africa, Latin America and South East Asia, this war is being fought in the Middle East. The rest may come later.

Potential conflicts exist in many parts of the world, but they will become real wars only if the markets so decide. Apart from studying those conflicts and making the participants aware of the international games they will be subjected to, it is important to make people aware in those countries that are not likely to go to war but benefit the most from the arms trade that many of the politicians they are voting for have interests in the arms industry. Allowing them to reach power is to help create a war somewhere in the planet. It is not enough for

---

[19] *The Guardian* April 22, 2003

politicians to disclose their financial interests after being elected if the issue of a conflict of interests arises in a parliamentary group. In fact it would be more correct if they disclosed them before being elected, even at the point of selection by their respective parties, together with a disclosure of the money donated to their electoral campaigns by lobby groups that represent the arms trade. Perhaps this is the right time to discuss whether those who have shares in, or are directors of, companies selling weapons, as well as those who have close relatives/friends who would benefit financially from selling weapons to other countries, should not be eligible for public office.

Wars are not only good for selling weapons, they are also loved by politicians as their careers can be helped by some of the following mechanisms:

(a) People who are worried about war watch more news programmes, and are more aware of the existence of politicians.

(b) The psychological profile of leaders can be easily changed to make the person appear stronger by the "sabre rattling" language that surrounds a state of potential or actual war.

(c) There is also for politicians in charge of making decisions a much bigger media exposure. This works by creating repetition of the "brand name" of the product, which is a basic marketing tool.

(d) During wars ordinary "critics" of the government's policies become "traitors" and everybody is forced to close ranks behind their leaders or run the risk to be seen as a "fifth column".

(e) During wars anything can be an issue of "national security", therefore shady deals can be hidden from the public.

(f) During wars a particular group becomes "the enemy", therefore discrimination (and hence scapegoating) becomes respectable.

(g) During wars people live in a state of fear and look for "strong" leaders to protect them. In exchange they are prepared to give up the civil guarantees and human rights they would want to take for granted in peacetime. For this reason a state of "war on terror" has been declared in the absence of anything that can give a real sense of being at war.

(h) During wars there is a shared experience that brings about solidarity, identity, and belonging. Wars can bring a sense of meaning to otherwise meaningless existence. It is a repeated observation that the suicide rate drops during wars. Whether this is an artefact created by the ease of getting oneself killed or a true reflection of the protective role of belonging and sense of community is probably too difficult to evaluate, but the point is worth noticing all the same. In fact, politicians know that unless there is a death in the family or amongst friends, wars can be quite exhilarating in a Roman Circus kind of way. They also know that wars can increase their chances of re-election.

(i) During wars some of the space normally occupied by celebrities, the role-models of the modern world, is given to members of the armed forces. This improves recruitment into a high risk profession that not many people in their right mind would wish to enter.

(j) The post-war period continues to serve the political marketing until the atrocities, the deceptions, the horrors, the civilian deaths, the environmental disaster, etc, all start to emerge, and yes, there is a change of government. But the damage is already done and the politician is sorted out financially and socially for life.

The Galileo Oath

It is essential that scientists in all disciplines agree on a common Oath of commitment to life, such as the one proposed by Dr Salvatore Puledda, the "Galileo Oath". Here is a fragment of his speech delivered at the opening ceremonies of the "2000 Without Wars" preliminary conference of scientists and academics held in 1996 at the University of California, Berkeley.

"… an enormous responsibility falls on scientists and their technicians. If they could say NO to the destructive use of science, if a great movement were created against weapons and wars, born out of universities and research centers all over the world, then, politicians and the military would see the space for warfare adventures of any type reduced to the limit."

Listening to this kind of idea, often we feel a flicker of enthusiasm which is, though, followed by a return to our everyday thinking: to the brutal reality of violence in far-away or nearby wars that television brings day after day into our homes. And then, once again we tell ourselves that that was a nice utopia, but that reality is this: wars are a part of humanity, they cannot be eliminated.

Now, I would like to quote the man who perhaps has been the greatest scientist of our times: Albert Einstein. In 1948, at the time in which the possibility of destroying all forms of life on the planet with a nuclear war appeared on the horizon of human history, he said:

"We, the scientists, whose tragic destiny has been that to make the methods of annihilation more horrible and efficient, must consider as our solemn and superior duty to do all that is in our power to prevent the use of those weapons for the brutal purpose for which they were invented. What other task could be more important? What other social commitment could possibly be closer to our hearts?

"Unfortunately, there are no indications that show that governments are aware that the situation in which humanity finds itself forces us to take a series of revolutionary measures. The present situation has nothing in common with that of the past, therefore it is impossible to use methods and instruments that have proven sufficient in the past. We must revolutionize our way of thinking, our actions, and we must have the courage to radically change also the relationship among nations. The clichés of the past are not enough today and, in the future, they will no doubt be obsolete. To make sure that all human beings understand all of this is the most important and decisive social function that we, as intellectuals, must carry out. Will we have the courage to overcome the nationalistic ties until we convince the citizens of the whole world to change their most rooted traditions?"

These words are extracted from the message that Albert Einstein wanted to address to the Conference of Intellectuals in Favour of Peace in 1948. The organising committee prevented him from doing so, and the message was published by the press on August 29 of this year[20].

I believe that the time has come to resume the path mapped out by Einstein, and later by Sakharov, to develop a science ethic, one according to which science cannot be used for destructive purposes and for the purpose of warfare.

In fact, today, science is riddled by an "ambiguity" that touches it in its most profound essence. On the one hand, science can make it possible, for the first time in history, to free a large majority of human beings from ills such as hunger, exhaustion and diseases, that have accompanied humanity along its long journey; on the other, it can transform itself into an even more dreadful evil, since now we have the

---

[20] Although Puledda quotes from an article he saw on 29 August 1996, Einstein had began in 1930 to exhort his fellow scientists not to work in war-related research.

possibility to create a global catastrophe, a nuclear war or an ecological collapse.

But it is in the so called Third World, in those countries that euphemistically are called developing countries, where eighty percent of humanity lives, that this essential ambiguity of present day science is lived day in and day out most dramatically. It is well known that many of the African countries South of the Sahara, for instance, assign to the arms budget large proportions of their internal gross product - including the assistance received from the richer countries. But where are these weapons purchased? In the First World, of course! There are weapon supermarkets. In Europe, we have the yearly scandal of the International Weapons Fair which is held alternatively in Paris and London. There, high military groups, particularly of the Third World, meet to go shopping, and, just like in a supermarket, there are various aisles - one aisle dedicated to aiming systems, another for intelligent bombs, a third one to tanks, combat helicopters, aeroplanes, and so forth. There are competitive prices, discounts for those who buy more, coupons, etc. An armoured tank costs millions of dollars, and that exact same amount could purchase all the medicine needed to eradicate malaria or infectious diseases that are the number one cause of death for the unfortunate African populations.

What can be done? In the last act of his perhaps most beautiful play, *Life of Galileo*, written during one of the times of greater tension between the West and the USSR, Bertold Brecht shows us the father of Western science, already old and sick, who ponders on the meaning and the future of his discoveries with his young assistant, Sarti. Sarti is about to leave Italy, where scientific research has become impossible owing to the condemnation of the Church, taking with him the unpublished manuscripts of Galileo's discoveries. Research can be continued in Holland and in Northern Europe where the conditions are more favourable. Looking towards the future, Galileo sees that from his work will emerge "progeny of inventive midgets", ready to sell themselves to the best offer, willing to be used for whatever purpose by the rich and powerful. But this progeny is born from his own mistake, his own example. If he, Galileo, had not surrendered to the Inquisition, if he had said no to power, perhaps his disciples, after him, would have done the same. Perhaps Science would have developed differently, perhaps it would have been possible to create something similar to the "oath" that Hippocrates, at the dawn of Western civilisation, created for doctors: the Oath of using Science only to benefit humanity.

Leaving aside the metaphor that Brecht's play proposes, I believe that this must now be the main pillar of a Science Ethic: the use of scientific discoveries only to benefit humanity. But, how to develop and implement this ethic? I think that the international scientific community must direct great efforts towards creating new and different organisational ways to put into practice that fundamental principle. It could be a solemn Oath taken by all those who enter the field of research. It could be the creation of ethical committees – similar to those in bioethics that already exist in the field of genetics – in each university, by which they denounce and reject research with warfare purposes, or the establishment of national committees to work in the political arena to fight against the armament lobbyists, etc. Basically, a creative effort to build the human science of the third millennium.

UNESCO and some universities are at present studying proposals by various scientific bodies concerned with ethical issues in order to ensure that the ethics of using scientific knowledge for the development of weapons of war and mass destruction, and other misuses of science, are clearly and effectively condemned by the scientific community."

In this way Puledda concluded his address. Since 1996 UNESCO has set up a website on the theme of an ethical oath for scientists[21], Prof. Joseph Roblat, Peace Nobel Prize winner proposed to Students Pugwash the creation of an Oath which has already been taken by many science students around the world and the AAAS (American Association for the Advancement of Science) appears to be *stimulating debate* about the issue.

---

[21]http://portal.unesco.org/shs/en/ev.php?URL_ID=6501&URL_DO=DO_TOPIC
&URL_SECTION=201.html

Chapter 9

THE BARBARIAN-ON-THE-WALL VIEW

Politicians use statistics like a drunk uses a lamp-post, for support rather than for illumination (Andrew Lang)[22]

We live in the first planetary civilisation in human history. Today, rather as it was among our prehistoric ancestors, the one with the biggest stick is winning, at least in terms of access to resources. However, if we look at what is happening to the "winners" from an existential view point we may reach a very different conclusion. Globalisation has not brought about a convergence of races, cultures and belief systems interchanging their goods and knowledge from a position of equality throughout the world. It has rather functioned as an imposition of one model of existence and one value, money, upon the rest of humanity by the international financial system that feeds the centre of the latest and largest empire to date: the USA's military and financial machine.

Old empires have come and gone, their rise accompanied by the bloody invasion of their neighbours and, later, as travel became easier, by shooting metastases to faraway places like spreading malignant tumours. They also took technological and cultural advances and inventions with them but the final balance was almost always for the benefit of the invaders. Their fall came as a result of internal decadence and external dissent starting at the periphery. The Romans could not control the hordes of Barbarians roaming and influencing the outposts of the empire at the time that its centre was also starting to decline in the midst of internal fragmentation, widespread corruption and decadence of values.

The European colonial empires of the XVI to the XVIII centuries had to resign themselves to the loss of their territories in the XIX and XX centuries when rebellion against their centres, also starting at the periphery, could not be contained. This appears allegorised in Aldous

---

[22] Who (mis) quoted from Mark Twain who had said "People use statistics...etc)

Huxley's *Brave New World* by "The Savage", a man born outside the established order of the Test Tube, dehumanising society who, in spite of his apparent weakness and cultural awkwardness, has the role of viewing a sick society from the perspective of today's right thinking people. In the film *Zardoz*, the same role is played by a barbarian-like character who arrives to destroy an apparently developed but all too misguided society as a way of saving it from itself. Redemption through destruction by the outsider's hand is the message: going up in a big cathartic blast that purifies the sins of a society that appears to be beyond redemption.

Constantine, Roman Emperor around 300 AD, converted to Christianity, the outsider's doctrine, to save the most powerful empire of the ancient world from its decadent and crumbling order. There are strong indications that he did more than convert, though. In fact he appears to have invested a great deal of creativity in the process. In the 1960's, there was a search again for the outsider's doctrine to save a decadent and materialistic society: Eastern gurus were imported into the West, bringing with them a different point of view. Sadly, the great success of the Capitalist machinery was to absorb them into a form of consumerism that promoted acquiescence rather than exciting activism amongst those who, dissatisfied with their own established order, practiced the imported doctrines. Far from stopping the decadence of Western civilisation, these imports ended up reinforcing in many, one of its most malignant symptoms, hedonistic individualism.

If we are to find our modern Barbarians, our outsiders capable of inspiring once more an evolutionary leap for human society, we must understand the mechanisms that have been at work in the creation of our present situation.

The arrival of the Multinational Company and the International Financial System has contributed to the development of an economic neo-colonialism that set the basis for this new phenomenon, the World Empire of the XX century. The military-industrial complex intertwined its geographical expansion, with the financial system giving raise to the giants of the Cold War, of which NATO (the armed wing of the American empire) emerged triumphant.

Whether by the sword or by the dollar an empire arises when the people of one place, let us call it a Nation, begin to expand, telling those they intend to subjugate that the conqueror's culture, lifestyle and sewage system are better than everybody else's. Since the times of the first imperial monsters, a few have come and gone in most continents. From ancient China to the Incas, from Egypt to the Romans, humanity has viewed those leaders of destruction, those Napoleons, Stalins and Hitlers with distaste, fear and awe, as they conquered territories and enslaved people to build their megalomaniac visions. And most importantly, they completed the physical occupation of territories by imposing cultural forms on others. They dismissed the way of life of those they invaded as inferior or primitive. Racial differences were presented as "natural superiority" just to make it crystal clear to their conquered subjects, who was boss and to justify to themselves and to their compatriots the right to oppress, kill and use as objects other human beings.

These are the times of The Big One. The tools for expansion of this World Empire show remarkable creativity. At the end of the Second World War the US established its undisputed military superiority (Hiroshima, Nagasaki, etc.) over the rest of the world. However, rather than going on fighting and annexing territories in the Roman, British, etc. style, this innovative invasion has taken place in much more subtle ways. It could be hypothesised that it was precisely the existence of two opposing and equally violent forces that helped and gave justification for the unprecedented expansion of both Capitalist and Communist Empires. The continuation of the war economy that so helped the USA recover from the 30's slump was established by means of the arms trade. The state could recoup the wear and tear of producing obsolete big guns by selling them to countries facing wars that they (the vendors, in this case both the Soviet Union and the USA) themselves promoted.

The centre of the empires always kept a few miles ahead in technology to ensure that nobody could challenge their power. NATO, rather than a defensive alliance, became the means to sell the better and more expensive stock to friendly powers. Countries that had not developed nuclear capabilities ended up agreeing to host bases containing nuclear missiles, and by doing so they also became targets for other, less friendly countries' nuclear missiles. The arms trade became the Arms Race, a hopeless attempt by The Other Empire, the Communist one, to catch up, which finally bankrupted it. Here humanity had its first wake up call to the globalisation of danger. For the first time in history human beings had the capacity not only to destroy themselves completely in the MAD (Mutually Assured

Destruction) option, but we also had acquired the ability to destroy the planet we inhabit. For the first time, truly and simply there was nowhere to run.

Both the Cuban Missile Crisis and the last days of the Nixon Administration impressed the public with the unpredictability of the two Imperial Giant's behaviour. With its victory over Communism, the Capitalist Empire became the only Super Power. The US President is (mistakenly) seen now as the only one with the real (mad) possibility to press The Red Button and blow up the world. Not surprisingly, humanity was shocked and horrified when it realised, by way of "Monicagate", that this super-being was just a guy!

Who is the Empire? All the citizen of the dominant country? Just its government? Their military? It can be perceived that what we call the World Empire, in spite of its apparent geographical concentration in the USA, is in fact a structure that stretches throughout the planet. Interlinked speculative financial institutions, arms dealers, secret services unanswerable to any elected body, government officials (most of them) who do not represent the people but rather the interests of the big corporations that pay for their campaigns, and media that masquerade as the voice of the people, the heart of the nation and even reality itself, whilst just vying to dominate the subjective life of the population for the sake of profit. This is the skeleton of the Empire. The people who live in the area where the Empire has accumulated most of its wealth have received through nationalistic rhetoric the illusion that they are also part of the Empire. In that way they are prepared to defend their country's "interests" abroad as if they were also their own interests. We can observe, however, that the less well off natives of any one country are made to live together with the migrants from other countries who are fleeing wars, poverty and famines. In some ways they are made to take care of, as neighbours, this very deprived population at the same time they have to compete with them for resources. It is not surprising therefore to see that those people most sensitive to xenophobic and racist concepts are sometimes those suffering the most economic discrimination in a nation. The great success of nationalistic capitalism is this identification of the poor with the country that oppresses them, rather than with other victims of the same oppression who come from different ethnic backgrounds or nations.

A very important tool used for the expansion of the modern empire has been the so-called "free" market. This is a form of Fundamentalist Capitalism which allows unlimited movement of capital (be it for investment or for speculation) and goods (but not people) throughout the world. Investment for rapid profit can be carried out without any commitment to production or to the people in the countries where speculation is taking place. It could be argued that abolition of trade barriers and restrictions against investment could be a good idea providing everybody started at the same time from the same mark, that is, from a position of equality. Since this is patently not the case, as those who proposed (or imposed) the system started from a position of advantage with the Multinational Corporations and the banking system already in place, "free" trade can only lead to increasing concentration towards the rich countries to the detriment of the worse off. Today, the policies imposed by the World Trade Organisation supported by the World Bank and International Monetary Fund in the name of "free" trade are draining poor countries in favour of richer ones and producing massive unemployment in "emergent economies" already burdened by unrepayable and artificially inflated foreign debts, contracted as a "favour" from the financial institutions of the Empire. This is the root of modern day neo-colonialism and the most important mechanism of concentration of wealth and resources into increasingly fewer hands.

Wars fuelled by the Arms Trade and economic disaster have produced huge movements of people. These are sometimes called "refugees" in order to criticise the situation of their countries of origin, sometimes called "economic migrants" to invalidate the justification for their journey, most often called "bogus asylum seekers" to excite the hatred of the local population and scapegoat them for domestic problems such as unemployment and violence. These masses of migrant workers form a fundamental body in the economy of the "free" market philosophy. They are the neo-slaves of the Empire. I shall examine more in detail the way this Planetary Empire has organised itself:

An interactive map of the world at the beginning of the New Millennium

International economic policies agreed by the most powerful economies, the G7, and imposed on poor countries give free reign to Multinational Corporations that move their production to where they can pay the least to the workforce. In this way, they exploit the population of countries with high unemployment and low incomes. Then they sell the cheaply produced goods in the rich countries at prices that cannot be matched by production employing workers who receive reasonable salaries. More firms take their manufacturing base away to the Third World, increasing unemployment and reinforcing the negative effects on the workforce in the richer ones. As Multinationals withdraw their profits from the poor countries and maximise their earning with total disregard for environmental damage, they contribute to impoverishing them, forcing in this way more waves of migrant workers.

Those who lose out the most in the present globalised capitalist economy are the countries that were also the most ravaged as colonies. Governments of ex-colonies tend to be "kleptocracies" (government by thieves), that is, those who join the political game hoping to enrich themselves. This is of course not exclusive to the poor countries, but the colonial structures left in place favour corruption. Also the system by which "loans" are agreed (e.g. from the International Monetary Fund) favours the corruption of officials who are seen as the agents of the "lenders", those in charge of making sure that their countries keep the rules imposed on them - such as the shrinking of the state and privatisation, even if that leaves most of the population bereft of services, health and education.

The "aid" those countries receive from the ex-colonial powers (which became rich thanks to the stolen resources and the slave trade) is imposing conditions that benefit mostly the lenders (mistakenly called "donors") and perpetuates the cycle of dependency and poverty. Characteristically, it has been described how aid to build five schools will come with a proposal for "structural readjustment", that is, the shrinking of the public sector budget through privatisation, which will lead to the closure of ten schools. Government officials in the "recipient" country will favour the loan and enforce the conditions imposed because they get financial rewards and contributions for their electoral campaigns for doing so.

"Aid" is always accompanied by conditions, for instance, buying products from the countries that are lending the money. This, added to the subsidising of food production in the developed world, is bankrupting the farmers of the developing world.

Developed nations make huge profits by selling weapons to the poor ones and benefit from their political instability. This is a manufacturing industry that tends to remain in the industrialised countries in order to keep the secrets regarding their production; otherwise there would be a risk of poor countries becoming as militarily powerful as the industrialised ones. Being in this way, one of the very few industries that does not move abroad searching for cheap labour, it is promoted amongst the workforce as a source of jobs rather than a source of violence, even if it is obvious that keeping a healthy market for weapons implies that there must be some wars around for others to justify the expense. This maintains the commitment to it of sectors of the population which would not be naturally in their favour. Furthermore, the buying and selling of weapons features within what has been generically referred to as "issues of national security" which ensures a degree of secrecy not allowed to other areas of trade. In this way a great many "shady money" transfers can take place away from the sight of ordinary citizens in the countries involved.

When workers in countries battered by persecution and poverty attempt to escape their plight by entering the industrialised nations they are qualified as "asylum seekers" and kept in legal limbo for long periods of time, during which they are forced to work in near-slavery conditions to survive. Much of the world economy is based on this mass of migrant workforce, which becomes also the focus of discrimination and scapegoating during political campaigning.

The availability of cheap (and desperate) labour is also used to weaken the power of the trade unions and reduce the cost of labour in general, to increase the profits of industrialists and the banks/shareholders. This leads to changes in the labour market, with an increase in the availability of manpower in such a way that if workers become more demanding they can be easily replaced. This increases the perception of local workers that foreigners are taking over their livelihood.

The hatred promoted against migrants by those who fuel the belief that "they are coming to take our jobs" leads to the election of governments with a more extreme "free" market stance, which also tend to appeal to the silently racist sectors of the population by exciting their worst fears of foreigners. This in turn worsens the situation of the migrants, strengthening the slave-like conditions of their existence. Marx had already pointed out that the differential between the real worth of a worker's task and his/her pay (the profit) promoted the accumulation of wealth. The migrant workforce provides the greatest opportunity for a maximum differential, as it is not protected by any law or trade union.

Profits are not reinvested in industry to expand the manufacturing base, nor are they channelled towards meeting the education and health needs of the population better, but rather they tend to be gambled in the speculative stock markets to make more profits without producing anything, to contribute to the concentration of wealth in fewer and fewer hands. When they are invested abroad they become "swallow capital", that is, they arrive when conditions are favourable for a speedy profit and are withdrawn when conditions change. In order to obtain permission from governments to behave in this way, they bribe them and/or pay for the electoral campaigns of the politicians who once in power will favour them, contributing in this way to the cycle of corruption prevailing in collapsed economies.

Professionals in poor countries that see their opportunities for employment and development curtailed by reductions in public investment tend to move towards the richer countries not only for further training and specialisation but also for better salaries. In this way, it is the poor economies that pay for the basic training of professionals, saving a great deal of money in education for the richest countries. The "brain drain" reinforces the poor self-image of the most oppressed economies, whose people end up believing that nothing good can be invented or created in their own nations. This phenomenon, coupled with intense advertising about products and the life-style of the rich countries, makes local people favour "imported" products rather than the locally produced ones. This is often taken to ridiculous extremes, e.g. a private neighbourhood on an Argentinean beach advertised that it counted on "imported sand"! Not surprisingly Argentina, being the country that embraced most enthusiastically the "free" market dream, was also the first one to implode into economic disaster. The most damaging effect of this deeply rooted belief system is the destruction of the national manufacturing industry, leading to increasing unemployment and leaving the field free for Multinational Corporations to bring in their exploitative production, whilst being regarded as the "rescuers".

Environmental damage and illness-inducing pollution produced by Multinational Corporations are not sufficiently recognised by International bodies. It is much cheaper to move factories to places where there is little risk of being held liable for deaths caused by pollutants, than to carry out the work in countries where there are regulations. Pharmaceutical companies take their research to the Third World to experiment on humans with their products much earlier or in conditions much worse than would have been allowed by the tough ethical constrains of their countries of origin. Most of the drugs that are researched, however, will not be affordable for those who are lending their bodies for this research, and more often than not the drugs that are seen as a priority for development are those that will make the most profit by fighting the diseases of the wealthy minorities in rich countries rather than the poor of the Third World.

Developing countries that rejoice at the arrival of jobs looking for cheap labour should not forget that by accepting the role of backyard of the developed world they are also likely to become the market for weapons produced in the industrial nations, as well as be the target of conflict that will create the need for that country to buy those weapons. It is of course true that conflict generally exists prior to the arrival of the market manipulators and the arms salesmen, but local conflict can be fuelled and exacerbated in order to create the market for weapons. Arms industries are a vital source of work in the industrialised countries that have moved all their production and even services to poor countries where the labour is much cheaper (i.e. Outsourcing, for instance: British Rail is moving its information service to India so when the customer wants to have the latest news about train delays in Manchester, they will actually be ringing Bangalor to get this information). We can see therefore that the enthusiasm following the arrival of a multinational factory to a country with high unemployment may be followed by paying a high price for those jobs. It may be much more interesting to create local industries that employ local people, without a snowball of side-effects that the local population will have difficulties to control.

There are of course a number of positive consequences of the trend towards globalisation. Fast communications throughout the planet allow a rich multicultural interchange of ideas and proposals, in such a way that people all over the world can link up to organise grassroots movements to learn to become independent from this vicious cycle of concentration and exploitation. In this way, local groups are connecting into international networks capable of looking at the global picture to propose alternatives to the present system. In fact, the anti-globalisation movement is completely dependent on globalisation for its very existence. Without travelling, the Internet, (a common language) and international communications it would not be possible to organise demonstrations that are synchronised throughout the world in order to protest against the effects of international trade rules, wars, etc. Through this rich exchange of experiential as well as socio-political issues some people are starting to realise that, contrary to what the world of advertising would have us believe, money does not give meaning to life and does not answer the basic existential questions of the human being.

Perhaps the most ominous quality of the new global empire is its success in conquering the minds of people far away from the centre. In previous times this would have been impossible, but Hollywood and TV have done what invasions and annexations had never achieved before. Values and a lifestyle alien to communities far away from the centres of power have been a daily dose of brainwashing for billions of people living in the remotest corners of the Earth. Television has introduced the American (yes, a country has appropriated the name of the whole continent!) way of life to all parts of the world. No wonder we can see people in jeans, trainers, baseball caps back to front and drinking Coke anywhere we go. TV has been presented many times as a vehicle for culture but as Quino pointed out in his cartoon *Mafalda*: "…if I were culture I would rather walk".

Paying attention to the contamination and cultural destruction induced by the mass media in certain communities should not be confused with the choices that such communities make about technology and their future. It has become a feature of well meaning people in the developed world to romanticise traditional lifestyles and criticise those who bring technology to them. The important issue is one of choice. If a people in the Amazon region decide that it is their choice to accept a life expectancy of 45 due to lack of running water, then it is their decision, but to deny information about the advances that humanity has made in terms of overcoming illnesses in order to "preserve" the culture of an isolated community is to deny also their intentionality. Salvatore Puledda pointed out in his Conference *"Globalisation, a threat to cultural diversity?"* that there is a tendency to consider culture as something from the past, fixed and unselective, with particular stress on the primitive. But culture is also the future project that unites a community and the choices that the community makes of their past experiences that need to be taken into that future project. An example could be the Maoris in New Zealand, bringing their dances and language with them into their modern lives but leaving behind cannibalism.

The art of story telling is probably as ancient as humanity itself. Stories by the campfire about the heroic deeds of those promoted as examples to be followed were probably soon seen as the best way to communicate to the new generations the values and the codes of a particular society. Whilst animals carry only their living memory and experience, human beings accumulate history and pass the teachings of time from generation to generation. History books in terms of the power to reach audiences' hearts have never replaced story telling. Later stories became also a way of resolving psychological conflict through identification with different characters in the Greek Theatre, and in the present day through the more-real-than-life-itself effect of the Soap Opera. Typically, characters in TV stories and films relate to one another in the same way that people relate in real life, that is, by concealing their real intentions and pretending to be someone else. But there are moments when the characters look directly at the camera and show their true intentions and personality, apparently hidden from the eye of the other characters. This is the moment when the more-real-than-life-itself effect sets in. This is what is missing in daily life which makes soap opera characters so dear to some people, to the point of addiction. It also allows individuals to work out, albeit in a very clumsy and not always positive way, their inner conflicts and troubles.

The TV and film industries have created a virtual world of beliefs and value judgements that has the appearance of being more real than life to millions of human beings. It has been the tool for the insidious conditioning of people with images and mental forms that penetrate our minds, well beyond our conscious awareness. Social stereotypes are as old as human society itself, but the present means of delivering them are the most powerful in history.

Today, this medium is used to neutralise the outsiders, to present them in such a way that all attempts to produce change, real change, will be met with horror or scepticism. The "make-believe" industry (including the media) has the power to present the rebels, the non-violent dissidents of the globalised Empire either as hopeless dreamers or as the worst scum on Earth. Nobody wants to see themselves like that.

Intentionality is at work though, through the growing independent media, alternative cinema groups and the Internet. With shoe-string budgets and truly human creativity, the barbarians are striking back.

Chapter 10

THE MOEBIUS REVOLUTION

It is not always possible to be aware of the way we have been influenced by stereotypes. For example, on one occasion when travelling by plane I was rather startled by the usual announcement: "This is the Captain speaking" delivered by a female voice. I saw then than in spite of my commitment to the liberation of my gender, I too had been successfully conditioned to see women in a stereotypical way, in this case not in the role of pilot in charge of a Jumbo Jet. Some time later, whilst reading Nelson Mandela's biography, *Long Walk to Freedom*, a passage reminded me of that experience. Young Nelson takes a plane. He's a little nervous and suddenly he realises with a start that the pilot is black. He then sees that he himself, in spite of his commitment to the struggle for the liberation of his people, has been somehow brainwashed. As he has never seen a black pilot either in real life or, most likely, in films, he is taken by surprise. We can see, then, that unless we become aware of the insidious effect of propaganda, the news, stereotyping in soap operas and simply growing up in a society that discriminates on the grounds of race, sex, religion, age, disability, etc., we will continue to recreate the society we are trying to change. In this way, it is healthy to realise that we are all not just victims but also in our own little way, agents of the sickening value judgements imprinted on our consciousness by the massive power of Education and the Media.

We have a choice, then. We can continue living by the values and intentions of somebody else's dream or to start to wake up to the alternatives. This means to intentionally devise ways to change the social structures that surround us, at the same time that we change our own structures of thought and feeling. Neutralising the years of learning from the education system, hours and hours of uncritically absorbed TV and words from the opinion formers can make us a little less conformist and a little more intentional in our choices. Many would fear becoming outsiders by embracing a position at the periphery. For most people this would be an unacceptable way of seeing themselves, because together with the values of society we have absorbed an image of how we should be to feel successful. This includes a position in society, money, a mortgage; all the things that keep us perfectly tied to the system. The 1960s enthusiasm for "dropping out" died in the 80s. But producing change does not imply a need to abandon all those things in life that are important to us. The image of the social activist as a sacrifice-junkie prepared to put "the cause" before family, friends and his/her own life rather works against an image of humanisation. Furthermore, those prepared to lay their lives to achieve an objective often feel reciprocally justified in taking other people's lives or demanding others to sacrifice themselves. This is not a criticism of the many heroes and heroines that sacrificed everything for the cause of non-violence. We are talking here about the *mental attitude* necessary to bring about a radical change in this inhuman system.

Let us begin by stating who are *not* the people capable of bringing about change, at least in the direction of humanisation of values and systems. There would be a temptation to look for angry-looking individuals who go around destroying symbols of the Empire and killing those living in its geographical centres in the process. In the wake of the September 11th assault on the World Trade Centre and the Pentagon it has become abundantly clear that the author of such atrocities has actually handed over the completion of the World Empire in a silver platter to those keen to expand their military-financial influence to all corners of the Earth. Never before have countries, traditionally mistrustful of the gigantic capitalist network, opened their espionage systems and markets to it as they did since the "war on terror" began. This war has become a justification for maintaining and enhancing a foreign policy that probably brought about this vicious terrorist act in the first place. Osama Bin Laden has been G.W. Bush's best friend. He has been the one who gave legitimacy to a rather dubiously elected government and united a nation behind a doubtful leader. He gave the opportunity to justify an increase in the military budget that not even the most powerful lobby groups representing the arms industry, that paid for the Republican campaign, could dream of. G.W. Bush has been Bin Laden's best friend, the man who transformed an obscure terrorist, persecuted in much of the Arab world into the inspiration and leader of many young Muslims as well as others who have felt oppressed by the American Empire. Paraphrasing Arundhati

Roy when she speaks about the violent clashes between Hindus and Muslims in India, "George W and Osama worship at the same altar".

Who would have said that the theme (repeated *ad nauseum*) of so many Westerns about a town hijacked by a bunch of bullies who dominate the terrified town's people through threats and actual violence would be a premonition of things to come? Those playing that role would of course be very surprised by this discovery, not unlike the WASPish character in the film *Falling Down* who comments in disbelief: "What, am I the bad guy now?" Far from being a recent phenomenon these activities have been around for some time. We can remember for example *The Other* September 11th, when in 1973 a democratically elected government in Chile was overthrown by a military coup backed by the USA. Much has been said about Henry Kissinger's participation in these events. As Tom Lehrer well put it, "Political satire became obsolete the day Henry Kissinger got the Nobel Peace Prize". We should see with certain nostalgia those times when interference in the affairs of a sovereign country was considered contrary to international law and there was at least some attempt to conceal it.

Violence cannot be a tool to fight the system, not just because it is morally wrong, but also because it is the very methodology of the inhuman system in which we are submerged. To justify violence for one side is to justify it for everybody else, and so the system thrives on guerrilla movements, terrorism, popular violent uprisings and wars. With the justification of self-defence, the need to calm down a situation, punish those responsible for atrocities and/or simply "prevent" further violence, military budgets are inflated, police forces get the go ahead for more and more restrictive and draconian practices, and painfully achieved human rights legislation gets bypassed. True dissidents from the present brutal system do not play its violent game but make a void to its violence. Opposing the system by imitating its methods is tantamount to maintaining it.

Perhaps there have been very few times in history when a whole country felt its heart sink as it did when Tony Blair decided to support the war in Iraq. So many in Britain felt betrayed because they had elected a Prime Minister with anti-war and antinuclear credentials. When he started arguing the case for war and playing Bush's advocate, so many felt dismayed and disgusted. What became clear was that as a good lawyer the Prime Minister could argue with equal passion the case for either side, and when he became convinced that war was more convenient for Britain at that particular juncture, he presented the case to his people as if the facts made it obvious that going to Iraq was the only possible choice. And he did so with the same determination with which he would have made the case for peace, when he was still a militant in the Campaign for a Nuclear Disarmament. The contradiction he imposed on his loyal friends, still unconvinced about the rightness or even the legality of going to Iraq exemplifies the type of damage to the human spirit that goes well beyond the silly political games that get played in the seesaw of "who is in power today".

It looks, then, that we shall not get a radical change in the system via the ballot box for some time. But eventually we need to find the new leaders of a democratic and non violent world. Who else is there? Those who rebelled against previous Empires came from the edges, but since the World Empire has no clear geographical edges this time they will have to come from the edges of the social structure. Not necessarily in a visible 1960's-drop-out sort of way, but they will have to make themselves known somehow. They will not be recognisable just for the things they say, since we live in the era of "double-speak" (an example of semantic violence) in which everybody seems to adopt the language, verbal and non-verbal, of their ideological opposites. In this way the New Left tend to dress like bank managers and talk in terms of economic markers and (sigh...) privatising everything. The New Right, people like George Soros, Mr Camdessus (the IMF's former Managing Director), the Tories, etc, talk about the suffering of the people, the social cost of structural readjustment, public services, the environment and the dangers of capitalism. Recently an oil company adopted as a logo a flower very similar to the sunflower of the "green" movement, to fudge its image as an environmental polluter. Furthermore, the biggest polluters are cleaning up their image by conducting research into clean, renewable energy, without actually changing their Modus Operandi. Governments should be warned that if they do not fund research into renewable forms of energy through public institutions, such as Universities, we will find that when the oil actually runs out the private oil companies will be able to hold the world at ransom through the patented use of clean energy technologies.

To confuse things further, it is not uncommon to see Management Consultants, those who advise companies on how to make more money for the shareholders whilst laying off as much as possible of the workforce, in jeans and pony-tails, back from the latest New Age-style seminar on the wonders of Caring/Sharing capitalism. So, how are we to recognise alternative minds, the seeds of the new society that will have to replace the present dehumanising system before it destroys us all? They are in fact easily detectable because they believe and live by something frankly scandalous (for present day thinking, that is). They go about, carrying out actions grounded in their conviction that people are more important than money! Surprising as this may seem, some dare state it and propose it as the basis for a new form of organisation.

One of the most important forms of awakening one another must be mutual education about the difference between information and propaganda. Propaganda comes in many forms. For instance, there was a campaign run by the makers of a vaginal cream to advertise in hairdressers in Australia, something forbidden by law. They did it, however, by writing the name of a website that in name related to the symptoms of menopause ("love hurts") in the hairdressers' caps. This connected straight away with the product they wanted to sell, aware that people confide more in, and attend more often, the hairdresser's salon than the doctor's surgery.[23]

Likewise, the way news is reported by different papers, presented as "the truth", in fact represents the ideology of that particular medium. Here follows an example of UK papers: the *Evening Standard* on 18 October 2002 published an article stating that children do better in Independent Schools; but the same study was reported by *The Guardian* as follows:

"Middle-class parents who send their children to independent schools in the hope they will pass more exams may be wasting their money, according to research published yesterday.

An Edinburgh University study has found there is little difference in exam pass rates between middle-class pupils at state schools and those in the independent sector. Although school league tables consistently show independent schools outperforming state comprehensives, the research indicates that when family background is taken into account there is very little difference in exam pass rates". (*The Guardian*, 18 October 2002)

---

[23] Reported in the British Medical Journal: bmj.bmjjournals.com/cgi/content/-full/325/7373/1180

Conversely, some books, even children's books, may contain eye-opening insights. The similarities between the Roman Empire and NATO in Europe were not lost to Goscinny, the creator of the French cartoon book series, Asterix. He described not only the relationship between European countries and their "friendly" invaders but also created a parody of American society by making scathing analogies between Roman and American customs. The fact that its meaning is largely lost to most people, who read it just as a children's story, speaks loudly of the power of the Empire's media in not making certain information that should be common knowledge available in a truly widespread way. The Gauls of the story were, of course, barbarians.

It is well known that the inability of the Roman Empire to conquer its most belligerent neighbours was not the only reason for its demise, and that many internal forces contributed to its decadence. Some would also say that it did not fall at all; it just transformed itself into a different kind of Empire, into a religious structure with a Pope where the Caesar had been, and a clerical hierarchy not unlike the Roman government. Perhaps this capacity for adaptation has not been lost on its modern day successor.

The culture of the World Empire is one of consumerism ("I shop therefore I am"), mass production and economic growth followed by periods of recession during which the most successful companies buy out or force the weaker ones to close in a process of progressive concentration never seen before in the history of humanity. Rapid speculative profit rather than long term investment creates a sense of uncertainty and instability where only having lots of money (never enough, in fact) can protect a member of this system's image of the future. In this way only money, a meaningless convention, rather than the creative process of production, acquires any weight in the scale of society's values. Human relationships are marked by relentlessly stressing the advantages of individualism, competition and success. Existential emptiness is filled by the progressive development of the entertainment industry. The senses are caressed by visual images, music, and the opportunity to live vicariously the life of heroes and heroines, celebrities and victims of atrocities, princesses and murderers, all from the comfort of our own living room. Ben Elton pointed out that we are moving further and further away from the 50's idea of the human being developing into a big brain with little feet.

Rather, the human being seems to be on its way to becoming a large stomach with a thumb for the fast forward button!

For those who feel frustrated by the apparent failure and slowness of progress on the road to change, we must say that failure is sometimes an indicator that we are on the right road - a little failure, and not total failure. It could be compared to working on an Intensive Care Unit. No mortality would mean that patients are being treated for dandruff or bunions. A very high mortality may indicate not that the unit is not working properly but that terminal cases, that should be allowed a peaceful death, are being vigorously and painfully treated to the last minute. The road to social change works in a similar fashion. If everything proposed happens very easily, then we are not changing anything, just the appearance of things. It means that change would have happened anyway, because the conditions were already present. If, instead, nobody gets even remotely interested in the alternatives that are being proposed, then they may be really off the mark. Real change means that new conditions that do not yet exist need to be created, and this means rowing against the current, but advancing. Nobody who follows blindly the creed that meaning is in the rapid success that is being promoted by the present system can actually change anything. Pragmatism leads to more of the same, a static impasse between two moments, an irrelevance in the history of human progress. Pragmatism teaches us that the ends justify the means. It tells us that it is all right to do something that goes against our principles, as long as it achieves the desired short-term objective. Contradiction is in this vision nothing to worry about; we all have to live with it, even if it means the death of the human sprit. Propaganda from the system seems to be saying that even the human spirit can be replaced by some bottled substitute, but the rates of depressive illness in affluent countries are telling us a different story.

There are of course attempts to give us via the Big and Small screens a vicarious taste of the human spirit. The lowly individual takes on the big corporation and wins. The shy adolescent defeats his bullies and gets the girl. Indiana Jones, Superman, Buffy... How many times can the Earth be saved from total destruction by my Hero(ine)?

Hollywood teaches us the way to separate the losers from the winners; there is no room at the top for gentle and caring people. Ruthlessness is the desired attribute of the successful. Faust is reborn: the moral conclusion in the cinema where *Wall Street*'s Mr Gecko and other produce-nothing speculators become the villains of the story, only to meet their well deserved punishment at the end is a short lived catharsis for their victims. Or consider the cinema story of Erin Brokovich, the woman who got the big bad polluting corporation to pay compensation for the lives it had destroyed (would it not be better to make pollution a criminal offence and Company Directors criminally liable?), only to hear later that in fact very little had been paid - but the triumphalist tone of the movie makes us believe it is all OK. It may be, but just in the cinema, not in real life. Make-Believe is the real opium of the people. Images direct human activities and if our images are manufactured in Hollywood we will create a world only fit for Donald Duck to live in.

The New Middle Ages

In the same way that irrationality dominated the post-Roman Empire era we see the growth today of the "magic consciousness" industry. When people have no future they turn to the gods, but if the gods are silent there are always people willing to speak on their behalf. In the heart of the World Empire lots of people are calling the gods. Not surprisingly there are at any one point in time about 15 million human beings involved in 12 steps programmes[24], not just fighting the alcoholism or drug addiction for which this helpful therapeutic system was designed but also using it to fight the effects of the very system they want to become more adapted to. There is shopping addiction, sex addiction and workaholism, all created by the Empire's lifestyle, all leading to large numbers of people learning to develop an external locus of control (God "as one understands it"). In this way millions of people are making themselves much more susceptible to accepting uncritically other external powers such as the words of politicians and tycoons as naturally superior to their own inner registers. If we add to this a large mass of people insulating themselves from geological and palaeontological studies on evolution, we have the perfect mix for the re-birth of the Dark Ages of Human History. Those who promote this, as "the will of the people", tend to use the media to marry belief and economic power, for instance through TV preaching.

---

[24] the core work of Alcoholic Anonymous

We have witnessed the power of the World Empire to dominate globally at the turn of the millennium. In the BC era - that is, "Before Computers" homogenised the whole world into accepting the calendar of the Empire - (in fact the Millennium for the Christian calendar was in 2001, the year 2000 was only important in the Bill Gates' calendar), there was no need for anybody else apart from the Christian community to consider the birth of Jesus the most important event in human history. We saw then that the usual apocalyptic nonsense that accompanies conventional time milestones had worldwide repercussions. Even Japan became very permeable to Nostradamus' prophecies. We should ask ourselves if this apparent desire in so many people to experience a little catastrophe might not be related to a wish to experience again something that affects us all equally, not just the poor, not just a human group of this or that colour. The Millennium bug (which was not a bug at all, but it sounded more threatening if it evoked images of epidemics like the Plague) got hip names (e. g. Y2K) that went very well with the big business it turned out to be. Not only were millions of perfectly good computers replaced by new ones on account of not being "2000 compliant", but also a variety of unnecessary programs were sold to detect if this or that computer was or was not compliant, when more often than not the only thing that had to be done was to change the date and see if it liked it. Was such a convenient money making scam affecting the whole world just an accident? But we did not hear the manufacturers of both hardware and software say "Whoops! Sorry! Faulty products, we'll recall it and fix it for you". It is rather curious that they are not being sued.

In summary, we are assaulted by the external procedures and the psychological forms planted on our minds by a kind of program. Not a computer program, but a structure that pervades in every aspect of human existence.

The current of thought known as New Humanism or Universalist Humanism begins from its very root, proposing the simultaneous (self) transformation of the individual and society. It does not make false splits between the internal and the external worlds. It does not put one before the other. If the consciousness-world is an indivisible structure, any revolution, albeit a non violent one, should address both sides of the structure at the same time. A Moebius[25] strip is a one sided tape that appears to have two sides. This is the perfect allegory for a kind of revolution that cannot be just external, political and organisational, nor just internal, psychological or existential. The methodology of non-violence offers also the best fit for this kind of radical change, for it implies the end of injustice, discrimination, war and violence in society and the end of violence within us.

---

[25] Named after Augustus Ferdinand Möbius (1790–1868), German mathematician and astronomer who designed the Moebius strip, that connects its inner and outer sides into a continuum

Chapter 11

GOODBYE SEMANTIC VIOLENCE
HELLO LANGUAGE OF CHANGE

Intentionality expresses itself in different forms. One of them is language. Through language we can glimpse the point of view of other people, their attributions of meaning and their intentions towards the future. Language is used to convince, persuade and threaten, altering in this way the point of view of others, but is also used to interchange and co-operate, developing collective points of view which are not the result of imposition but of joint activity. Language can be an instrument of violence or of development, and it is human intention that guides it in one or other directions.

Many people have studied language from the point of view of meanings, structure, the way words relate to object, etc.

The feminist movement unearthed centuries of conditioning through language, into the belief that women were inferior to men or just mere appendages of men. Words like "chairperson" and the tedious but absolutely essential "he/she" are winning their way painfully into the literature and the boardroom. There are, however, examples which just do not sound right, like "hangperson" or "hitperson", as they are associated with activities women would probably not wish to be involved with, but here is where the limits of non-sexist language become somehow blurred.

Another attempt to curb semantic violence is the so called "Political Correctness", that tends to point out the presence of sexism, racism and any other kind of discriminatory "ism" in language. Its main difficulty is that when applied with extrem"ism" it can become a form of violence in itself. Sometimes the fear of not being PC enough leads to it acquiring a different meaning than the one officially intended and accepted, closer to "Poor Communication" than to Politically Correct. PC language has also been used euphemistically (a newspaper referred to Paul MacCartney as "philosophically challenged"), showing once again that is not the tool but the intention behind it that is responsible for the insult.

Throughout history, descriptions of mental states have furnished language with the largest variety of insults, simply because as soon as a name is applied to a mental illness or deficiency it becomes a form of insult for people who do not suffer from it. The old classification of morons, imbeciles and idiots as forms of intellectual impairment, lost its original meaning a long time ago and new names are proposed all the time trying to find friendlier denominations, which are not stigmatising. This is of course a hopeless task because only a change in the intentions of the general population, i.e., a more compassionate attitude towards those suffering from mental disorders, can reverse this trend. An alternative strategy has been to apply names that do not roll easily on the tongue. Thus we can see some success in the absence of drivers shouting from their car windows, "Hey you, Learning Disabled, where do you think you're going?" Less fortunate is the choice of the word "schizophrenia" to describe the contradictions induced in individuals by a fragmenting society. It derives from the misconception that schizophrenia is a form of "split personality", a lay term that in fact describes non-psychotic dissociative disorders such as hysteria. It is thoroughly unfair on people suffering from schizophrenia, one of the most stigmatising disorders (so much so that some have even denied its existence in an extreme attempt to protect its sufferers), to have to carry also the stigma of a brutally dehumanising social organisation. Since society's attitude may not change soon enough, perhaps it would be wiser to change the illness' name to honour the scientist that best studied it. It worked for Alzheimer's disease.

Language, like any other human activity, develops in the context of intentionality. There is an intention present in any attribution of meaning, and as we saw in the previous chapter, the intentionality of those in power tends to charge everything they touch with their meanings and directions. Language develops, therefore, perpetuating that line of power.

The following are some examples of recent distortions in the meaning of a small selection of words and the way in which such distortions serve certain interests and intentions, not surprisingly related to the acquisition and retention of power.

"Anarchy": this word was born meaning "no government", indicating an ideology that proposes a society where individuals and groups organise themselves, without authorities. The word was then converted into a synonym of "chaos" and this was soon incorporated into dictionaries and crosswords. The media use them indistinctly to mean disorder and social disturbances. Perhaps the adherents of such ideologies may think there is today a kind of poetic justice in the fact that mathematicians and physicists are now talking about Chaos as a form of spontaneous order!

"Individualism": originally meaning the rights of the individual immersed in a social environment and the uniqueness of each person, this word was revamped within the model of free market economy to glorify self-centredness and selfishness (leaving "Individuality" to carry some of its original meaning). Popular expressions of this shift in the concept of individualism such as "to look after number one", "greed is good" and "the Me decade" embody the joy with which hedonistic capitalists welcomed their freedom from compassion and consideration. The suggestion that selfishness and individuality are the same thing, also creates the tacit understanding that their opposites, solidarity and uniformity, are also synonyms. In other words, if we were to start to help one another we would end up thinking all the same and wearing the same clothes. This imagined danger was somehow enacted by Communist China by adopting a rather uniform style of clothing, which did nothing to dispel the myth of uniform minds.

The word "individualism" (equated with selfishness) has produced an increasing deterioration of the fabric of society as communication becomes more difficult and is actively discouraged, being as it is a source of empathy and solidarity, which opposes the neoliberal economic model. Prof. A.H. Halsey, Emeritus Professor of Sociology at Oxford, has blamed individualism for the decline in the family, as parents become unable to think in collective terms and children are treated as objects to be possessed in divorce cases. The desirability of individualism has had also as a consequence a sense of dehumanisation, as a process of objectification of "the other" takes place, accompanied by a sharp drop in the capacity for empathy, which is one of the mechanisms that make it difficult for human beings to hurt one another. This opens the door to interpersonal violence, war, torture and the upsurge of ideologies such as neo-Nazism, all based on the objectification of individuals of human groups, which are regarded as "alien", "foreign" or simply a "thing".

"Cynicism": a cynic is a person who sees little or no good in anything and who has no belief in human progress. In a situation not unlike today, the Schools of Decadence of ancient Greece counted amongst their expressions the Cynics who were, together with the Stoics and the Hedonists, a response to a decaying society. Cynicism has remained throughout history as a cul-de-sac for human consciousness; a bitter refuge that signals the death of intentional life for a cornered individual who feels that the only possible choice left to him/her is the intention to deny or to destroy hope. In the past few years, the word "cynical" has undergone a kind of refurbishment in the "educated" circles and has acquired also an air of "intellectually stimulating" and "sophisticated" added to its original meaning. This creates also a feeling that the opposites of cynicism, faith and enthusiasm, are some kind of coarse naiveté and stupidity. Cynicism is a form of self-fulfilling prophecy: if I believe that nothing can improve, I will do nothing to make things better, therefore nothing will change. To be right becomes more important than to try one's best in order to create the possibility of improvement, accepting that our efforts may succeed but may also end up in failure. The added dimension of lack of sophistication for those who do not show at least some degree of cynicism discourages even further those who would be prepared to attempt to introduce changes from taking the initiative, for fear of being seen by others as artless or gullible.

When did "peasant" lose its meaning? Surely some time ago it must have meant someone involved in rural tasks. The association of this word with lack of intellectual and social abilities today is so strong, at least in the UK, that it probably creates an immediate prejudice towards people employed in country tasks, reinforcing the trend of migration towards the urban centres. This is true, in particular for young people, at the height of their preoccupation with their self-image and aspirations of opening opportunities for their future.

"Pragmatism" was the ideology developed in the USA by James, Pierce and Dewey who applied James' original work on beliefs and ethics to a "problem-solving" type of education also known as "Instrumentalism". In its application to wider fields of human activity it became synonymous with a definition of what is right on the basis of the consequences of the proposal. In other words "success" (preferably immediate, although the long term results should also be considered, at least in theory) is the only measure for assessing whether one's actions are worthwhile or not. Not surprisingly, one of the worst insults in the North American vocabulary is to be a "loser". The pragmatic view supports the belief that the ends justify the means. In economic terms, profit has become the main indicator of the effectiveness of one or other policy.

In ordinary language "pragmatic" is often used to mean "practical" (as opposed to "theoretical"), which is concerned with the applicability of an idea or project but which makes no assumptions about the rightness of such action. The consequence of this confusion of terms is that many policies which are perceived as being morally wrong or having long-term deleterious consequences are carried out anyway because they are "practical". Political opportunism (policies that go against the party's traditional ideology but are adopted all the same because they are "vote winners") and dumping nuclear waste in the sea for future generations to worry about, are the direct result of the words pragmatic and practical being used as synonyms.

"Natural", the buzzword of the 1990's, continues to exert its magic misrepresentation in the new millennium. Following a tremendous, but still not serious enough, move towards environmental issues, the word "natural" became synonymous with everything that is good and right in every field. Natural substances in soaps and creams suddenly cropped up in every shop as a sort of guarantee of the effectiveness and goodness of the product. The fact that some natural phenomena like earthquakes and hurricanes, or natural substances like strychnine, or naturally occurring illnesses like rabies, are not particularly good for people has been glossed over by many who found in the word "natural" a perfect justification for concepts that are otherwise very difficult to sustain on moral grounds. On 2 May 1990 Professor Michael Novak (one of the "gurus" of free market economy) told *The Independent*: "...differences in the endowment of nature, in talent and in the pursuit of happiness exist and it is the first task of justice, and hence, of government, to preserve them." In other words, not only are the profit making companies and financial institutions now dedicated to increasing the widening gap between rich and poor, and between long and short life expectancies, but the Justice system and even Governments should be involved in the task of stressing these "natural" differences that exist between people, without taking responsibility for contributing to create them in the first place. They do so by promoting the unequal distribution of wealth that creates differences in childhood education, nutrition and illnesses. These conditions combine with more deterministic factors, which are nevertheless highly modifiable by the action of the environment such as the genetic makeup, to form the "natural endowment" of an adult individual.

In the same vein "Human Nature" has also been applied to justify a vision of human beings that betrays them. Since nature is used here to mean something fixed and unchangeable, it is in direct opposition to the concept of intentionality. Human nature is used in general to imply negative aspects in humanity. Greed and violence are "explained" (with a sigh) because "Oh, well, it is human nature". At the time of proposing solutions to human problems this concept is utilised to tell us that we need to find something outside ourselves, like gods or market forces to guide us because human nature is bad, flawed and unreliable. But who presents these solutions coming from "outside" humanity, if not other humans, possessing the same "nature"? In 1998, soon after becoming UK Prime Minister, Tony Blair gave a speech in Paris. He recounted how in his youth he had worked as a waiter in a Parisian café. All the waiters had agreed to put the tips together on a common dish for equal distribution. After a while he discovered that he was the only one doing so. He stopped and called this his "first lesson in applied socialism".

Whilst we all remember the (oh, so many!) experiences that made us lose faith in humanity, this is the keystone of the future: either we foster a belief in the unchangeable nature of human beings in such a way that what has happened will continue to happen regardless of any efforts made - in other words, the success of the lowest common denominator for ever - or we take the decision to nurture a belief in the possibility of change. We may be guided by clear images of better forms of organisation and supported in our own experience of intentional modifications in our lives and in history. Giving in to corruption, to the absence of solidarity, to the Enron brand of "creative accounting" and so many other examples of betrayal of our fellow humans on the basis that "everybody does it" marks the end of hope, the end of trust and a humanity of isolated individuals who feel completely on their own in terms of ensuring their own survival.

In market economies, it is supposed that competition (dictated by the markets) will balance greed (human "nature"). However, it is not unknown for competitors to reach agreements that benefit them and not their customers, neutralising in this way the supposed external control (in the UK cars cost about 17% more than in the rest of Europe, by common agreement between manufacturers, because having the steering wheel on the right creates a captive market). This is one more example that shows that intentionality is the strongest force that regulates human behaviour, and that generally what is presented as coming from outside humanity, as well as what is described as "human nature" are simply manifestations of somebody's intentionality. In this context, we could say that there is in fact no such a thing as human nature. Let us review a statement that supports this insight:

> "Human beings are historical beings whose form of social action changes their own nature".

We can observe that from this awareness stems not only our responsibility, but also our freedom. As time goes by the human being is progressively more and more immersed into a world of human-made objects and human intentions. Difficulties in controlling other people's intentions have created a nostalgia for the times when hunting or fighting the elements rather than trying to tame the London Underground in the mornings, or one's boss, was the rule rather than the odd weekend exception. Many feel that a return to a more "natural lifestyle" is the only way out of the city inferno, but the main characteristic of anything natural is that there is no choice. By choosing to go "back to nature", to stop wearing clothes and using electricity, or to eat with our hands instead of cutlery, we get even further away from Nature as selecting one possibility above others, which are offered mechanically to our consciousness is the quintessential intentional act.

"Freedom" is probably the most abused word in the dictionary, used and misused to sell from the most diverse ideologies to tampons. Perhaps we should see in this trend a symptom of the lack of it experienced by people and their shared aspiration to achieve it. However, this can hardly justify calling one's enemies "terrorists" and one's friends "freedom fighters", when they are using the same violent methods in their activities.

Expressed as in "Free Market" the word provides an illusion of freedom from regulation, something that only happens in the "Free World" and not in socialist countries where State interference leads to a difficulty in amassing a well deserved fortune. We know very well, however, that the 1996 meeting of the G7 (the seven most industrialised countries), concluded that while the liberalisation of markets throughout the world would benefit the richest countries, it would probably be catastrophic for many developing countries, and that was just tough. Two years later, the by then G8 (having admitted Russia as one of the big players) corroborated that the vicious circle of debt service and further borrowing by the poorest countries contributed to the spiral of poverty, but the banking nations remained unmoved by the popular pressure to cancel debts - other than in a token way and mainly to avoid complete bankruptcy of some countries that would then default on future debt repayment - even if most loans had already been repaid several times over in interest.

An article in a Kenyan newspaper pointed out the tendency of these industrialised banking countries that live off the interest on the loans they make to less developed ones to call themselves "donors" rather than "lenders", suggesting a humanitarian rather than for-profit intention to their actions.

A particularly worrying trend we witnessed during the war in Bosnia was the tendency of the media to use the term "ethnic cleansing" to refer to the activities of the Bosnian Serbs killing Muslims and raping their women. The correct term was of course "genocide", but the language of the aggressor became the official denomination in this case and it was used again in the Civil War in Rwanda, and again in Kosovo, showing how we can "get used" to a term which was at first used sarcastically and in horror, but was later incorporated as the normal way of referring to those attempts of extermination. This term is also used instead of genocide as officially, the UN has the obligation to intervene in cases of proven genocides. "Ethnic cleansing" also cleanses their hands.

A word that should be considered suspect of semantic violence is "discrimination", applied both to the description of good taste and intelligence in making choices and to the violent and objectifying segregation of individuals and groups on the grounds of their ethnicity, religion, gender, sexual orientation, etc.

Another form of semantic violence is the use of a word that completely changes the perception of the subject. For example, when Sir William Rees-Mogg[26] wrote about the world economic crisis in his

---

[26] *The Guardian*, Monday 7 September 1992: "Hurricane warning that Germany should heed"

usual precise, attractive and well-researched style, after a long analysis of the state of the markets and the economic markers, he dedicated about 5% of the article to the human suffering this crisis is bringing, and in particular to those who are losing their jobs, their assets and homes. However, he did not allow our hearts to swell with sympathy for the poor victims of the system being discussed, at least not for long, as he finally stated with complete certainty, "These people are always dangerous". Just with one word, "dangerous", the perception of the dispossessed changes completely, from poor victims deserving our solidarity to an unmistakable threat to our safety, our livelihood and our comfort.

Language can transform another person into "the other" or into "the enemy". When we speak of somebody as a person who feels, thinks or suffers (as in Sting's Cold War song *The Russians Love Their Children Too*) we identify with them and that humanises "the other". Instead those who refer to "the foreigner" or "the alien" as someone coming to take their jobs, rape their women and contaminate their purity create a perception in others of the foreigner as "the enemy" and close any possibility of compassion or communication.

During the 1980's and 90's, we heard two related words combined to give a rather distorted picture of the economic situation. One of these words was "recession". Massive lay-offs followed privatisation of public assets, small businesses failed, large companies merged and take-overs were rife. Ordinary people heard from the media, "We are in a recession". We imagined that what was happening to us was happening to all. Nothing could have been further from the truth. In fact it should have been called "concentration". What happens during so-called "recessions" is that with the fall of production many companies fail, which gives other bigger or better-placed companies the chance to take them over. Some financial groups carry out this also. They are simply concentrating in their power more and more of the world's assets. The amount of resources has not changed. Simply, some have taken more of it, so everybody else has less. These are the mechanics (but very much intentional mechanics) of the cyclic pattern of expansion and contraction of the economy, the "bubble and burst" or "boom and bust" economics that characterises global capitalism. If we add to this that, thanks to developments in tools and technology humanity needs fewer and fewer people to produce what the rest of us are going to consume, it is clear that unless we reduce working hours unemployment is going to continue to increase. But companies demand "maximisation of resources" (euphemisms for exploitation in "managerese"), because paying one worker to work for many hours is cheaper than paying two, to work half that time each plus holidays, sickness, maternity leave, etc. Increasing profit is the only accepted criteria for a successful business. In fact, recession is used to justify all around the world the loss of every conquest that trade unions and workers in general have made in the past few decades.

Next to recession comes "rationing". Once this was almost unthinkable when talking about absolutely essential things such as health, the care of the elderly and education, but today its inevitability is no longer questioned as health services state they must ration in the face of "limited resources", starting with treatments that are not "cost effective".

Real rationing is something that happens after shipwrecks and wars, when there is not enough to go round, so everybody agrees to use an equally reduced amount of food, water or services, etc. It evokes images of catastrophes and solidarity. It is a good word, an emotive word. But it cannot possibly apply to reductions in the budgets for health and education, whilst directors of privatised public utilities are at the same time paying themselves obscene salary increases or bonuses, some banks announce record profits, the casino that is the Stock Exchange renders its rich gamblers even richer whilst producing or creating nothing, and the arms trade continues to yield almost unimaginable profits. Not to mention the unnecessary and destructive expenditure of war.

Even if it were true that new developments in medicine will necessarily create increasing costs or that a longer life expectancy will demand more from health services, it should be the hallmark of a civilised society to increase the percentage of its budget in the pursuit of the well being of the population, at the same time that it reduces that which works against it, such as the production of weapons.

Rationing of health services in any case only applies to the poorest sectors, as those who can afford it are encouraged to take up private health insurance. A quick look at countries that have had this system for years (e.g. the USA) shows that it is not only substantially more expensive as per capita expenditure but also does not guarantee all sorts of treatment, as Insurance Companies apply ruthlessly the principle of cost effectiveness and that which does not yield profits is excluded or provided exclusively to those that can pay ridiculously high premiums. A large sector of the population lives without any form of health cover and the lawyers fuelling lawsuits at every step of the way run away with much of the money that should be dedicated to health care. Rationing is one of the cornerstones of Social Darwinism in the capitalist culture, the survival of the richest.

Euphemisms are rife in this intentional misrepresentation of meanings. We have already referred to politicians who announce that their country has been given a contract to build a particular weapon by giving the numbers of jobs that such contract will create, that is, the contract is given to the public as a way of cutting down unemployment - rather than expressing the figures of how many people can be killed by the product of this successful bid.

Semantic violence applies both to verbal and to non-verbal forms of communication. Fashion has evolved a situation of power that discriminates against women, but this has been more or less well disguised as an intention to make "the fair sex" more attractive. Women were given high heels that increased their fragility; skirts that imposed a tense body posture, legs tightly closed or crossed, and a handbag to carry their belongings so as not to spoil their figure with bulky wallets and cosmetics in their pockets. This also imposed the need to pay attention to not losing an object outside one's immediate person. Men instead were given flat shoes to put them in a more solid standing, trousers to be able to relax the legs and big pockets to be able to forget keeping an eye on their belongings, so they could concentrate on more important things such as protecting the fragile, tense and preoccupied women. It is no wonder that in old Hollywood movies, it was always the girl who fell whilst being chased by the monster and the guy who saved her. This inequality, presented as seduction has divided the feminist movement almost from the very beginning: should a woman who aspires to her independence and development of her full potential wear pumps, comfy trousers and baggy pocketed jackets, and compete with men on equal terms, or, should she take advantage of the sexual power that a tight miniskirt and stilettos can contribute in the pursuit of passive aggressive manipulation? As usual, the answer probably lies in not allowing externally imposed and conventional values to contaminate the decision making process, and making choices based on attitudes that are both internally coherent and externally compassionate, as well as capable of opening the future. An indicator of finding a sense of freedom in making some choices would be diversity, since any attempt to regulate or codify how women should behave is bound to be an expression of oppression of female intentionality, whether rooted in old male or new female power structures.

The great paradox of female liberation has been that as women have struggled for equality in order to be accepted and heard in situations other than their roles as wives and mothers, they had to show that they could do the same things as men. Only then could they start the real process of contributing to the liberation of humanity as a whole, by starting to celebrate the slight differences that exist between male and female thinking processes. In fact, one of the most important elements that allow us to hope that the cycle of endless violence that has characterised human history can actually change is that this new component has come to join the old structures of thought. Since male and female thinking are only slightly different, with huge areas of overlap, by joining them together we have something similar to the process of binocular vision, where two slightly different images produced by the left and right eyes overlap. The resulting picture has a new quality that the separate sources are not capable of producing by themselves: it has depth. In the same way, the acceptance of the role of women as thinkers and planners for the new human society that is being built at the present moment, renders the future three dimensional, more complex and full of new possibilities that were unknown or unthinkable before this additional element came into play.

A predilection for a type of metaphor to indicate the real quality of an idea has been seen recently in relation to monetarist ideologies. Whilst they are presented as sciences in an overt way, covertly they are introduced as religions. We have heard enough of the "gurus" and the "High Priestess" (Margaret Thatcher) of the Free Market suggesting we must have faith rather than question or try to understand its esoteric language. Goscinny's Asterix in *Obelix & Co* beautifully depicted this. A young and recently qualified Jacques Chirac arrives in the dissident Gaulish village to try to defeat its rebellious population with market-forces-speak. When the puzzled villagers do not understand he reverts to explaining his complex economic plan with a caricature of the way American Indians were supposed to speak English.

Jerry Brown, former Governor of California, colourfully depicted these mystical connotations of the Market Economy in his statement:

"There has never been a religion with as many believers with fewer doubts than the free market dogma".

Metaphor is generally understood as a way of bringing out the beauty of apparently dull or neutral situations, such as in poetry. An acrimonious divorce may be described as "the dying embers of love" and having to make painful decisions may be allegorised as "crossing the Rubicon", but metaphor can also insult, for example by calling someone "Einstein" when we really mean that they are stupid. It can also be used to conceal ugly truths. Massive lay-offs may be described as "company slimlining" and the loss of labour gains may be called "flexibilisation of the workforce". When the economy is described as being "leaner" and "fitter", in reference to what is in reality a further concentration of resources in the hands of an increasingly shrinking wealthy minority, the words are opportunistically taken from the fashion of dieting and keeping fit. In "lean cows" Biblical times (or during a famine) the terms would have had rather different connotations.

Metaphor may also be the language of de-humanisation. Language that qualifies machines is used to describe phenomena of consciousness, even when Artificial Intelligence is still very far away from resembling human thinking. Those working in the mindless mechanical routine of the production line are referred to (and probably feel like) Robots. Unfeeling, un-empathic people are described as Androids and many have the sensation in the streets that Zombies, those who look human but have lost all capacity for conscious awareness, surround them. All these ways to appraise "the other" are evidence of the loss of the capacity of and desire for even attempting any form of human communication.

A metaphor is the substitution of a term for another, which is heavily contaminated by a value judgement, that is, it carries an intention. In this way the same thing or person may be described with reference to different aspects. For example, Margaret Thatcher was metaphorically described as "the Iron Lady" during the Falklands war, but she was later referred to as "the Bag Lady", in relation to her onslaught on the British welfare state.

Even the word "globalisation" carries an apparent meaning that suggests an interconnected planetary civilisation, a humanity living in a global village, (albeit with a number of global village idiots, as mentioned in an Editorial of the BMJ magazine) and a melting pot of cultures, systems and beliefs. Millions of people around the planet register it in reality as the imperial overpowering of the world by one culture, one lifestyle and one economic system that advances bulldozing all other diversity of opinions and ethno-cultural existence into a uniform subjugated magma. Interestingly enough, the words *"mondialisation"* and *"mundialización"* that refer to precisely that convergence of humanity into a network of countries and cultures in a more equal footing, exist at least in French and Spanish, but not in English.

New generations always invent new words, not only to refer to new concepts but also to exclude the older generation, which is regarded as obsolete or oppressive, from participating in the discussion. In the BC era (Before Computers) there was a whole generation who had the potential to learn to use them although they had not been invented. The use of computers brought a new language to all aspects of life. Some of the older generation declared themselves "computer-phobics" but others launched themselves into the cyber culture with enthusiasm, although knowing all too well they are doomed to learn "new-generationese" with an accent.

The acceleration of technological developments announces a growing gap between the language of the new generations and those whose formative landscape did not include virtual reality, the Internet and who knows how many other forthcoming dramatic changes in our daily environment. Such a language gap is not a superficial difference; it describes a whole new set of experiences that, acting on the developing brain, produces actual neuronal differences of a kind that cannot be predicted in advance. Those who were taught science with a well drawn dividing line between particles and waves in subatomic physics had to struggle with the concept of a particle/wave duality, but those who were brought up with the latter, simply think of it as the most obvious and natural concept. The threat of becoming obsolete leads some older people to seek ways to impose a language that includes a code of conduct and a legal framework onto those who will have to live with a completely different set of experiences to which today's concepts and perspectives will not apply.

We may conclude that language is the way in which ideologies, concepts and points of view about the world are transmitted throughout generations and the form and content of language tells us a lot about who is winning in the eternal power struggle. Perhaps it would be interesting to find language expressions that do not lead to those struggles, but there again; seeking power is only "natural"...

If language is to help to move humanity in a developmental non-violent direction, it must concentrate on intentions rather than forms and roots rather than appearances. We must move away from simply delivering information in a one-way system between the individual and the media. This transforms every human being into an island, isolated from others with whom discussion could take place in order to critically receive such information. The present scheme is increasingly at the service of a power structure that does not consider the human being as the central value or concern, and that leaves us divided, ruled and dehumanised.

Language should be the means for seeking consensus, stimulating empathy and creating real and direct communication.

Chapter 12

WHICH HUMANISM?

A brief history of some of the currents of thought that have been inscribed under the term "Humanism" can be found in Dr Salvatore Puledda's book *On Being Human*.[27] Some highlights of this history are important to understand the different meanings giving to the word Humanism.

Fifth century BC, Greece: Protagoras, "Man is the measure of all things", meaning that mortals are the arbiters of the human condition. Socrates: Human existence rather than the gods is the matter for philosophy.

1126: Averroes (Ibn Rushd). Arab philosopher, astronomer, and writer on jurisprudence; born in Cordova. Translated Aristotle's writings. Greek Humanism was in this way reintroduced into Europe by Arab philosophers to form the substratum of the Renaissance.

XIV to XVI centuries: The Humanist Renaissance. Petrarch recovers ancient texts from Greece and Rome. Artistic expressions become concerned with human existence and emotions, rather than the divine. Puledda reproduces a text from Pico de la Mirandola as follows: *"Oration on the Dignity of Man* was conceived as an oration to be read at the opening of the projected great debate in Rome, in order to give direction to the event and define its scope. At its beginning, Pico presents his conception of the human being, doing so with a rhetorical figure of great effectiveness: God explaining how He has created man. Here is the relevant text:

> "We have given thee, Adam, no fixed seat, no form of thy very own,
> no gift peculiarly thine, that thou mayest feel as thine own, have as
> thine own, possess as thine own the seat, the form, the gifts which
> thou thyself shalt desire. A limited nature in other creatures is
> confined within the laws written down by Us. In conformity with thy

---

[27] *On Being Human: Interpretations of Humanism from the Renaissance to the Present*, forward by Mikhail Gorbachev. Latitude Press, 1997

free judgment, in whose hands I have placed thee, thou art confined by no bounds; and thou wilt fix limits of nature for thyself. I have placed thee at the centre of the world, that from there thou mayest more conveniently look around and see whatsoever is in the world. Neither heavenly nor earthly, neither mortal nor immortal have We made thee. Thou, like a judge appointed for being honorable, art the molder and maker of thyself; thou mayest sculpt thyself into whatever shape thou dost prefer. Thou canst grow downward into the lower natures which are brutes. Thou canst again grow upward from thy soul's reason into the higher natures which are divine."

Not surprisingly this text has been hailed as a true first Humanist Manifesto. It contains in fact a remarkably modern description of, and invitation to exercise, Intentionality.

Erasmus of Rotterdam marks the more religious aspect of Renaissance humanism. His critique of the ways of the Church of his times helped pave the way for the Reformation. His friend Thomas More, in his work *Utopia*, expresses a new concept way ahead of his times: a moral society based on human (rather than divine) intentions.

Other important names were: Galileo Galilei who contributed to setting the basis for the scientific method; Francis Bacon who described with great precision the "idols" that taint the vision of the consciousness, no doubt a great advance in the understanding of the subjective quality of intentionality; and Giordano Bruno who was burned at the stake not only for his adherence to Copernicus' heliocentric theory of the universe but also for his alternative views about human spirituality.

During the XIX century Humanism identified itself with rationalist and secular currents of thought in such a way that its name becomes synonymous with atheism. This view has been criticised by William James who proposed that humanism cannot be exclusively identified with its scientific and secular versions, any more than religion may be monopolised by fundamentalism. (*The Variety of Religious Experience*, 1902)

In his early writings Marx considers the human being as the active part in the development of history. Later, his *Historical Materialism* relegates human consciousness to a second place, giving the Productive Forces the central role, and moving away in this way from the humanist position.

Jacques Maritain developed at the beginning of the XX Century his Theocentric Humanism (as opposed to the Anthropocentric one, as he describes other forms) in order to update the Church into a more modern relationship with its environment.

The 1st and 2nd Humanist Manifestos of the American Humanist Association state the basis for tolerance and non-violence in society, supported by ethics that have their roots in secular rationalism. Heidegger's Humanism mainly criticises other humanisms for accepting metaphysical assumptions about the world into which humans come to spend their existence and stresses the quality of Being-in-the world, that is, the situational hallmark of Being. In Existentialist Humanism Jean-Paul Sartre brings up the theme of Husserl's Phenomenology that sees consciousness not as a passive recipient or reflection of the world but as the active force that structures and creates the social world in the process. He takes this view to the idea of political commitment or "engagement", in this case leaning towards a socialist perspective.

As we can see, there have been many attempts to position the human being in the Universe. What is quite clear is that we live in a world of human intentions and that whatever belief we may have about the beginning of the world or humanity we can only count with any certainty on our human intention to take us wherever we want to go, or even more importantly, to decide where we want to go. It is also more or less clear that we cannot make decisions in complete isolation from other people because everything we do has an influence on others and everything others do has an influence on us. Therefore a certain level of co-ordination of intentions for the common well being is necessary. We could say these are the roots of our "social contract". (Sigh...) If everything were so simple.

If we can agree that Humanism is about achieving a better comprehension of the meaning of "being human" we need to observe how it is directly related to the concept of intentionality. The understanding that we see the world from a human point of view and that we cannot rid ourselves of such subjective vision has led science to a search for its neutralisation through the statistical method, double blind studies and computer programs for random assignation. However, what cannot be randomly determined is what subject is to be researched; therefore science has to accept that it can never be completely objective and that its direction is given by human intentionality. Slowly, we have been becoming aware that there is no observation without an observer and that the observer is part of the observation. In the studies of quantum mechanics this has been seen to be more poignantly stressed than in other areas of science. This realisation is penetrating our way of thinking, clashing against the rigidity of a belief in "an objective reality". Upon this rests, in addition to many intolerant perceptions of the world, the whole power structure.

Science fiction, in particular in the post-war 1950s, tried to produce supra-human characters, mutants or visitors from other planets, possessing special powers like telepathy and teleportation. They had different values and different senses. However, not many authors tried to imagine them without intentionality, without a subjective vision guiding their actions, demonstrating in this way how difficult it is for writers to conceive mechanisms other than those of their own consciousness.

Husserl pointed out that we do not see the world from the outside but always from the centre of our own mental space (which Silo[28] developed later in his study of the space of representation). However, we see others "from outside", therefore we use a different point of view to see ourselves and to see others. This does not necessarily lead to an insurmountable alienation since by means of the simple mechanism of communication we can obtain information about how others see themselves "from within" and we can verify similarities and differences. We can put ourselves in "other people's shoes" and we can make choices between individualism and solidarity. The educator Jaime Barilko expresses this in a paraphrase of Descartes:

"I think, therefore, you think".

Perhaps some of the most important experiences that seem to establish this communication, the connection between two different conscious individuals, are the most "unusual" phenomena lacking a clear rational explanation, from *"déjà vu"* to unexplainable coincidences. We tend to be relieved to discover that our "strange" experiences are shared by others. Such connection is largely emotional

---

[28] *Contributions to Thought, Collected Works*, by Silo. Latitude Press, San Diego, USA, 2002

but also touches on a sense of meaning. In these circumstances, the variability in landscapes is replaced by the commonality of mechanisms of consciousness, which gives us a taste of humanity, distancing us from other live and inanimate entities in which we do not recognise such commonality. However, the smallest glimpses of rudimentary mechanisms that remind us of our own immediately connect us to other external nonhuman entities. So we talk to our computers as if they could think or have a will of their own. Frequently we project human qualities onto animals and interpret their behaviour according to our own mechanisms of consciousness. Not surprisingly, many people feel more "connected" to their pets than to their neighbours, as the pets have been taught to please their owners and to reflect somehow their owners' preferences, whereas the neighbours insist on having their own particular and not always friendly intentions.

If we can take a structural look at the world that surrounds us we can see the action of a similar intentionality upon different aspects of the social spectrum leading to concomitant changes. For example, in the last few decades the hidden or secret tends to become visible: *Glasnost* (openness or transparency, in the ex-Soviet Union), investigative journalism uncovering conspiracies and scandals, in architecture buildings like the Pompidou Centre and the Lloyds building in London externalising pipes and structure that used to be hidden and, in Popular Culture, the singer Madonna created a trend characterised by wearing underwear on the outside. Superman had done the same many years before but the intention seems to have been to conceal rather than to show. The cinema industry echoed this trend by equating ugly and horrific with visible skulls, guts and muscles and oozing body fluids. TV gave access like never before to the contents of other people's minds, allowing close-ups of the joys and sufferings of others, not just friends or relatives but people from different races and cultures as well as those who had been traditionally concealed from the general public. Around the time of Queen Elizabeth II's "*annus horribilis*", one daughter-in-law showed her breasts and the other (tragically) her emotions; then the future King confessed his unfaithfulness in an unprecedented interview, all in a sort of Royal *Glasnost*.

Some philosophers remained, however, unmoved by this wealth of evidence about consciousness (or intentionality) in "the other", and so the "problem of zombies" became much debated. In essence, the issue is that we only have direct access to our own consciousness and others may behave as if they also have it but there is no way to tell for sure. So, for all we know, we may be surrounded by zombies acting as if they were human. It is unlikely that anybody would actually believe this, but many times an absurd concept is created in order to facilitate disproving it rationally. Absurd as it may be, the theory of zombies reflects the trend towards the subjective register of dehumanisation that accompanies some social processes.

We have seen earlier in this book the relationship that exists between the denial of intentionality in others and violence. Unlike the philosopher who muses about zombies in general, the individual who uses "zombification" as a form of violence is highly selective, reflecting an intrinsic ideology. If somebody feels that only bank managers and private entrepreneurs are truly human and that the workforce is largely zombie-like, it is likely that this person will adhere to neo-liberal schemes. If, instead, we observe somebody who feels that only those who participate in the productive forces are worth of human solidarity, this person will probably be a Communist. There are, of course, degrees of dehumanisation and there is a huge gap between simply avoiding thoughts about the suffering of others and going out deliberately to destroy them. The "problem of zombies" also opens the question of the extent of responsibility of thinkers who may create a theory or model that gives credence and respectability to violent dehumanisation tendencies. Very few people would try to justify the social Darwinism of the Nazi regime in Germany, but the social Darwinist state of affairs being created in the name of individual freedom in market economies appears to be doing just fine.

Philosophers and their models may have a much deeper effect on social tendencies than we realise. Karl Popper wisely criticised the exaggerated claims of the scientific method, but later he went on to develop his Three Worlds Theory which, in my view, takes humanity a step further into a dehumanised path. In short the model proposes the existence of three worlds, or fields: World 1 is the objective world of material things, World 2 is the subjective world of minds and World 3 is the world of the products of those minds, which after being created acquire independent existence. That is, once knowledge is created it is stored in books, CDs, etc. and it is no longer part of the subjective world of mind. This model is not *wrong* because models are rarely wrong, as the mind has the plasticity to adapt to the shape of most models. However this model is *harmful* because it denies that we all carry in our minds other minds or at least parts of other people's minds, since it tells us that once the product of somebody's creativity becomes imprinted on an object for storage, it becomes divorced from the original processes that created it. The model also contributes to the view that the contents of one's mind only belongs to the self. We can observe, however, that we carry in ourselves the accumulation of thousands of years of evolution in human thinking, and if any one of us had been born at any other time the contents of our minds would have been completely different.

It is, of course, possible to acquire a great deal of knowledge without knowing anything about the minds that produced it originally, but connecting the knowledge to the mind always adds something to it. Recently, I let my mathematically challenged mind struggle through Roger Penrose's *The Emperor's New Mind* and the Turing Test immediately caught my attention as the problem of Artificial Intelligence is so closely linked to the problem of zombies and consciousness in general. In this test a series of questions is given to a human and to a computer. If the computer manages to deceive the listeners into believing that they are hearing the answers from a man (or a woman) then one must assume that the computer also possesses consciousness. Later on I came across some biographical notes about Alan Turing, one of the pioneers of modern computing who, being a homosexual in 1940s Britain, had more than a fair share of problems (in fact he was forced to take female hormones and ended up committing suicide). Apparently, he originally designed the Turing Test to prove that it was not possible to tell the difference between answers given by a man from those given by a woman. It seemed to me of utmost importance to see how knowledge often arises from a quest to overcome suffering, in particular when suffering is created by oppression. In this sense, I have to disagree with Popper's sterilised World 3 and conclude that the mechanisms of consciousness involved in the production of knowledge are as important as the knowledge itself. But in order to perceive this, one must be prepared to connect with the human quality of "the other" and with their needs, something that leads to a sense of solidarity.

If ideas become disconnected from the people who produced them, then it is possible to support the kind of furious competitive individualism (again, Social Darwinism) that characterised Popperian social thinking. Another problem in this model is that it refers to knowledge that has already been produced. During our lifetime new knowledge will be manufactured by others, some of it undoubtedly of some benefit to us, and there is no guarantee that it will be done by individuals belonging the social class, the race or the culture we feel naturally inclined to help develop. So our attitude towards different social groups will contribute to determine the quality and quantity of intellectual production that will eventually make it into books and CDs. Severing the connection between others' production and their intentionality is also self-destructive.

The divorce between people and their production is also involved in the process of dehumanisation that began with the Industrial Revolution. Artisans manufactured things for others who knew who had made them. In the industrialised society the production line became completely anonymous, so it is not difficult to see how we may forget that the objects we use are the products of human work. Art has preserved this relationship between the producer and the production, and large amounts of money are paid for this insight into somebody else's mind, feelings, etc. Nobody contemplating Munch's *The Scream* can deny the strength of feeling of the author, even if we are also making our own subjective interpretations. Designer clothes, sunglasses, watches, etc., came to recreate that feeling of "I know the person who made this" but only for the artist, the designer. The production line remains anonymous. Separating the scientist, the thinker and the inventor from their production can only reinforce the trend towards dehumanisation. We can feel that our need of other people decreases as the knowledge we seek can be found in books and CD ROMs. Would Stephen Hawkins' adherence to the "Big Crunch" theory (that the Universe will collapse after expanding for a while longer) be the same to us if we did not have an image of the man himself undergoing an equivalent experience? Theories have the capacity to affect the way people feel about the world in which they are living, just as much as artistic production does. Optimistic theories fill people with hope and energy to go out and construct. Apocalyptic scientific predictions fill them with gloom and dismay. The assumption that scientists' theories are not affected by their personal lives, wishes and failures, as well as believing that scientists are "objective", leaves us open to the influence of the ups and downs of their personal lives.

Perhaps the most important lesson we may derive from the awareness of the creative process in others is to stimulate the creative process in ourselves, that is, our own intentionality.

The effect of the location of one's mind amongst other minds can be dramatic enough, but the influence of images about the location of one's body in space (and space has been changing a lot since Galileo discovered that other planets also had moons) can also suffer extreme expansions and contractions, accelerations and sudden stops, a little like going on a bus.

Not that long ago the Earth was, at least for some people, a still flat disc alone in the Heavens. A few centuries later we are travelling at an unimaginable speed in so many directions (spinning, orbiting, and moving towards some unknown point in the Galaxy, hopefully not a Black Hole, wobbling on our Earth axis and rushing away from the Big Bang epicentre) pushed and pulled by close neighbours and far away cosmic enigmas. This is not the best system of images to feel any kind of self-control over one's own body. However, just before humanity's threatened to shrivel into insignificance, the Anthropic Principle came to the rescue. It suggested that this carbon-based universe in which we live could only be the way it is because if it were any other way we would not be here living in and observing it. Some went even further by proposing that this universe is so unbelievably improbable that it allows us to assume that it was created the way it is *in order to* allow consciousness to develop - a jump with great style from physical theory to metaphysical teleology. It is not difficult to see the fingerprints of intentionality all over such a radical leap. Human consciousness was again firmly placed at the centre of the universe but this time not in a way as self-assured as the belief that Man had been chosen from above by a humanoid to reign over all other creatures. This new central role rather seems to stem from awareness that we can only perceive the universe the way our consciousness construes it and that a better understanding of the world(s) "out there" requires changes in our very own consciousness, including the way we connect with our spiritual life or God.

So much stress on the power of our intentional consciousness made many people uncomfortable. In his book *The Dice Man*, Luke Reinhart creates a character that decides to live by chance. He makes a list of actions to carry out during the day and lets the dice choose for him. Inevitably, he is unable to eliminate altogether his intentionality since he himself must choose the items of the list, or the person who will elaborate the list, etc. In other words, in order to liberate himself he feels he must give up his freedom of choice but, as Sartre had already pointed out, this is no easy task.

Intentionality also makes us responsible for the direction of our viewpoint and our value judgements. For this reason there have been attempts to neutralise it in our judicial system, assuming that the decision of many is less biased that the decision of one, e.g., in trials by jury, of which Pontius Pilate may have been an unwitting predecessor by allowing the people of Judea to take the decision from his hands.

Socio-economic systems have been designed in which it is supposed that intentionality does not exist. In Communism it was assumed that every aspect of the organisation sprang from the shape of the productive forces and the State was given all the power and property (including human beings). There is little doubt today that the intentionality of those operating in the name of the State gave direction to the process or, in other words, any system is as good or as bad as the intentions of the people operating within it. During a TV interview Mikhail Gorbachev criticised precisely such contradictions exemplified in Stalin's flags full of wonderful slogans of Equality and Freedom whilst the human being was being subjected to the most horrific oppression. Similarly, in the Market Economy everything is left to the wisdom of the market forces without acknowledgement that they are manipulated and directed by a minority in control of international financial capital and intent on continuing to increase their profits. In these systems of assumed external control some social situations are seen as inevitable accidents or consequences of the general order. There is, however, good evidence that unemployment in market economies is not only seen as desirable but more precisely as essential to curtail the power of trade unions and "flexibilise" the workforce. This was "confessed" by one of Margaret Thatcher's aides in an interview with the press.[29]

One of the most interesting failures of the predictions made about the Industrial Revolution - at least in the UK, for which Marx had described the inevitable liberation of the workers after a few

---

[29] The Observer 21/6/92 Alan Budd *"Maggie's man: We were wrong"*

predictable victories up the class struggle and a new Revolution - was the failure to foresee that it only liberated the aristocracy and led to only a partial improvement in working conditions. In creating a strong class of entrepreneurs locked in permanent battle for wages with the working class it distracted attention from the fact that the landed gentry could continue to live off the ground rent paid by just about everybody living in their extensive territories. In fact the Feudal System never quite went away; it just went out of people's awareness and/or priorities. The next step in this dehumanising saga was the advent of the shareholders, who diverted the attention from the struggle between owners and workers, both emotionally and personally committed to the future of the company, to the much more detached decision-making process guided by a discussion between the Assembly of Shareholders and Management, both capable of walking away without much grief if the Company got into real trouble.

Erich Fromm pointed out that the horror of dehumanisation is not a Right or Left political problem and that there have been people in both tendencies who raised their voices to denounce the dangers of human objectification in the industrial society. However, the two sides differed in the proposed solutions, which he qualified as Romantic for the right and Radical Humanist for the left. His own desire to complement the spiritual/psychological with the socio-political existential needs of the human being led him to syncretise Marxism and Psychoanalysis, not always with happy consequences. Others used the term Humanism to refer to the most varied doctrines, already mentioned at the beginning of this chapter. Thus Christian Humanism, Existential Humanism and so many others came about, so many contradicting one another, but in the common name searching for something that can describe, define, comprehend once and for all the human phenomenon.

Humanism encourages us to form an Identity that expands to include all human beings. The expansion of identity is generally a mechanical process that starts in childhood, when identity is given by a sense belonging to one's parents and home, one's toys and favourite foods. When children begin to go to school they are presented with national symbols, class, grouping by intellectual abilities and race. Some schools will also provide a sense of belonging by means of uniforms and pride in the name of the institution itself. Other identities that emerge at this time are preferences for one football club and the exclusion of (even hostility to) others.

As we grow up, identity continues to expand to include other interests and clubs, profession (or lack of it) and one's general social role. Identity may continue to expand to the rest of humanity through travelling, learning other languages, trying other ethnic groups' food or admiring their art. Identity may also start shrinking at this point if the future is felt to be threatened by competition, hostility, war, etc. In this case taking refuge in a particular group or nationality, or race, even profession, and excluding from one's identity the more general human species is a very mechanical and mostly animal response of retreating into one's territory in order to feel stronger and more protected. This seems to work for a while but more often than not it strengthens the threat. What works for animals does not work for humans in the long run. We can see from history that security is best created by not having enemies, rather than by raising the highest fences.

When identity expands to include oneself as a member of the human species, we can look at designing policies and forms of organisation that do not exclude anybody and that do not create resentment and desire for revenge. This ideal state of things is of course very difficult to achieve, because of fear (reinforced *ad nauseam* by those who profit from all forms of violence) and because we are starting from a position where a lot of centuries-old resentments and enmities are already playing an important role in social organisation. We cannot sweep aside the pain that is already there and claim a clean slate from today. Nor can we justify continuing the long line of retaliatory existence that ensures violence and destruction in our times and for future generations. Becoming part of the human species as an identity demands a re-accommodation of certain images in our minds and this implies a very courageous effort. Many will be asking themselves "Why should I be the first?"

Since most people in a situation of conflict feel sincerely that they are the injured party, that is, the victim, being the first one to let go and extend a hand in friendship or simply call a truce is unimaginable. It might be seen at best as a show of weakness, at worst as a betrayal of their own identity and their people. "A fight to the death", "victory or death", these are battle cries that ensure nobody will question the wisdom of going into that battle in the first place, or consider the alternatives. A cartoon character in the Mafalda series reads in a book:

"It is better to die standing than to live on your knees", and wonders, "What about just subsisting sitting down?"

So why should I be the first to adopt this extended identity, this universal inclusion of every human being on Earth (and beyond, perhaps in the future), why should I be the first one to stop the violence?

(1) Because choosing to intentionally produce the termination of an age-old conflict over the default mode, that is, the mechanical continuation of the cycle of violence and revenge, is an act of great courage and it embodies the essence of humanity over purely animal instinctive behaviour.

(2) Because it opens the future for oneself and for others, sometimes for many millions of others and surely for one's loved ones.

(3) Because in a seemingly materialistic and meaningless world, in which happiness is as long-lasting as our interest in a new car, a new house, a new relationship or a new toy, taking humanity into a new positive era, being able to effect a positive change produces a much more all-encompassing sense of inner satisfaction. It is also an antidote against the stress induced by the sense of lack of control over our environment, since we can gain the register of faith in our capacity to influence it.

It is difficult to see how violence can be ended just by somebody giving the order to do so, no matter how charismatic, mystical or rich. Only the extension of one's own identity as "human-like-you" will be able to help us identify with enough elements or other people, no matter how different their colour, customs and beliefs, to trigger the empathy mechanism in which we can feel the pain we inflict on another person. It is a process that begins with a decision, a resolution. Such a decision is, however, not enough because we will always revert to the default mode when we are tired, not paying attention, daydreaming or angry. It is necessary to make an honest and thorough examination of one's mechanical tendencies and the images that are linked to them that trigger violence or discrimination in our reactions. Recognising them, softening them and intentionally modifying them may take time but it is a shared work that strengthens our sense of community and belonging. Education also needs to contemplate how to promote the extension of identity prospectively for the new citizens during their formative years. Much good practice is already available, but it often depends on the goodwill of teachers already busy and forced to prioritise the academic curriculum over all other concerns. When the real dimension of the potential benefits that the end of social violence may bring to the world community as a whole is taken into account, perhaps education that prioritises this extended identity, inclusive of all diversity may become a reality.

Chapter 13

THE SPACE OF REPRESENTATION
IMAGES FOR CHANGE

In phenomenological terms consciousness is always consciousness "of something", an interaction between the function of perceiving or experiencing the internal and the external worlds and the objects belonging to those spaces available to our perception at any particular time. We do not, however, perceive them "as they are in themselves" but rather "as we see them". Therefore a more precise definition could refer to those worlds by calling them Internal and External Landscapes[30], to imply the presence of our own subjective point of view in the description of these spaces.

We link these two spaces by means of images, either as the final stage of the process of perception in the presence of external objects or as a representation of real or imaginary ones in the absence of external stimuli. These images happen within the Space of Representation and their study provides an interesting basis for the understanding of the interaction between individual and social phenomena as well as the nature of intentionality.

Although our consciousness has no extension in itself (or at least not beyond the extension of our bodies) it has the capacity to contain the representation of the whole universe. In this sense consciousness performs its functions as the perfect unlimited interactive virtual reality. As it does not structure its representations as passive reflections of the "real world" but rather always carries an intention, we could see consciousness as virtual reality with an attitude.

Many have expressed their worry about using the language of technology to describe phenomena of consciousness, such as calling the brain the "hardware" and the learning of incoming data the "software". In my view, far from this being problematic, it is extremely telling of what we are doing by creating technology, that is, we are projecting the capabilities of our own brains and our bodies in general into the

---

[30] *Humanise the Earth*, by Silo, Looks and Landscapes. *Collected Works*, Latitude Press, San Diego, USA 2002

outside world, to perfect them, enlarge their capacity and perhaps also in order to understand them better. A simple example can be found in the way levers, developed to move heavy weights, helped understand how muscles, tendons and bones work. In many ways this also applies to computers. They now come to complement the study of animal behaviour that has allowed our ancestors to discover rudimentary forms of human elements, which are easier to understand in a simpler way, without the complexities they acquire when we move to study them at human scale.

Description of the space of representation

If we close our eyes, we become aware of a space in front of us. This is not a flat screen. We can imagine an object in it, moving right or left, forwards or backwards, up or down. This is a three dimensional space where we can represent forms, colours, memories, sounds, yellow submarines, the smell of freshly baked bread, etc. In fact we can represent images originating in any of the senses, as well as others that come purely from our imagination. Now, if we open our eyes this space disappears and we see "the real world", but it is still possible to imagine that there is somebody behind a door when there is nobody there, the imagined presence being real enough to produce fear. We can also "see" someone else's expression as bored, friendly, hostile or indifferent according to our own particular mood.

Let us revise now our perception of "reality". Since Immanuel Kant and other Transcendental Idealists[31], it has become more or less clear to humanity that we do not see reality "in itself" but rather our perception of reality. Phenomenologist thinkers enriched this concept with their detailed studies on the nature of perceived phenomena. Silo in particular described how what we see as reality has been filtered through the senses, associated with memories, tinged by our emotional state as well as our intentions and hopes for the future and by whether we are fully awake or half asleep.

The perception of the external landscape overlaps with the space of representation when our eyes are open in such a way that it is possible to add elements to the perception which are in fact representations. In general we realise quite well that such elements are imaginary -

---

[31] *System of Transcendental Idealism* (1800).

psychosis and altered states induced by some drugs (i.e. hallucinations) being the most obvious exception. However, when the mind is invaded by powerful emotions, differentiating what is coming from the "outside" from what is being added from the "inside" may become a more difficult task. Going back to the example in Chapter 1, if I see two of my friends laughing, telling each other something in a whisper and looking in my direction, I might infer that they are talking critically about me when in reality they are simply sharing an embarrassing secret. It is not unusual to see meanings in our perceptions that are just in our imagination. Intentionality, our wonderful capacity to complete the picture and give meaning to everything our consciousness interacts with, sometimes gets it very wrong. Contradictions in the form of strong internal struggles between thoughts and feelings reduce our capacity to perceive with clarity by adding the contents of such struggles to any experienced phenomenon, as a sort of haze that clouds our understanding and makes us act in the social world on faulty information. The feedback from the social world that follows this inevitably inappropriate and misguided behaviour may tend to confirm the individual's mistaken interpretation of events. In this way, somebody who permanently accuses (wrongly) others of persecuting him/her on account of a strong personal belief or climate will get in the end rather unfriendly reactions from their social environment. Our own attitude towards others is more often than not a self-fulfilling prophecy. This works not only for paranoia but also for a positive outlook, as zillions of self-help manuals would attest.

The space of representation overlaps with, and manages to imitate in many ways, the perceived world. This is not surprising since perceptions condition the space of representation. We are born into a three dimensional space, lit at the top by the sun and dark at the bottom. Throughout our formative years our nervous system develops anatomically and functionally to live in it. It is known from animal studies that if a kitten is brought up in a space that only contains vertical lines, as an adult the cat will not recognise horizontal lines. In a similar but at the same time much more complex way, the space we perceive in our childhood and adolescence (the formation landscape) conditions our space of representation that will accompany us throughout our adult lives.

Human beings are, however, different from cats. The critical period for the development of specific functions of the human brain is much longer than for most animals and for many abilities it is only relative. This means that even if a function is not developed during the critical period, it may be learnt later, albeit in an imperfect way: languages get spoken "with an accent" if learned after the ages of 11 or 12, when the critical period for the acquisition of a "mother tongue" ends.

Another fundamental difference is human intentionality, which actively modifies the environment in response to the attribution of meaning it gives to perceptions. For instance, although our space of representation is fundamentally three dimensional in response to the sensory data accumulated since childhood, physicists today rebel against this limitation and force themselves to "think" in more dimensions. New generations are presented with this concept in the course of their education and in science fiction literature, so what for one generation is "created" for the next one is a "part of the given environment"; this leads to real differences in the way members of a society relate to the concept and in the very way the brains of different generations are organised. It is important to stress here that the wiring of the brain is not a static anatomical structure that gets fixed at a point in time. Far from it, the phenomenon of brain plasticity continues to evolve throughout our lives and new neuronal connections appear and disappear in response to stimuli, experiences, plans and hormonal and other biochemical changes. Likewise, and partly as a consequence of this phenomenon, consciousness is not a fixed container that houses objects like an empty box, but rather it has been described as a "stream" which, like a river, is never the same in two different moments.

The projection of the contents of our space of representation into the social world reminds us of conditionings acquired from the physical one: to be at the "peak" of one's career, "on top" of the world, that "sinking" feeling, achieving "stardom". The social environment further shapes the internal one in continuous feedback creating the illusion of an "external, objective reality". Let us consider some expressions of this: morality, religion, and the class system.

The human being has developed the historical and atavistic sense that good things come from the heights and bad things happen at the bottom. Perhaps this image has been enhanced by the position of the sun, above, source of life and warmth, worshipped in the form of various gods, beacon of light ever present in most mystical currents. Down below there is darkness (probably primitive humans were more vulnerable to predators at night) and soil, hidden things, where the body goes after death in many cultures.

Also the body has in the upper part the head, with ideas, aspirations, intelligence, and the domination of animals bigger and more powerful but less clever. Our eyes and ears, our main connection with the world, are also at the top. At the bottom of our body we find sex and mechanical functions like walking, excretion, etc. It is interesting to imagine our view of the world if our eyes were located on the tips of our big toes!

Erect walking, which allows a view "from above", is considered by many, together with human sexuality (i.e. the "missionary position"), and speech, quite "natural" to the human being, but these are three characteristics that humans only learn when brought up in a human environment, that is, they are the result of social learning.

The physical world has lent our history the language to express that good things come from above. For instance, let us take the power structure. The class system has the "upper class" as the best, the one with more privileges, the most respected. Our internal landscape has its upper part occupied by ideas, aspirations, the future, guides, religious figures, gods and angels, idols and mystical experiences. The overlap of these with the class system lends the upper classes the glow of the other occupants of the region, so that we "look up" to those we admire or feel our superiors. This makes us subservient to them, we copy their hairstyle and try to "ascend" in the social ladder to rub shoulders with the great and the good, escaping with horror from the "lower" classes to which the language of discrimination attributes what is instinctive, mechanical, irrational, or uncontrollable in the depths of our internal world: low passions, dark motives, wanton sexuality, absence of "discrimination".

The real disadvantages created by this vision, such as bad health, poor housing and a shorter life expectancy for the poorer layers of society, give a rational justification to the struggle to "climb" the social ladder and to "look down" on those we see below us. During the French Revolution and in the writings of Karl Marx and others who made egalitarian proposals we see again the rebellion of human intentionality against this mechanical and unjust vision. Their failure in practice makes us aware of the difficulties in overcoming the "pecking order" without an understanding of these internal processes. Revolutions of external structures that are not accompanied by a reorganisation in the images we carry in our space of representation are doomed to fail, as people will recreate the same society over and over again, albeit giving different labels to the same social forces. They relate to the way images are organised in our consciousness, because these projections are imposed on us early in our lives and are then endlessly reinforced by the propaganda of the interested parties.

The power structure is further reinforced by attributing to the existing or imagined "powers" (Gods, Nature, Extraterrestrials, The Stars and the Market Forces) the capacity to control, regulate or punish humans. Sometimes the self-appointed priests of these "powers" elevate themselves above other human beings in the name of the "sacred" or "specialised" function they fulfil, often creating an esoteric language that ensures a closed shop and excludes the uninitiated (e.g. legalese in the complex and very power orientated Legal System; in the same way Mass in Latin used to stress an intermediated relationship between the congregation and God).

In this way a class system and power structure which are presented to us as "natural" or, at least, historically determined start to feel much less deterministic, in fact basically a consequence of human intentions and, therefore, much more amenable to change. In the words of the Indian writer Arundhati Roy, we are looking at "human history masquerading as God's purpose".

Social classes are also defined by the amount of money people have. In the ideology of monetarism money acquires value in itself, in other words it is no longer a convention, or a practical way of simplifying barter, but it becomes the coveted object itself. It becomes a myth, the universal expander, the means to get not only material goods but also that subtle something which will make us complete. It becomes the means to become that sought after image of the perfect self. It becomes the only reward for a person's effort. It becomes the value of a human being. It becomes the only god, with banks as its churches, the "gurus" of the free market economy as its prophets and bank managers as its priests. It can only work as long as consumers, producers and dealers have "confidence" in the system, that is: faith.

Where are religions left in this space of representation with its top hijacked by Mammon, pop "idols" and film "stars"?

A search for the purpose or meaning of human life has been quite widespread in unconnected civilisations. Often this meaning has been made explicit in the particular creational history or myth of a human group; for example, in the Judeo-Christian tradition suffering is connected to meaning as humanity is supposed to be atoning for the Original Sin, whilst the inclinations of presiding gods in other traditions set the direction for the mortals they allegedly created or regulated - aesthetic in the Greek civilisation, hedonistic and war-oriented for the Romans, deeply rooted in the forces of nature for American Indians and original African doctrines.

Religions may have appeared to cope with the unknown, amongst other things with death. For whatever reason, the gods came to occupy the upper part of our space of representation, perhaps following deification of natural phenomena like the sun, the moon, etc., reinforced by the original intimation of the potential of the human being to become something different, to know, located as a register in the head. Some religions may have been started by the experience of special states of consciousness described today as "experiences of light" or "peak experiences". Unfortunately we cannot rule out also that some religious phenomena may have derived from hallucinatory experiences, either chemically induced and brought on by mind altering substances or by the elevation to the role of priest, witch doctor or prophet deranged members of ancient societies. The expressions of some or all of these experiences have been then surely projected into the human landscape in ways that were pertinent to their cultures. Soon some people must have discovered that manipulation of others "in the name of the gods" was much more powerful than simple brute force, setting the scenario for a happy marriage between the development of powerful religious hierarchies and the class system, both living off the glow of a more profound and meaningful spiritual search.

Morality also responded to the projections of internal regions. Above: the "elevated", the "spiritual" paths, high aspirations, ethereal activities disconnected from the body; below: the mechanical, sexual, passion driven, eschatological pursuits. A morality was created that extolled fasts, physical pain and sexual abstinence and condemned the pleasures of the body and sex as sinful, the works of the devil who lives below in the "underworld", bringing a person down through temptation, the "fallen" woman and the man of "low" passions.

Even in a more updated scheme like Sigmund Freud's we draw the rational conscious at the top separated by a dotted line from the unconscious *below*, full of messy instincts and unmentionable desires. Jung, instead, located the unconscious (or at least a part of it) closer to the gods, mystical experiences and the stars. In view of the clear differences in registers given by this opposing location of images it is not really surprising that those two founders of the Psychotherapy School could not understand one another. We can also see the difference in registers produced by the morality and the social forms that stem from rigidly vertical and patriarchal religions when compared with those that arise from the cult of "Mother Earth", typically showing flattened hierarchies and a friendlier attitude towards sex and the body.

Gravity adds its weight to these correlations of bodily sensations and representation of values. No doubt it feels good to "climb" the social ladder, the effort makes it even more worthwhile, but in order to go down one only has to "let oneself go". Economists tell us that if we have faith in the market forces and let them do their job properly and without interference wealth will accumulate "at the top" and then it will "trickle down" to the less able. For those waiting in vain at the bottom of the social hierarchy wealth might appear as the first element capable of defying gravity.

Concepts appear in the space of representation as images which may be conjured up as an effort of imagination, or they can arrive into consciousness fully formed from memory. Often they correspond to translations of impulses coming from the inner body, such as thinking of food when we are hungry, craving for a cold shower when we are hot, or dreaming about being persecuted and not being able to run when our legs are entangled in the bed sheets.

Literature provides us with many examples of this translation of impulses from the body into images that appear in the space of representation.

In *Lady Audley's Secret* by Mary Elizabeth Braddon, one of the characters says: "Come out of the room, Alice. I believe it's damp, or else haunted. Indeed I believe all ghosts to be the result of damp. You sleep in a damp bed - you awake suddenly in the dead of the night with a cold shiver, and see an old lady in the court costume of George the First's time, sitting at the foot of the bed. The old lady is indigestion, and the cold shiver is a damp sheet."

Cyrano de Bergerac, who was later to be made famous by Rostand's play in which his large nose becomes the focus of tragedy in his life, wrote in the XVII century a book called *Journey to the Moon*. In this book the inhabitants of the moon measure their intelligence by the length of their noses, which they also use as a sort of sundial. By pointing the nose to the sun they can read the time on their teeth, no doubt a very interesting attempt to see the source of his unhappiness as an asset. Not only does he give his big nose a raison d'être but he also locates it in the "heights", next to the moon, the sun and intelligence in the space of representation.

A telling example of the confusion of responsibility in locating images in the space of representation is that when we fall in love we "put that person on a pedestal", but when our feelings change the person "falls" all by him/herself.

Not only visual images and bodily sensations can evoke different regions of the space of representation. Music can "elevate the spirit" or lead us to the "depths of hell". It should suffice to observe the faces of people listening to their favourite musical pieces; the way eyes roll upwards to follow the chords of certain passages. This phenomenon was not lost on religious institutions which have used music to evoke feelings in their congregations akin to "mystical" states, strengthening in this way the connection with the religious experience.

The predominant Eurocentric vision of the world can be seen in maps where the Northern Hemisphere is the one containing the dominant culture. Quino depicted the rebellion of a child living in the Southern Hemisphere against the idea of being "underdeveloped" by turning the globe upside down.

It appears then that in this complex space of representation there is an overlap of representations of bodily sensations, perceptions from the physical world, the representation of the social world and the representation of our internal world or psychological space, each component lending qualities to its neighbours in the same region. They can express themselves in the shape of images, which allow our consciousness to become aware of its own contents and produce interesting intentional modifications within itself, and in its relationship with the external world, by either transforming those images or re-locating them in a different region.

Structural thinking erases the dotted line between high and low and integrates these spaces in a dynamic relationship where the movement of images is free and devoid of moralistic prejudice. In this context the integration of psychological contents not only helps us to feel better but also devolves the structure energy that was stuck at the "top", in the "middle" or at the "bottom". It can then be used by any part of the individual's psyche to feed aspirations, to search for its own meaning or to transform his/her own environment, all part of the same structure.

Influence of levels of consciousness[32]

The space of representation is not a topographically rigid container, but rather its shape and the movement of its contents are influenced by the level of consciousness of the whole structure of the mind. During sleep images are believed as if they were in fact happening in reality. We say then that dreams have a high power of suggestibility. Also we tend to locate ourselves in dreams as part of the scene. Dreams may be allegorical (or symbolic), indicating the complex processes of integration and re-accommodation of contents and memories that is taking place during sleep. They may also be completely literal and many observers have pointed out that this is common in nightmares where conflicts present themselves painfully and crudely, in a way similar to daily reality. During sleep sensory input is transformed into imagery that protects this level. When a noise appears in the environment, such as the alarm clock, it may be translated into the image of someone shouting within a dream. If the stimulus continues the person wakes up and realises where the noise is really coming from.

In the level of semi-sleep or daydreaming we may be awake but only partially aware of our surroundings and engaged in some kind of imaginary story or fantasy. The suggestibility of these images is much lower than in true dreams and we know perfectly well that what we have in front of our eyes is not real. However these stories tend to be compelling as they serve as compensations for uncomfortable realities (those without a house may daydream about palaces, those without

---

[32] More detailed descriptions of the Space of Representation and levels of consciousness can be found in *Contributions to Thought,* by Silo in Collected Works, Latitude Press.

love think about princes in shining armour and everybody else dreams about the lottery and all the things we would do if we won it!). On the other hand, sensory input (seeing, hearing, etc) also impresses our consciousness in this state without any kind of critical selection, appearing to our minds as reality itself. This is due to a complete lack of awareness of the mechanisms and instruments of perception when we are rather caught up in the state of daydreaming.

This is the level of optimal sexual functioning where fantasies have the highest level of suggestibility to set in motion sexual activities and bodily sensations. This is also the level to which advertising tries to bring us down, as our critical power is much lower than when we are completely awake. In this state we are also much more suggestible and ready to believe any dreams presented to our vision either by our own consciousness, by the TV screen or by posters in the Underground. The fact that so many scantily clad or sexually provocative women are used in advertising reveals the intention of the advertisers to create an atmosphere that will lead us as deeply into semi-sleep as possible, seeking that high degree of suggestibility that will make us believe their claims about the advertised product. It is not difficult to detect in political advertising also an appeal to semi-sleep in the type of imagery that is presented to the electorate, which is not at all surprising, considering that political parties are more and more contracting advertising agencies to run their campaigns. In this way information is replaced by manipulation and representative democracy by "spin".

A particular state of heightened suggestibility, hypnosis, seems to be helping us understand the effect on the brain of "believing". A recent report of research carried out in the US appears to suggest that the brain reacts more to what it believes to be reality than to the stimuli presented to the senses. In this way, if a black and white picture is placed in front of a subject's eyes but he/she is hypnotised to believe that it is a colour picture, the part of the brain that "lights up" in a highly sensitive scan is the one related to the perception of colour, and vice versa.[33] This does not mean that belief is everything, since if we jump from a 15th floor we will die, no matter what we believe, and people who live below the poverty line will starve if they are deprived

---

[33] "How hypnosis can colour the mind", *The Guardian*, Monday February 18, 2002

of food even if they are hypnotised into thinking that the World Bank is looking after them. This all means that there is a "real world" out there, but it is also important to acknowledge the power of faith and belief in human behaviour.

A more awake level of consciousness is characterised by a stronger capacity for attention and concentration on a selected object or issue, an increase in criticism that reduces the suggestibility of images and a better awareness of their location in the space of representation, as well as more intentional activity. This is the optimal level for daily activities such as study or work. However, here we are still convinced that what we see is "the real world" as we tend to concentrate on the object that demands our attention rather on the mechanisms of, and effects on, our own minds. In this wakefulness or vigilic state we have enough access to an intentional direction of mental activity as to be able to reject daydreaming and external stimuli unrelated to the task as "distractions".

A higher level of consciousness is related to an increase in the capacity for attention not only to the object impressing our consciousness but also to the mechanisms of consciousness themselves, increasing in this way the intentional content of those mechanisms, also known as reversibility. In sensory terms seeing is replaced by looking, hearing by listening, and there may be an awareness of temperature, touch, taste, kinaesthesia (awareness of the position of the body) and coenaesthesia (the general sensation of the body as a whole). In memory remembering is replaced by recalling. Suggestibility drops to a minimum. Insight about the functions and shortcomings of one's own mind, and the way our perceptions are shaped by it, is at its highest in this state of consciousness of the self. It makes people less suggestible to dreams, political and social manipulation and advertising. It also makes us aware of the existence of consciousness in others and promotes empathy reducing our capacity to hurt others, as we can see more clearly that in doing so we also hurt ourselves. We can perceive here our own Space of Representation in action, its mechanical conditionings, its levels, and its confusion with "reality".

Totalitarian and authoritarian regimes may use overt force to control the people, but the so-called "open society" may be in fact as authoritarian and controlling as its blunter relatives when it uses the hypnotic power of semi-sleep. Fashion, image making, spin-doctors, celebrities as models, archetypes, pressure to conform, stigmatisation of dissent, and advertising in general are all part of the mechanisms of power that rely on control of people's subjectivity. A society that is seeking to become less violent and more intentional, ensuring individual freedom in the context of social co-operation and practicing not just tolerance but rather celebration of diversity requires ways to promote access to higher levels of consciousness for its inhabitants as part of their basic education and daily participation in the social contract.

Many people find it difficult to believe that the end of violence is possible since it fulfils so many roles in society. What will replace it? They ask, unaware of the universe of new activities that will open to everyone, such as creativity, involvement in decision-making, inner development, life-long learning, sports, leisure and many others we will discover when we are no longer so busy dreaming about freedom.

Chapter 14

NEW HUMANISM

Knowledge about the mechanisms of consciousness and the laws that rule the physical world grow, but human suffering does not seem to be diminishing significantly. Is this not a contradiction? Or at least, should it not be so?

This awareness may be the door to move towards a new type of society. The trouble is that old activists are tired and new generations come into a world that promotes disbelief that massive change could happen as a consequence of human effort. Those who question the global system are marginalised as an irrelevant nuisance, or their activities only reported when they involve violence.

Fragmentation is the sign of the times, internally and socially. This is the legacy of the apparent triumph of Capitalism over Socialism and the post-modern revolution, the one that questioned everything and left us submerged in a miasma of moral relativism. This is the perfect ground for pragmatism to take hold of the would-be new idealists. Pragmatism and idealism do not mix well. If a person is capable of imagining a better situation, there will be energy to move in that direction. But if the only parameter used to decide the direction of one's actions is immediate success, then nothing truly new can be created.

By definition, anything that can be delivered *ipso facto* demands that the conditions for it should already exist. Ideals act in the world by creating such conditions. They produce transformations that could be more important than the ideal itself, even if the ideal is not to be achieved in the end. It has already been mentioned that Immanuel Kant proposed the creation of something akin to the League of Nations as a way to attain lasting peace in Europe. Surely he did not live to see it happening; nor did he live to see it failing. However, this ideal worked for more than two centuries upon people's consciousness in such a way that it led to attempts to find new ways to link up with other countries which in the past had been their enemies. An ideal cannot be undertaken pragmatically, becoming dependent on its immediate results. This acceptance of the short-termistic mental frame by those who consider themselves idealists is an important point in the paralysis experienced by so many disillusioned activists, prisoners in the belief that the only good ideal is the one that can deliver immediate results. Idealists should also learn to recognise the critical moments, the windows of opportunity, the bifurcation points in the chaotic systems, where concrete actions may position the direction of the process closer to its objectives.

So many speak today of confusion, moral relativism and lack of fixed and permanent points of reference, cynicism, the materialist life, a lack of models...

Beliefs are about having a sense of control over one's environment (we have already seen the way that absence of control is registered as stress). Cynicism is therefore the ultimate form of control. Cynics are right more often than idealists because things do not change unless we believe they can, unless we put the energy to make them change even if this means taking the risk that we may fail. Change can also be the result of accidents in ways that are seen as uncontrollable. Being right does not mean being happy, in particular if what is seen as unchangeable is a bad situation, but it may feel safer: "...better the devil you know..."

Beliefs, alas, change throughout our lives. We believed in Father Christmas. We believed that our parents were infallible, that happiness was having that house, that car, that partner. We believed that voting for this party or that politician would create a better society, one that would make us feel well. Beliefs cannot, therefore, be our guiding light, and yet it is impossible not to have beliefs. Phenomenology offers an exit door to this conundrum by proposing that the beliefs we encounter on the road to knowledge should be made subject of an *"epoche"*, or *"*bracketing*"*. In this way we can concentrate on learning from experience rather than being unduly attached to our assumptions.

Perhaps a scene from the film *Life of Brian* made by the group Monty Pythons, where a crowd of followers run after a reluctant would-be Messiah demanding a Sign, has done more for an understanding of the mechanisms of believing than centuries of scholarly philosophical discussions.

We need beliefs to exist in the world but we also need the flexibility of our belief systems to adapt to new situations and accept evidence of the contrary that comes from experience, unlike some famous politicians, and lemmings. If we did not believe that we are going to be alive tomorrow, then nobody would set the alarm clock to go to work. However, if we believed that our journey to work would always take the same time, traffic jams would be an unbearable challenge to our sense of reality.

A frame of reference is a set of beliefs about our surroundings that produces familiarity and expectations about the world, for example, finding the Post Office and the Supermarket always in the same place; that a certain pattern of behaviour more or less consistently will lead to the same outcomes. When the frame of reference collapses everything appears to be a little surreal, eerie, "Kafkian". This is exactly the kind of scenario that many authors alluded to when the acceleration of the historical tempo started to exercise its effects over a slowly adapting brain. They all described characters that suddenly found themselves in situations for which they were not prepared. Kafka's *The Trial* and *Metamorphosis*, the British TV programme *The Prisoner*, the American series *The Twilight Zone*, as well as science fiction stories of being transported to parallel universes where the rules and assumptions we take for granted in this one do not apply, all created these settings.

What makes these stories scarier than other fantasy worlds, such as *Alice in Wonderland*? Choice does. Unlike their eerie counterparts, fantasy worlds are generally presented as places where the protagonist of the story can enter after passing a certain threshold, but retaining some degree of control over moving forward or staying put. They are journeys of exploration, intentional. It could be compared to the different experience of planning to go on a holiday to China or waking up in a hospital bed in China, but without knowing how we got there.

Beliefs are necessary and useful to provide an infrastructure to our daily and more mechanical functioning, but they may not be so useful to define the way we want to live in the future. Only Intention can give us that. We live at present in a world defined by beliefs and assumptions. It is as safe as it can be, except for wars, famine, terrorism, crime, the approaching environmental disaster, etc. Believing that everything is the result of human nature or the will of God simply leaves us where we are. Arguments about the existence or not of God are sterile as they put the debating parties in a mental position that moves further and further away from the possibility of the type of meaningful experiences that are available to believers and non-believers alike. Even if the disagreeing parties always interpret those experiences according to their cultural background (some will think that a sense of elation and connection to everything that exists is caused by God, others that it is produced by a little squirt of endorphins in the temporal lobe), sharing the experience can help identify "the other" as a fellow human being, to understand that they are capable of connecting to the same meaningful state, and yet, construe them according to their own landscapes. Being a vociferous atheist demands the same amount and strength of faith as being a religious fanatic. A belief in Science as the solution to all our problems or in Money as the great regulator of human behaviour will leave us in the same place, that is, denying that whether we like it or not , even within pre-existent conditions we have not chosen, we create our future. Science and Money are the tools of our intentions; they do not have independent existence.

If the only permanent thing in the human being is change, the only assumption worth holding on to is that there is a lot yet to be discovered and created.

Post-post-modern re-renaissance

We know now enough about the human consciousness and the factors that have shaped our cultural background to attempt to live, from now onwards, intentional lives.

Which direction shall we give to them? Is there anything solid and permanent to take as reference? Post-modern thinking tells us that everything one's mind creates is just another model, and therefore everything is relative to the culture that gives birth to that model. Most models are deeply based on belief systems, which are, of course, epochal and cultural. So, for instance, a social organisation based on a "superior race" dictated by the power of the gods will tend to enslave and impose such power over the "inferior others" and because of this belief such a level of oppression will feel completely right, a given. To the oppressors, that is.

Another belief system which could create a model of existence would hold that the world is going to end on a particular day; this might affect people in different ways, some might develop a hedonist lifestyle dedicated to numbing the awareness of the approaching end, whilst others would dedicate themselves to a saintly existence to achieve together an idealised afterlife.

It is true that both Socialism and Capitalism are models. There is nothing inevitable about the way production and trade are organised, nothing "natural" that favours selfishness above solidarity or vice versa.

There are, however, other kinds of models that extrapolate mechanisms of consciousness rather than beliefs into the social environment. An example is the knowledge that when we hurt others we hurt ourselves because we form an image of the other person's suffering that acts upon our own body. This awareness would produce a model of social interaction containing a kind of solidarity which is not really epochal and does not depend on geography or culture. Whether we allow ourselves to register the other's pain or not is immaterial. Training, numbing, desensitisation, they all detach us from the register but not from the effect. It has been happening to all of us since the beginning of humanity. Those who work with violent criminals know that developing empathy towards potential victims is a better safeguard than the threat of prison to prevent re-offending.

A form of social organisation based on learning to reinforce our empathy towards others would be a model based not on belief but on a principle that arises from experience. Principles, however, are abandoned in pragmatic existence. "A man has got to do what a man has got to do" to reach a certain objective. If this man has to betray his own principles to do so, how can he live with himself afterwards? Self-betrayal is the most painful experience. It is fragmenting. It makes us lose respect for ourselves. It leads to an existence of self-justification, trying to put the pieces together. And we are forced into this type of action every day in a society full of contradictions. Who will trust a person who betrays his (or her) own principles at every step of the way in order to climb the ladder, to reach an objective, to get one up on everybody else? In this state of affairs we not only mistrust others because of competition but also because we see others betraying their own principles. We recognise it in others because we are doing the same. Would you buy a second hand car from Dr Faustus? If this process of self-betrayal has been allegorised as the sale of one's soul to the devil is because at a deeper level it marks the death of a part of us, the death of the human spirit. Pragmatism may be, as a model of short term production and consumption, reasonably efficient. As a model of existence it leads to a dead end.

It could be argued that fragmentation, contradictions and self betrayal are personal choices and that we should do nothing to influence others. Whilst this is true we must also take into account that contradiction does not remain a self-contained individual activity, but oozes towards the social environment. Those who are angry with themselves project that anger onto others because it is more tolerable to think we are under attack from outside forces than from ourselves. We cannot run away from ourselves. In this way internal violence becomes external violence and, therefore, a social concern. We must balance an understandable desire to march people forcibly into therapy against the right to self determination. It is compassionate however to impart knowledge and offer tools for change in an indiscriminate way, knowing that those who become aware of their own negative role in the social environment will be grateful for your help and will put them to good use.

Pre-post-modern models were first questioned at the periphery of the old empires. In the same way the new planetary civilisation gets its strongest critique from those it assimilates and invades. Models are more clearly seen for what they are, rather than the "objective reality" they pretend to be, by those who live with two different models in their minds: the traditional model of one's culture and the one imposed by the imperial power. For those born at the centre of the empire there is only one model and it just feels like reality itself, like the absolute truth. It has been said that the only animal not aware of the existence of water is a fish. It is not surprising then that new models for the transformation of the planetary empire may well be coming from the edges, from the outskirts, from those who can compare the advantages and disadvantages of different worlds.

No proposal for a better or more coherent human society should become a rule, a law to be followed blindly, no matter how good it appears to be, since in its application it would then become the opposite of what it tries to achieve. Neither should new guidelines of behaviour make the pretence that this is the "natural" way for human beings to exist. It must be always present in our minds that what a society does is to encourage the development of certain potential in its members, but that the potential to do the opposite is always present. There is no "natural way" for us to be. Choosing to live in contact with nature, rejecting technology or modern medicine are intentional acts available only to human beings, just as going to colonise distant planets would be. Nor are those choices completely free, since the moment of our choice is the consequence of an infinite number of other choices made by others before us. However, the types of choices we can make can be grouped more or less as follows:

1. Not to choose (and there is always going to be a Hitler going around collecting discarded choices);
2. Choosing the conventional or the primeval (traditionalism and fundamentalism);
3. Choosing the opposite to the conventional (adolescence);
4. Choosing that which opens the future for oneself and for others, regardless of whether it follows conventions or opposes them (new humanism).

Two positive modes of behaviour arise from the analysis of both historical and personal experience: Coherence and Solidarity. The awareness that our relationships could improve by treating others the way we would like to be treated, putting oneself in other people's shoes, loving one's neighbour like oneself, not doing onto others what we would not like done unto us is very ancient, it turns up in different forms in most cultures and religions as the product of experience and wisdom. It also seems to be universally ignored.

This principle of solidarity, also known as The Golden Rule is rather tricky and not as simple to exercise as its repetition has made us feel it should be. It can be interpreted as an invitation to sacrifice, that is, to put (shock! horror!) other people's needs before one's own. Good as this may seem it can lead to a sense of expectation, in the one who makes the sacrifice, that the others should be grateful, or reciprocate, or change for the better as a consequence of the good deed delivered to them. It could also lead to resentment when they do not respond to those high expectations. Nobody wants to "sacrifice in vain". Instead, when other people's needs are seen to be, at least, as important as our own, then there is less room for subtle obligations and more for interpersonal freedom. In any case, when the choice of action (whether the other is seen as more important or just as important) is made by a person who is acting on the basis of the register of his/her action, solidarity leads to a sense of satisfaction which gives meaning to it regardless of whether it is appreciated or not. When sacrifice or even solidarity is imposed by a rigid external system or a promise of reward and punishment here or in the afterlife it is almost impossible to act on them without expectation or in a truly selfless way and, very often, it is done grudgingly.

As we have seen earlier, there are mechanisms of consciousness that support the tendency towards solidarity. Images of what is happening to others are represented in our space of representation in such a way that they produce registers similar to those being felt by the person actually having the experience. In this way, if we see somebody being hurt we may feel a tension and a tingling in the area where the other person feels the pain, or we may simply feel sick or develop a tension in any part of our body as a non-specific reaction to an image of pain in others. One of the most famous photographs of the Vietnam War was that of a naked little girl crying and running covered in napalm. This was an image that had physical repercussions in those who saw it and this in turn influenced their thinking about the war. Many people have the experience of starting to feel an itchy scalp just by knowing that somebody else in the room has head lice. Following the same principle we have seen the general sanitation of images in the media reporting on wars, since if people actually saw soldiers and civilians being blown apart nobody would support any kind of war, the arms trade or anything harmful to people. This identification with the pain of the other is a safeguard against interpersonal violence, but not a complete one. Training, habituation, objectification and dehumanisation of ethnic groups and strong emotions of hatred and desires for revenge can override this identification. It can also develop deficiently in those who are not given warmth and affection or are severely physically, sexually or psychologically abused during their formative years. We all have the potential to develop empathy but making it happen is a function of good attachments (according to Bowlby's theory) or at least being the recipient of empathy from another human being at some point of our lives. Many children growing up in war zones are deprived of this experience and it is clear afterwards that they cannot adapt well to living in peace. Numerous studies have focused in particular on child soldiers and the extensive damage to their development.

It is also well documented that most genocides, whether they led to military intervention to protect the victims or not, never happened suddenly, although they may have been reported in the world press that way. In fact all atrocities committed against a particular ethnic or political group follow a campaign built up over years during which such a human group becomes a scapegoat for all the ills that happen to befall the country or society where they live. Acquiescence and rebellion are both incorporated into the slander. Escaping from discrimination into a progressively more isolated group becomes interpreted as a desire to differentiate themselves from the wider community. Aggression is seen as confirmation of all the slander piled up on them. Genocide never happens from one day to another. People's minds need time to dehumanise others so completely as to accept it is right to kill them. There is always time to introduce programmes of learning how to integrate and stop discriminating a particular community, and training can be given to that community to respond in ways that will neither isolate them nor make them fall into the trap of the self-fulfilling prophecy by responding with violence. It is the responsibility of the international community, which appears to be so keen to condone military intervention (as long as there is oil or other strategic valuable assets in the area) after the massacre has already begun, to monitor the likelihood of such phenomena arising. It is necessary to detect the signs early enough to prevent these kinds of atrocities. Pre-emptive military strikes should have no place in a civilised social order. Educational interventions for the prevention of violence are our best option. In my view the European Union is at present the best placed to develop a Rapid Response Unit for the prevention of genocide, to be deployed in places where the signs point to increasing discrimination of an ethnic group, to work intensively with the population.

The representation of the image of pain (or joy, or any other personal experience) is one of the fundamental mechanisms of action of empathy. The closer we feel to the other the easier it is to empathise and feel solidarity. The expansion of empires to lands in close proximity before the development of long distance communications implied that conquered and conquerors were essentially alike. The colonial empires that developed when long distance travel became easier put peoples that looked very different and had very different cultures in close contact, adding to the violence of the conquest the violence of dehumanisation. One of many examples that springs to mind is the discussion in colonial Spain about whether the natives of the new continent had a soul or not, after the "discovery" of America.

Solidarity (but only amongst the workers) has been extolled by the left wing movements that sprang up at the end of the XIX Century and was demolished by the neo-liberal ideology. The latter interpreted the lack of a "feel good factor" as basic unhappiness about the amount of pocket money in the population, not realising that perhaps a much more important factor in making people feel good (once basic needs are covered) is a sense of belonging, of being cared for and accepted by others, of being able to love and feel close to others, of having a future with others. Savage individualism and cut-throat competition as the sole form of human interaction can only lead to paranoia as it becomes clear that we can trust nobody because nobody can trust us.

The free market myth of: "first wealth concentrates in the most able hands and then it trickles down to the poor" has been now clearly dispelled by the progressive and unlimited concentration that is threatening to transform society into a few small islands of rich people living in private estates and protected by private armies, whilst the rest of the population become neo-slaves, survival criminals or police. In this widening gap of wealth, privilege and life expectancy feeling good is not contingent on the number of consumer goods a person may attain (although advertising makes us feel it is), but on the relative situation we find ourselves in when compared to others. Not having one's basic needs covered is bad enough, but those who flaunt their obscene wealth in front of the dispossessed are adding psychological torture to the physical sense of deprivation. Furthermore, the perception that a great part of the gains made by the super-rich is the result of speculation in the world Stock Market casinos leaves those who participate in production and services for the growth of their communities submerged in a sense of injustice that another promise of a little tax reduction cannot lift.

What would an anthropologist from Mars think of a species that balances its global economy on the whims of a few gamblers? And are these financial giants truly happy? Are they not afraid that the market will collapse, or that someone may come to rob their possessions? Are they never disturbed by a (quickly suppressed, no doubt) twitch of guilt about the suffering they manufacture? The proliferation of expensive therapies and sophisticated alarm systems, instruments to spy on potential competitors, security gadgets and private armies of Security Guards for fortress-like private neighbourhoods are the tell-tale signs of a growing awareness that having so much more than others may make the lucky ones feel close to the gods but also very unsafe.

Solidarity in this context is not just good because it is dictated by a higher power but because it leads to a more satisfying existence from an experiential point of view. Its main enemy is fear of becoming the dispossessed.

The second part of the post-post modern humanist equation is Coherence; a register of agreement between thought, feeling and action in such a way that our deeds in the world develop with a clear direction. Its opposite, contradiction, carries a painful sensation of internal division that paralyses action. In an ideal world we should have total freedom to make choices that only lead to internal agreement such as "I think these people are great and I also like them" or "I feel like helping in such and such situation and I also think is the right thing to do". If we observe this less than ideal world we live in there is still some room for making coherent choices, and in this sense we retain a rather high degree of responsibility for our own progressive happiness or dissatisfaction. In this way some "false steps" we may have taken in our lives are remembered with a bitter taste of self-betrayal and we return to them over and over again in front of new experiences and at decision making times in painful re-enactment of That Horrible Moment.

There are other situations in which social contradictions permeate into our lives limiting the freedom of our choices and making us feel trapped. A short anecdote will illustrate this point. A friend of mine works in an Intensive Care Unit in a country with a high degree of corruption. Some time ago money was made available for a much needed expansion of those facilities. After inviting public estimates from several companies my friend noticed that the Director of the hospital had chosen the most expensive proposal, no doubt responding to a bribe by the selected company. My friend immediately denounced the offending behaviour but the Hospital Director remained in post, backed as he was by an equally corrupt Minister of Health. The ICU expansion never happened. The Coronary Care Unit, which was going through a similar process did undergo improvement, as those involved accepted the overpriced development, looked with distaste at the Director taking his cut and then looked the other way. Walking around the beds of a well-equipped CCU my friend mused whether he should have done the same for the benefit of his patients, knowing deep down that he could not. This kind of personal contradiction can only recede in front of a profound social change.

Our daily lives are filled with less dramatic contradictions which stem from a violent system of economic organisation. Many people feel they must be extra nice to their bosses or simply to "management", even if they think they are horrible people, lest they lose their jobs. In times of low unemployment there is some freedom to change jobs but when so many people are queuing for so few posts the sensation of being trapped increases, because employees have families to feed and mortgages to pay. Workers in such a climate eventually accept lower wages and feel unable to practice solidarity, as everybody will be trying to be the one who does not lose their job in the next readjustment. This is the scenario of inescapable personal contradiction for millions today as they contemplate with a heavy heart their laid off colleagues as they leave the office/workshop, etc., whilst thinking with a mixture of relief and shame "Well, at least it's not me!"

Overcoming contradiction is vital for a sense of internal growth and self esteem. There is no moral relativism that can justify wishing other people's destruction for our own survival. In the same league we can find more subtle examples that somehow fail to impress our consciousness in our daily existence. We know that many rich countries are engaged in the manufacture of instruments for torture to be sold to other governments who use them on their citizens. Torture may well be banned in the UK and a private firm over here that makes and sells those instruments over there is not exactly everybody's preference. Similarly we know that UK companies and Government are selling weapons to countries that are invading their neighbours and engaging in all kinds of human rights violations of their own populations. We know, and try not to think about, female genital mutilation and the killing of baby girls in other parts of the world. We may feel helpless in our lack of capacity to influence events that are taking place far away. This exacerbates the contradiction but we cannot deny the effect in our lives. Every time we feel that something is too horrible to think about we develop a sort of numbness, a little black hole where the mind refuses to go. As the unthinkable horrors grow so does the anaesthesia, until this numbness is large enough to start to include other things, other people whose suffering we could but do not do something about, and so the numbness expands until we no longer care about our own suffering. Then we decide that cynicism is intellectually stimulating and continue to exist as if we were alive.[34]

---

[34] From concepts developed in *La Mirada del Sentido,* (The Look of the Meaning) by Dario Ergas

The process of working intentionally towards personal coherence by learning to make decisions with a clear direction towards internal unity may be difficult enough when we are carrying the weight of a myriad of past wrong steps, but it cannot be completed unless we also attempt to eliminate the roots of social contradiction. We must create models for a human society that allow equal rights and equal opportunities for all; that fulfil the basic proposals of New Humanism:

- Placing the human being, rather than money or power, as the central value in society;
- Affirming the equality of all human beings in such a way that nothing is above the human being and no human being is below another;
- Recognising personal and cultural diversity without any kind of discrimination;
- The continuous development of human knowledge beyond any dogma or belief accepted as the absolute truth;
- Sustaining freedom of ideas and beliefs
- Rejecting violence in all its forms, whether physical, economic, racial, religious, psychological, ecological, gender-related, etc.

Certainly, the balance between freedom and control has been the theme of reams of paper in studies and political proposals. Humanity fluctuates between insistence on the rights of individuals, whatever the cost to the needs of a balanced society, and the possibility of a reasonable sense of justice and equal opportunities for all, which implies a degree of commitment from every individual not to demand complete freedom. At the extremes of these two factions we have the two rigid images of the end of history, Marx's socialism and Fukuyama's liberal democracy. Both create some degree of horror in those who analyse their consequences. Communism terrifies with the disappearance of the human rights of the individual submerged in a dictatorship of the interests of society (in practice the dictatorship of those who achieve control of the state), the latter threatens, and to a high degree is showing in action, the oppression created by the tyranny of the lowest common denominator, be it greed, individualistic compulsion to succeed and have power over others, or the dictatorship of money.

All sorts of third ways spring up here and there to try to combine the best aspirations embodied in the extremes, but without their drawbacks. We want freedom but we (at least some of us) also want equality. Anarchism worked hard at making such combination, but it assumed a human nature that romanticised the aspirations and instincts of human beings. The huge gap between its idealisation of the process to achieve it and its real possibilities turned to violence and destruction, at least in some quarters.

The European social democracies and economists like J.M. Keynes have attempted a model of benign capitalism that preserves the basic tenets of liberalism and democracy. They tend to regulate at least part of the economy in order to prevent the malignant concentration of wealth and resources that has become in itself a violation of human rights. The psychological and also physical torture of parents who see their children die of malnutrition or of a treatable illnesses for lack of access to basic nourishment or medical attention, whilst being exposed through a globalised media to the opulence and waste of their wealthier '"fellow" human beings, does not stop when the torturer leaves the room. Was the relative loss of individual freedom a price worth paying in Cuba for that country's reduction of infant mortality to a level only comparable to the richest economies of the world? The chronic American embargo on Cuba, trying to cripple its economy to show that "it does not work", says NO. The parents of children dying of malnutrition elsewhere would not be so sure.

We speak of freedom and human rights as if they where absolutes that can be achieved from one day to the other by the simple imposition of a system, by this and not that political party winning the next elections. Or by a violent revolution that so radically changes the social order that all vestiges of the previous one fade away, forever, completely.

The creation of a new society that works towards freedom and equality is a process, not a point in time. Evolution v. revolution is a pointless argument. There will be moments in the process when change happens in a gradual and measured way. There are moments when people get fed up and explode. The difference between a revolution and a riot is the previous homework. Neither can be planned but clear images of the world we want can guide a moment of social unrest towards important changes. Without those images more of the same ensues, with a better justification for repression by the oppressor of the moment. We cannot anticipate at present at which times people will get fed up and explode. The only thing we can do is to be prepared for such moment with clear and coherent images and proposals for a better form of organisation that can lead to a better world. In the meantime we must begin the elimination of the cruellest forces that contribute to the suffering of humanity at the present moment. The following list does not pretend to be comprehensive (there is no "blueprint" of the perfect humanist society, rather it is something that should evolve guided by basic principles and with full participation of everybody involved), but rather it attempts to reflect the main points of the proposal of New Humanism in terms of social organisation.

These are the factors that contribute to concentration of wealth and resources that will have to be profoundly modified in a process of change towards equality and social justice.

(1) Progressive elimination of speculation: The stock markets and the flow of capital that move freely around the world searching for the best dividends without reference to production or social needs detract from the profits that could be reinvested by companies to improve their working conditions and their products. The amount of speculative capital is today so unimaginably large that were it to be taxed at an infinitesimal rate it would be enough to solve the problems of health and education over vast parts of the planet. The Tobin tax earned its author a Nobel Prize but it turned out to be "not applicable". Moreover those who accumulate the most are often exempt from tax by special agreements and tax havens.[35]

(2) Regulation of the activities of multinational corporations: These companies are the root of the globalised economy. They move production where it can maximise profit in a way completely divorced from the needs of the workforce or the population of any country. They destroy the environment with complete impunity in the developing countries. They pay exploitative wages to workers and sell their products for maximum profit in the developed world, but raise the unemployment rate in that world. They tend not to pay tax in any country.

---

[35] *A haven right here on earth*, Judith Larner and Patrick Collinson, Saturday February 21, 2004, *The Guardian*. "So you are rich enough and desperate enough to become a tax exile. But where should you head for? There are now 70 tax havens across the globe, and many are far from glamorous".

(3) Workers' participation in co-management and share of the profits: Labour is within the present economic system a commodity that can be bought or sold, valued by market standards of offer and demand rather than as the unique contribution that each human being can make to the social whole. In this way poverty is a concept created by the "evolution" from community living to the compartmentalised organisation of the capitalist society. In the floated company the interests of the workers clash with the shareholders'. In companies where the workers *are* the shareholders conditions tend to improve.

(4) A decentralised not-for-profit banking system: The geographical distribution of the banking system puts the most powerful banks in the so-called developed world, so that the flow of capital in the form of profits for lending, the raison d'être for the traditional style bank, is also towards the developed countries.

(5) Changes in patent laws: Seeds from the Third World are modified, patented and resold to poor countries, often ensuring that plants will be sterile and unable to produce seeds for the following year, so that farmers are forced to buy seeds year after year. Patent laws for pharmaceutical products exclude the less well off from access to reasonable healthcare. Gene patents are also threatening research in all areas of medicine and biology. Double standards are applied with impunity by those in power, e.g. we have seen the US absolving itself from patents laws on grounds of *national interest* but imposing heavy penalties on others who attempted to do the same. And we are only just beginning to see the patents of the technology for clean energy developed by private (many of the Oil trading) companies which will end up making the outcome of this life saving research only available to affluent people and countries.

(6) Changes in trade agreements: The WTO has been an accomplice of the bullying of the least developed economies to make them sign "agreements" which bind them to more exploitation. This situation cannot remain in its present form. Balanced regional trade agreements must be the beginning of fair and just trade.

(7) Progressive demilitarisation and proportional arms reduction across the world: The arms trade is one of the biggest promoters of war and poverty. The highest technology is the most expensive. Countries that are basically producing raw materials have to dedicate great part of their land to the production of "cash crops" such as coffee and tobacco, to buy weapons. In this way the land dedicated to feeding

people is also dramatically reduced. The reduction of the arms budgets throughout the world is an urgent necessity that cannot be postponed. We should begin by effecting nuclear disarmament in *all* countries as proliferation can only lead to disaster. The dividing line set up by international conventions that mark what is permitted or not in war has already been broken. Depleted uranium based anti-bunker devices leave radioactive debris that can seriously affect the health of soldiers and civilians. War is already a little nuclear. It can only get worse. In the words of Robert McNamara attending a conference hosted by Medact[36], the Medical global health Charity, "the greatest threat to humankind is nuclear proliferation …Britain should not develop a new nuclear weapons capability and …the development of new nuclear weapons is insane and a waste of money". We are paying for these arsenals of death *with our taxes*. Therefore, we may have a choice.

(8) Regularisation of the situation of all the refugees, wherever they may be: The movement of refugees and economic migrants has already been described amongst the mechanisms by which this apparently unwanted workforce is in fact keeping the economies of the developed countries afloat. The provision of basic needs for them is a huge task that cannot be left to the individual countries. An international coordinating body must be properly funded to break the vicious circle of poverty and discrimination in which refugees live.

(9) A revived sense of self worth for people and goods from the developing world: Sadly a thoroughly unfair consequence of colonisation and its modern equivalents was, and is, not only the material dispossession of the invaded countries but also the destruction of the sense of worth and self reliance of the subjugated peoples. Recovering the lost self esteem is also a function of recovering their culture and sense of community.

(10) A stricter code of conduct for the Media: Raising awareness of the differential reporting of events which reinforces the view that the rich and powerful matter more than the rest of the world. The introduction of more opportunities for alternative media as well as a more ethical formation as part of the Journalism curriculum. Although censorship is not the best way to give direction to the film and TV industries, it is important to promote as part of the education system a critical view of this material from an early age.

---

[36] www.medact.org/wmd_nuclear.php

(11) Encouragement of family education and planning for all: The composition of the family and methods of birth control are an important part of cutting the circle of poverty in some parts of the world. The nuclear family concentrates, the extended family spreads. Women with access to birth control can develop careers and therefore a family can become a two income family. This also improves the quality of life and the education of other generations of women.

(12) Education: Not only does education increase the capacity to gain access to profitable employment, it also increases the awareness of one's own exploitation. Perversely, the brain drain created by selective immigration of well-qualified people into the developed world deprives those who most need it of this essential resource. The money immigrants send to their families is seen as a kind of redress, balancing the books with this unofficial aid, but that still leaves their countries of origin bereft of their skills.

(13) Prevention of the disappearance of the State and its replacement by Private Companies as its manager and NGOs/Charities as providers: The use of charities and NGOs to transfer the roles of the state to non-elected bodies, often used by multinationals to widen their influence, is part of the global agenda. There are of course many such organisations that work sincerely in the best interest of the people they serve, but groups that represent other interests and directions have adopted the format of the NGO. Moreover, no matter how well-meaning and dedicated an NGO, it can only cover the territory it is trying to help in a piecemeal manner. Only the state of each country has the capacity to organise health, education and development programmes at national level. The two basic considerations that can determine the direction of an NGO are: Who defines the priorities (the NGO administration or the people at the base)? and Money comes with conditions.

(14) Freedom from social control through psychological manipulation: There is no stronger force to control the behaviour of others than the key to their fears: fear of death, fear of loneliness, fear of foreigners, fear of illnesses, fear of pain, fear of the future, fear of fear. Fear is not a good advisor and it is a ruthless lord. Developing ways to deliver us from fear is paramount whether through solidarity or an existential or spiritual search for a meaning in life. The Media, often the tool used by the social manipulators, has a clear responsibility to review its role in this respect.

(15) Real rather than purely formal Democracy: The recurrent parody of democracy we call elections is leaving more and more people feeling unrepresented and betrayed by their politicians. Only a real opening of the political process to the people without imposing monetary restrictions on their participation may revitalise this process. Amongst the main areas in need of radical changes we find:

(i): Lobby groups and party donations. These are ways for commercial interests to buy the cooperation of politicians who see themselves not so much as the representatives of the will of the people who elected them as the voice of the funds that brought them into the position of power.

(ii): The focus groups. In order to stay in power parties try to detect vote winners. If people are prepared to vote for an issue contrary to the principles of one's party, it becomes incorporated in some disguised format. Since the European population seems to be moving to the right because of the propaganda of neo-fascist groups, the mainstream parties are adopting their policies in subtle ways rather than making an effort to educate the population about the fallacy of the scaremongering arguments.

(iii): The process by which candidates are registered for elections. In the UK access to participation in Parliamentary elections, domestic as well as European, is secured by large sums of money per candidate, a deposit that can be recovered as long as a candidate obtains more than 5% of the votes. This has been justified as a way of excluding "crank" and extremist groups but in actual fact ensures a monopoly of the political process for the parties already in power and excludes new ideas from being put to the electorate. It certainly does not exclude rich cranks and extremists as can be seen by observing the list of candidates in recent elections, and in fact it sends a strong message that no matter how bizarre or fanatical an idea may be, money can make it respectable.

(16): Massification of access to renewable forms of Energy and investment in research of alternative Energy sources by Universities and other National bodies: The excuses given by many Governments to delay the introduction of clean Energy and at least attempt to stop the impending environmental disaster is that it is still too expensive. In reality very little is done because Oil Companies and the Nuclear Industry are very powerful lobbies.

Finally, it is important to remember that from confusion and disorientation to witch-hunt only one step is needed, someone who points the finger at a convenient scapegoat. Then, all is "explained" and fascism raises again its ugly head. It is imperative to develop an internal reference so that we can plan a future of freedom for all human beings. The rising awareness of the power of consciousness to shape the world puts humanity at its best position to create the type of habitat most conducive to its development. *Homo sapiens* could think. Later *Homo sentiens* became aware of thinking. *Homo intentional* can choose how to think.

Joy is contingent on the perception of an open future. Those who attempt to live intentional lives at every step open the future for themselves and for others. Armed with the tools of experience and communication a new humanism is awakening and pointing to the fact that not only is the Emperor naked, but his Empire is also a lie. Wherever we live, whatever our beliefs, whichever our present conditions, building a world fit for human (all humans) existence is possible, necessary and meaningful.

Chapter 15

EDUCATION FOR NON VIOLENCE
(In collaboration with Tony Robinson)

The World Health Organisation initiated a campaign against violence in 2002. It proposed the creation of programmes to deal with violence at personal, social and institutional levels.[37] UNESCO also initiated a campaign to dedicate the first decade of the millennium to Non-Violence Education.[38]

This Chapter contains the Courses based on New Humanist thinking launched to provide practical tools to those who wish to carry out activities to counteract the growing violence in their lives, their immediate environment and the world at large.

The following two courses of Education for Non Violence in 12 sessions are part of the programme to produce changes at social and personal levels. The courses are given as guidelines and we recommend their adaptation to the particular circumstances of those who receive them and also those who deliver them.

Course 1

Introduction

Violence is complex and difficult to eradicate. In this course we are approaching the roots of violence from a variety of personal and environmental factors. We do not give these workshops as lessons to be followed passively, but rather participants are invited to take active roles, look at their own experience, help others overcome violence and, if they feel motivated by the theme, become instructors themselves. For this reason these workshops are ideal for educators, community leaders and workers as well as NGO members who wish to educate the

---

[37] www.who.int/violence_injury_prevention/violence/en/

[38] UNESCO Culture of Peace and Non Violence campaign: www3.unesco.org/-iycp/

communities they serve on non-violence as a complement to other projects of health, general education, development, etc. They can also be useful to groups suffering discrimination such as women, minorities, the young, etc., and all those who wish to create a different and intentional environment for their lives.

We can find the roots of violence in factors that derive from:

1. Personal Factors: Tensions, lack of self-esteem, impulsiveness, compulsions, frustration, painful memories, contradictions, the absence of a meaning in life.
2. Factors of our relationship with our environment: Individualism, competition, resentments, isolation, lack of communication in the family, at work, social fragmentation, etc
3. Factors of the Global System: Dehumanised social values, unreachable models of "happiness", the cult of celebrities, social injustice, discrimination, loss of cultural roots, the institutions that keep an unbalanced international order, territorial invasions, etc.

The Course deals with all three fields of violence and the factors that influence them:

The following diagram shows that violence can be experienced at a personal level, in one's relationships with people in one's environment and at a global level. The violence can also be connected or overlap, for instance, if we feel depressed about wars in the world this can make us treat others around us unpleasantly. The workshops cover a number of topics that are applicable to counteracting violence in one or all of those fields.

Personal

Personal experience of
violence: registers
Learning non violent problem
solving strategies
Relaxation, breathing, body
postures. Personal Virtues:
Self esteem & Coherence

Valid Actions: (Empathy
and internal reference)
Non-discrimination
Recognition of other
people's virtues.
Communication
Self-Organisation for
the development of
projects for social
change. Solidarity

Types of Violence in the
world: Humanisation of
Values and Institutions
Communication through
international networks
Non Violent Alternatives
to the present System

Relational   Global

Workshop 1

Introduction to Education for non-violence

The first six workshops of this Course aim to give us a better understanding of the personal (tensions, compulsions), environmental (a culture of violence), and global (inequalities, free-market dogma) forces that interact to produce violence. Today competition and individualism are promoted as the ideal forms of human interaction by the forces in power, creating isolation and fragmentation in communities. We will develop strategies to modify situations of violence that arise in our own lives and we will discuss what changes are necessary in our immediate environment and in the global system to lead to a non-violent society.

Forms of violence

(Conference organised by the Community for Human Development, San Francisco, 18 September 1982):

"We denounce violence as the fundamental problem of the present moment.

All individual and social conflicts stem from a situation of violence.

We distinguish between numerous forms of violence and we are not just referring to its most evident manifestation, physical violence, which we find in wars, torture, terrorism, assassinations, assaults and physical punishment.

There is also economic violence known as exploitation.

There is racial violence known as discrimination and segregation.

There is also religious violence, know as fanaticism or intolerance.

And there is also a psychological violence that begins within the family, it continues to be found in education, and it ends up putting the young to sleep and turning them into nihilists. This in turn opens up an abyss between the generations and this abyss threatens the stability of the individual and society.

So let us not be surprised when someone responds with physical violence if we have subjected them to inhuman psychological pressures or the pressures of exploitation, discrimination or intolerance. And if this response should surprise us it is either because we are an interested party in the injustice (in which case our "surprise" is also a lie) or because we only see the effects without noticing the causes that determine this explosion.

If suicide or mental illness is the road that someone has taken in order to escape their daily reality it is because that person has been subjected to a situation of violence. It is true that there are organic mental illnesses and there are suicides that occur when a person has an incurable disease. But the statistics are swelling; the number of cases is increasing by the day and they do not refer to these physiological problems.

These tragic eruptions that seem to us to be simply individual cases are manifestations of a system of violent tensions that pressures human society. Someone might believe that their isolation or lack of communication with others is simply their own personal problem, but the fact is that today isolation and non-communication affect enormous groups of people. How could this then be just a personal problem if millions are feeling the same non-communication and the same isolation?

Yes, we are against physical violence. We also have manifested our opposition to the bomb in Europe, in Moscow and in New York, as millions of pacifists have done in order to show the world that there still exist enormous moral reserves of peace and hope. But we are not concerned only with this problem.

The antinuclear marches and manifestations are fine. But they are not enough. It is necessary to clarify oneself and clarify others. It is necessary to take on a courageous commitment and to define the positions that we, and others, have with respect to violence. It is necessary to dismantle the bomb that we carry within ourselves."

The point being made here is that violence takes on many different forms. The definition of violence that is used in New Humanism is anything that causes pain and suffering in others and anything that denies the intentionality of others and treats them like objects.

Exercise – Personal experience of violence

1. Brainstorm as a group what you consider to be violence from an experiential point of view.

2. Write down about your own experience of violence, whether as victim or as perpetrator. Classify the experience according to the type of violence.

3. Describe the types of violence that worry you the most, whether you are directly involved or not. Describe how this affects your image of the future.

4. Group discussion and advice from the group to each participant on developing new attitudes in the situations described.

5. Conclusions: What are the common elements that make violence an important issue in people's lives? What are the common elements that make violence recede?

6. Plan for the week: Make a plan to start to affect, positively, a situation of violence that is troubling you at the moment. Present the plan to the group.

Workshop 2

Relaxation, body postures, breathing & moods

(From *Self-Liberation*, by Luis Ammann[39])

These are techniques we can practice in order to be capable of giving different responses to situations of violence as well as developing better control and a more intentional relationship with our environment.

Relaxation

Exercise 1 – External physical relaxation:

In this exercise we will study the ways to relax our bodies. But before beginning this basic practice, you need to learn to recognise the most tense areas of your body.

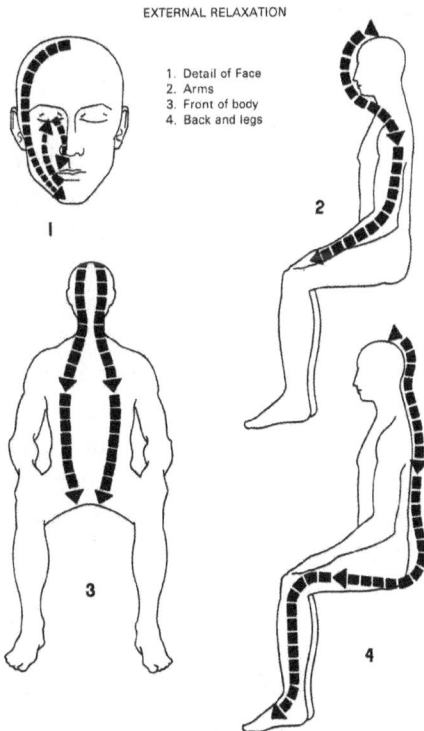

EXTERNAL RELAXATION

1. Detail of Face
2. Arms
3. Front of body
4. Back and legs

Figure 1

Which areas of your body are tense right now? Pay careful attention to your body and discover those tense areas. Perhaps the back of your neck or your shoulders are tense? Or perhaps the muscles in your chest or your stomach?

To relax these points of permanent tension, you must first begin to observe them. Observe your chest, your stomach, the back of your neck and your shoulders, and your face.

Then, wherever you find the most tension, strongly increase this tension. Hold this tension for a few seconds

[39] Latitude Press, San Diego, USA. First English version: Samuel Wiser, 1981. Revised Spanish version, Editorial Altamira, Buenos Aires, 2004

until the muscles become tired. Then, abruptly release the excess tension. Repeat this process three times. Tighten the tense areas, hold the tension for a little while, and then abruptly release the tension.

You have learned how to relax your most tense muscles by doing something opposite to what you might expect; you have tensed your muscles even more in order to relax them.

Once you master this technique, proceed to mentally feel the external muscles of your body in a symmetrical way. That is, always feel both sides of your body, for example, both eyes, both shoulders, both hands, etc. at the same time. Begin by feeling your head, your scalp, your facial muscles and your jaw. Feel both eyes at the same time. Then attend to both sides of your nose, the corners of your lips and your cheeks. Next, mentally move down both sides of your neck at the same time and focus your attention on both your shoulders. Now, gradually move down your arms, forearms, and hands until each of these areas is completely loosened up and relaxed.

Now, return to your head and repeat the relaxation of your face. But this time when you finish your face, instead of going down your arms, go down the front of your body. Move symmetrically down the front of your body as though you were following two imaginary lines. Move down the front of your neck, your chest, your stomach. Continue until you reach your lower stomach and the bottom of your trunk. Feel the whole front of your body completely relaxed. Next, return to your head, and go down the back of your body. Start with your scalp, with the top of your head and follow two symmetrical lines down the back of your head and neck through your shoulder blades and out onto your back. Continue to follow the two lines down each side of your back until you reach your lower back and the bottom of your trunk. Continue to move down both legs until you reach the tips of your toes, leaving the whole body very well relaxed. When you finish and have a command of this exercise, you should experience a good external muscular relaxation. (See Figure 1)

Exercise 2 – Internal physical relaxation:

Review Exercise 1, and repeat it until you master the technique. Try to do the relaxation faster each time without losing the quality of your relaxation.

In order of importance you should first master the relaxation of the facial muscles, the neck muscles, and those of the trunk in general. The

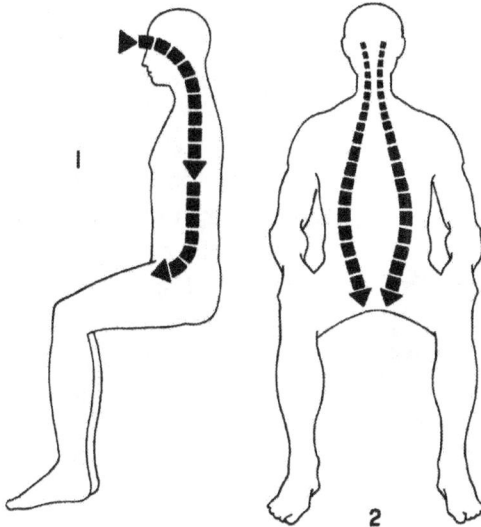

INTERNAL RELAXATION

1. Side View
2. Front View

Figure 2

relaxation of the arms and legs is secondary. People often believe the reverse, and thus waste a great deal of time working on secondary areas such as their arms or legs. Remember that your head, neck (especially the back of your neck) and trunk in general are the most important areas to relax.

Now let's go on to the internal relaxation. First, relax externally, and then feel your head. Feel your eyes, and try to feel very well your eyeballs and the muscles that surround both eyes. Now feel the inside of both of your eyes at the same time. Experience an internal and symmetrical sensation of both your eyes, and then move your attention toward the inside of your head, relaxing your eyes completely.

Continue to move toward the inside of your head, letting yourself slip toward the inside while relaxing completely. Continue as though you are slowly "falling" down your throat toward your lungs. Symmetrically feel the inside of both lungs and relax them. Then, continue to descend inside your stomach, relaxing all your internal tensions as you go. Keep moving downward, relaxing the inside of your lower abdomen until you reach the bottom of your trunk. Finish with the whole inside of your body perfectly relaxed.

We have not covered the arms and legs at all in this second type of relaxation. You go from the eyes back toward the inside, and move as if falling towards the bottom of your trunk. Practice this exercise several times. When you finish, check to see whether any external muscles are still tense.

All the external muscles should now be perfectly relaxed, and of course, you should also have achieved a good internal relaxation. This

185

will allow you to advance to the next exercises, which are somewhat more complex. (See Figure 2)

Exercise 3 – Mental relaxation:

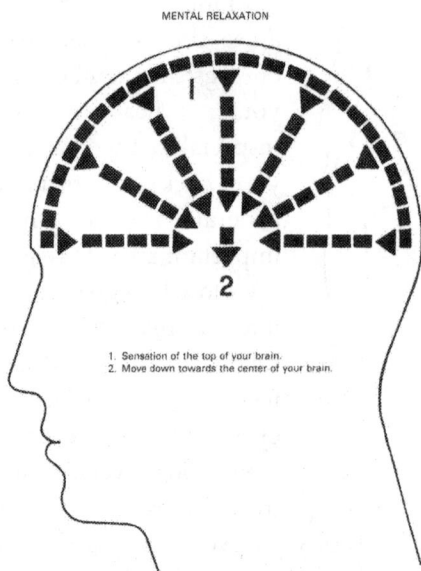

MENTAL RELAXATION

2

1. Sensation of the top of your brain.
2. Move down towards the center of your brain.

Figure 3

Practice Exercise 2 again, and try to go at an even, constant pace, not spending more time in one area than in any other. Repeat the exercise and speed up your internal movements without losing the sensation of depth. When you have a command of the exercise above, continue with this exercise.

In this exercise we will work with mental relaxation. Begin in a state of external and internal relaxation, that is, go through the external and internal practices in Exercises 1 and 2. Then, feel your head again, feel your scalp, and below it your skull. Begin to feel your brain inside your scalp.

Feel your brain as if it were "tense". Then, let that tension loosen up and "flow" inwards and down, towards the centre of your head. Concentrate on this and move inward one layer at a time. Continue lowering the tension with a sensation of "falling" as the top of your brain begins to feel very soft and pleasant. Always move down, down towards the centre of your head, down below the centre, lower and lower. Feel a soft, warm, and fluffy sensation.

Repeat this exercise several times until you become proficient at it. (See Figure 3)

Exercise 4 – The Experience of Peace:

Repeat exercise 3 several times until you can quickly experience mental distension.

To check your progress, first relax externally, internally, and mentally. When you finish and have the internal register of mental relaxation, stand up and walk around the room, open and close the doors, pick up several objects and replace them, and finally return to your seat. Are you just as relaxed as when you finished your external, internal and mental relaxation?

When you can master the above exercise, try to quickly return to a mentally relaxed state after more complex everyday activities.

You have now mastered three forms of relaxation: external physical, internal physical, and mental relaxation. You are ready to begin to apply these quickly and efficiently in everyday situations.

So far, you have worked basically with muscles and internal sensations. In this exercise, you will begin a different type of work. You will learn to train your mental images.

Images are what mobilise tensions, and similarly, they generate relaxations. For example, imagine a fire, and imagine you are there at the fire. Notice how your muscles become tense.

Conversely, imagine that you "put out" the fire and observe how your external muscles relax and you register a relaxation in your internal sensations.

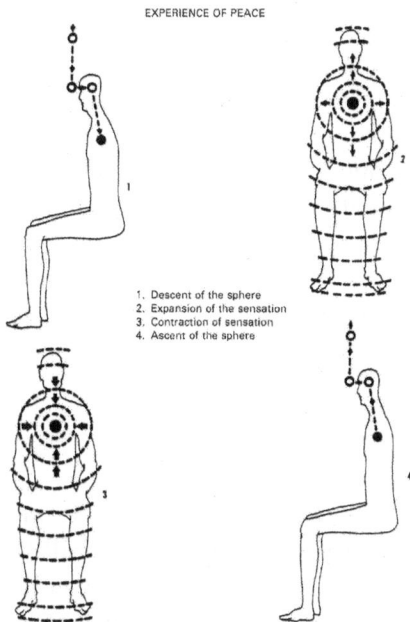

EXPERIENCE OF PEACE

1. Descent of the sphere
2. Expansion of the sensation
3. Contraction of sensation
4. Ascent of the sphere

Figure 4

In this exercise we will begin to manage a particularly useful image for the rest of the work in what we call the Experience of Peace. To begin, relax externally, internally and mentally, and then imagine a brightly shining transparent sphere up above you. Let it descend from above, enter your head, and lower it until it is inside your chest at the level of your heart. (See Figure 4)

When first trying this practice, some people cannot imagine the sphere very well. But this is not a real obstacle because what is important is that they experience a pleasant sensation in their chest, even if they do not have the supporting visual image of a sphere. And with practice they will eventually be able to correctly visualise a sphere that descends and rests in the centre of their chest.

When this image is resting in your chest, begin to slowly expand it or "let" it expand so it gradually grows until it fills your whole body. When this sensation that starts in the centre of your chest has expanded throughout your whole body, a warm sensation of peace and internal unity will appear which you should let operate by itself.

It is important that this sensation extends to the limits of your whole body, that is, that it radiates from the centre of your chest, increasingly filling your body, until you achieve a sort of internal illumination. When the sensation reaches the limits of your body, the relaxation will be complete.

Sometimes your breathing will become deeper and positive emotions will appear pleasant and inspiring emotions. However, pay no attention to your breathing; simply let it accompany your positive emotions and keep your attention on the expanding sensation.

On other occasions, memories and very vivid images may arise, but you should always have greater interest in your growing register of peace and calm.

When this register has diffused throughout your body, you have mastered the most important part of this exercise, and the Experience of Peace will arise. Remain in this interesting state for a few minutes, and then slowly contract the sensation and the image back towards your chest to your heart. Then, raise it to your head, and gradually let this "sphere" you have been using move outside and disappear. This completes the Experience of Peace.

Remember, if you have not relaxed correctly as explained in the previous exercises, you will be unable to carry out this important experience.

Body Postures and Mental State

If you have ever noticed the difference between the posture of someone who is depressed and someone who is happy, you will easily grasp the relationship between posture and mental or emotional states. The important point is that just as a given mental state leads to a certain bodily posture, a given posture will also induce a certain mental and emotional state.

We distinguish two kinds of bodily postures: (1) static positions, which are most commonly standing up, sitting down, and lying down, and (2) dynamic positions such as walking forward, walking backward, bending over, and changes of pace, and transitional movements.

Exercise 5 – Static body postures

(A) Stand as you do normally. Imagine a vertical line passing through your head and body to the ground. Using this straight line as a reference, notice whether your head is badly positioned, whether your chest is sunken, your stomach is out of line, or if you hold your lower stomach in and thus push your buttocks out of line. Do not yet try to change any incorrect positions; simply keep them in mind and remember all the details. Then, draw your body in your notebook just as you remember it, both the side view and the front view. Mark any incorrectly positioned points, and see what you need to correct.

Now stand up and start to correct your posture. Notice that this isn't easy because for years you have formed incorrect posture habits. Change back and forth several times between your usual incorrect posture and the correct posture.

Once you think your posture is correct, check it by standing with your heels and spine flat up against the wall. Note any areas where your body does not touch the wall, and correct things so you stand with everything in a vertical line.

(B) Sit in a chair as you normally would. Again, imagine the vertical line passing through your head, and note the errors in your posture. Then, correct your posture. Finally, put your buttocks and spine up against the back of the chair. Then return to your normal incorrect position. Change back and forth between your normal, incorrect position and the correct position several times.

(C) Lie down and relax your muscles. Observe which parts of your body are incorrectly positioned and cause strong tensions. Pay special attention to the position of your head and back. Correct your posture, and then change back and forth several times.

<u>Exercise 6</u> – Dynamic body postures

(A) Walk as you do normally, and observe any errors in your posture. Next, keep walking and try to maintain the correct posture you established in the previous exercise series.

(B) Walk, sit down, then stand up and walk again as you would normally, and notice any errors in your posture. Repeat this, but this time use correct posture.

(C) Open and close a door, trying to keep correct posture. Notice whether you lose your correct posture as you do this. Repeat this several times.

(D) Walk around the room, and then lean over and pick up an object from the floor. Keep walking around, and lean over again and put the object back on the floor. Notice whether you abandon your correct posture as you do this. Repeat this several times.

(E) Walk around and greet the other people, shake hands and talk briefly. Walk around again and notice the moments when you "abandon" correct posture. Repeat this several times.

(F) Write down your observations and exchange comments with the other people so you can help each other improve incorrect postures.

IMPORTANT: Make it a point to correct your posture in everyday life until the next meeting.

Breathing and moods

When a person's emotional state changes, this changes many things inside the person including their breathing. An emotionally aroused person's heart begins to beat faster and their breathing becomes higher in their chest; their voice comes in uneven gasps, and may also become higher pitched.

Just as specific internal states are related to certain bodily postures, they are also linked to definite ways of breathing. Knowing this, a person can modify their negative emotional states by adopting correct postures and changing the way they breathe. Of course, these modifications do not occur instantly. When you change your breathing or posture, the corresponding change in your internal emotional state will occur only after a delay of a few minutes. Let us explain this further.

When we are in a bad emotional state, we will have confused thinking, use incorrect posture, and breathe inefficiently. If we now stand up and walk using correct posture, the negative emotional state will still continue through inertia for some time. However, if we keep a correct posture, we will find that a few minutes later our emotional state will in fact begin to improve.

Our emotions will also improve in the same way if we correctly control our breathing. But, before changing it, we must first observe how we normally breathe, and only then learn to modify it.

Being able to improve one's internal state in these ways is a valuable tool that gives us more control over our responses to the environment.

Exercise 7 – Complete breathing

Sit in a chair using correct posture. Close your eyes and relax your muscles as completely as you can. Exhale completely, without forcing anything. Then, extend your stomach, stick it way out, and begin to inhale air. Try to have the sensation that you are "filling your stomach" with air. When your stomach is "full", hold your breath a few moments, and then exhale. This is called "lower breathing".

Once you have mastered this, again inhale, filling your stomach with air, but next "pull in" your stomach. This will give you the sensation of the air rising to your chest (this sensation can be reinforced by expanding your chest and pushing your shoulders back). Hold the air in your chest for a few moments and then exhale. This second phase is called "middle breathing".

Begin the third phase by filling your stomach with air up into your chest in "middle breathing", and finally, move the air to the upper part of your chest, towards your throat. Reinforce this final upward movement by lowering your shoulders and extending your neck slightly. This is called "upper breathing".

Now go through the whole breathing cycle; lower, middle, and upper inhaling only once. Exhale at the end of the exercise.

To summarise complete breathing, you sit with correct posture, close your eyes, relax your muscles, and follow this sequence: exhale completely, expand your stomach so air enters the lower part of your lungs, raise the air to the centre of your chest, move it to the upper part of your chest, and finally exhale.

At first, you will find you do the different parts of this exercise in a disconnected or jerky way. But as you repeat it several times, you will develop a harmonious rhythm. You smoothly and continuously inhale and exhale using all three levels of your lungs so that by the end of the technique your lungs have been fully exercised. Make sure your complete breathing gradually becomes gentler until you completely eliminate all effort in it.

IMPORTANT: Practice complete breathing several times. Take notes on any difficulties and resolve to practice this exercise two or three times a day. On the basis of your experience you can use this way of breathing both as a daily exercise, and also at special moments when you wish to balance your mental and physical states.

It is recommended to begin all successive workshops with a relaxation and Experience of peace to set the tone of the work.

Workshop 3

Valid action

Is it the same to do one thing or another? Are all actions the same? Or if we ask in another way: Do all the actions we do have the same value? If this is not true, how can we know what action has more value, what is better and what is worse or what is "good" and what is "bad"?

In our experience, not everything is equal. There are neutral actions that make us neither better nor worse - they are more or less habitual or pleasant. There are others that harm us, which are contradictory. And finally, there are other actions which are very positive and which we call "valid actions".

In New Humanist thinking, the foundation of valid action is neither given by ideology, nor by religious commandments, beliefs or social legislation, even when these things may be very important. The basis of valid action is not given by any of these things. It is given by the internal register of the action.

And what is the register of a valid action? The register is one that we experience as unitive. We feel good and in agreement with ourselves because we are thinking, feeling and acting in the same direction and we are treating others, as we would like to be treated.

The register also gives us the sensation of internal growth: the sensation that something has improved in us when we acted that way. And it is also something that we want to repeat, something that we would do a thousand times over if we could. It extends into the future and gives us a project for the future in the sense that if we could repeat this action something would continue to grow and improve inside of us.

To summarise, valid action is characterised by thinking, feeling and acting in the same direction; treating others, as we would like to be treated; a desire to repeat the action and a feeling of personal growth.

Exercise 1 – Coherence:

Overcoming contradictions is essential to reduce violence. An internal struggle does not remain in the individual but it projects itself into the world as violence.

If my thoughts, my feelings, and my actions are in agreement, if they all go in the same direction, if my actions do not create contradiction with what I feel, then I can say that my life has coherence. But though I am true to myself, this does not necessarily mean I am being true to those in my immediate environment. I still need to achieve this same coherence in my relationships with others, treating them the way I would like to be treated.

Of course there can also be a destructive type of coherence, which can be seen in those who are racists or fanatics or in those who are violent or exploit others. It is clear, however, that their relationships with others are incoherent, because they treat others very differently from the way they desire to be treated themselves.

When we experience differences between thinking, feeling and acting many different emotions arise, some of which are described in the following table:

Thinking	Feeling	Acting	Internal register	Examples
True	False		Hypocrisy	An employee despises their idiotic superior but pretends deference in order not to lose this job, needed to feed the family.
False	True		Stupidity	Liking a leader to the point of following them without applying a critical enough perspective to the proposed policies.

False			True	Regression of the Action	Doing the right thing for the wrong reason, e.g., participation in Save the Children to meet the Royal Family
	False		True	Humiliation	Accepting charity from those who violate our rights or put us in a situation of poverty, disadvantage and dependency.
True			False	Emptiness	Being aware of the need for profound transformations in an unjust and violent system but feeling too busy or tired to do anything.
False	False		False	Vengeance, Envy, Disheartenment, Boredom, Nihilism	Allowing negative mechanical tendencies like cynicism to dominate all aspect of one's life and making others responsible for all our difficulties.
True	True		True	Coherence and a sense of Meaning	Making intentional positive choices that can open the future in any situations we happen to find ourselves in, always trying to find the most positive aspects in others.

Use the table below to chart the level of coherence/contradiction present in various aspects of your life. In this way we can detect those areas than require attention to developing a more coherent attitude.

	What I think	What I feel	What I do
Home			
Partner			
Work/Study			
Friends			
Society			

Exercise 2 – Solidarity:

The universal principle to "treat others the way you would like to be treated" appears today to be totally ignored as competition and individualism promote social fragmentation. This principle exists in all cultures and religions in their most humanist moments, as we can see in the following examples.

"Blessed is he who preferreth his brother before himself. - Baha'u'llah, tablets of baha'u'llah, 71

Don't create enmity with anyone as God is within all. - Guru Granth Sahib

What is hateful to you, do not to your fellow man. That is the law: all the rest is commentary. - Talmud, Shabbat 31a

When you treat others as you would have them treat you, you liberate yourself - Silo

In Happiness and suffering, in joy and grief, we should regard all creatures as we regard our own self. - Mahavira

Do unto others as you would have them do unto you. - Matthew 7 v.12

No one of you is a true believer until he desires for his brother that which he desires for himself. - Prophet Muhammad

This is the sum of duty: do nothing unto others which would cause you pain if done to you. - Mahabharata, XIII:114

Do not hurt others with that which hurts yourself.- the Buddha"

a) List moments when you treated other people in a negative way. Then, list moments when you treated other people in a positive way.
b) Imagine yourself at the receiving end of both positive and negative actions described above. Compare registers.
c) Group Discussion.

Exercise 3 – Valid action:
a) Make a short list of actions you regret.
b) Make a short list of actions that fulfilled the four qualities of valid action.

c)   Compare registers.

d)   Group Discussion.

e)   Plan for the week

Workshop 4

Discrimination

A teacher in the USA, called Jane Elliot, created racism in her class[40] by telling children with brown eyes that they were better than the children with blue eyes. The blue-eyed were excluded from games and eating together with the brown-eyed. On the second day she reversed the roles and sure enough it was the brown-eyed children who were excluded. On the third day she explained that there were no differences and that she had done this as an experiment to give them an experience of what it is like to be discriminated against.

Twenty years later the now grown-up subjects were filmed stating how important that experience had been for them, to learn about how not to discriminate. One of the most important conclusions was that Jane proved that children performed at their worst on the day that they were discriminated against, dispelling in this way the myths created by so-called "scientific research" about differences in IQ in various ethnic groups.

Consider the following riddle: A man and his son are run over in a car accident. The father dies at the scene and the son is rushed to hospital for life-saving surgery. The surgeon arrives at the operating theatre and says "I cannot operate on this child, he is my son". How can this be?[41]

From whose book does this extract come?

"We put down briefly in Khartoum, where we changed to an Ethiopian Airways flight to Addis. Here I experienced a rather strange sensation. As I was boarding the plane I saw that the pilot was black. I had never seen a black pilot before, and the instant I did I had to quell my panic. How could a black man fly a plane? But a moment later I caught myself: I had fallen into the.... mind-set, thinking Africans

---

[40] She did this the day after Marin Luther King died.

[41] The surgeon is female.

were inferior and that flying was a white man's job. I sat back in my seat, and chided myself for such thoughts......"[42]

These two questions allow us to see that we are conditioned by stereotypes, and that even those who are fighting against discrimination carry in themselves certain mechanical assumptions which, if not tackled, could become part of the violence of the system.

Exercise – Personal experience of discrimination

1. Write a list of characteristics that you have which you sometimes feel are a source of discrimination:

2. With internal honesty, write a list of characteristics that others have which you are prejudiced against. (reading optional!).

3. Write down a short list of events in which you were either the victim or the agent in any form of discrimination.

4. Group discussion, interchange of experiences and words of advice from the group to each member based on positive experiences of how others have managed to overcome situations of discrimination.

Meditation on the following principle:

"It does not matter in which faction events have placed you, what matters is for you to comprehend that you have not chosen any faction".[43]

5. Plan for the week with the aim of being more pro-active when realising that someone else is being discriminated against.

Workshop 5

Virtues

It is common for human relationships to be based on criticism, since the prevailing system is based on competition. It is not only common but even expected that people will put each other down in order not to be left behind. In this way we all fear what others think of us and our positive qualities go unrecognised. This contributes to the

---

[42] From *Long Walk to Freedom*, by Nelson Mandela, Abacus, 1995

[43] From *Humanise the Earth*, by Silo, Chapter XIII, The Principles. *Collected Works*, Latitude Press, San Diego, USA, 2002

sense of dehumanisation and isolation created by our environment. If there is no trust between people, working together becomes almost impossible.

A very entrenched kind of discrimination is the one we direct towards ourselves. When we believe the stereotypes created by this system we initiate a process of self deprecation and self-censorship that leads us to expect less from ourselves, not believing in our own capacity, seeing ourselves through the eyes of others also conditioned by stereotypes. In "A class divided" Jane Eliot demonstrated that believing in our own capacity affects performance. Undoing the psychological damage created by stereotypes is the most difficult task in the process of rehabilitating a person or a group that has been discriminated against.

In this exercise we will learn to focus on our and other people's positive characteristics in order to improve our communication and sense of solidarity towards others. This also gives a sense of self-worth and self-esteem, which we mentioned before as one of the elements that, when missing, can be a source of violence.

Exercise – One's virtues

1. Each participant writes down a list of their own best qualities.

2. Then the group tells each participant the virtues they see in them. If the participants do not know one another, they can write down a list of things that others told them are their positive qualities whether believed or not.

3. Each person compares the list they wrote with the qualities that others see in them and makes comments to the group. Try to remember how you feel when you are treated by others on the basis of criticism or on the basis of your virtues and compare registers.

4. Write down a list of people you know in the following table, according to the headings, and list their virtues.

	List of virtues in people around me (a list for each person)
Family: mother, father, siblings, others	

Work/Study	
Friends	
Partner others	

5. Write down a couple of projects you are interested in focusing on with your virtues. Choose which of your virtues you can support yourself with to develop these projects. (Break into groups to interchange.)

6. Plan for the week to pay attention to and acknowledge the positive qualities of those you meet in your daily activities and family, friends, etc

Workshop 6

Organisation

Why do we need to organise ourselves?

We live in a system that creates pain and suffering in millions of people who feel isolated because competition and individualism are given as the desirable models of personal interaction. The system is very well organised and it promotes divisions ("divide and conquer") to prevent a change in its direction.

Only people who manage to work in cooperation, in an organised way that nevertheless maintains a sense of individuality and personal growth, can develop alternatives that will change the direction of the system and their own lives. Since violence is the sign and methodology of this system we need to create an organisation capable of demonstrating that the methodology of non-violence can lead to radical transformations.

Given the dangerously irresponsible and irrational behaviour that is observed in today's world leaders, it is important to create a movement of people who become leaders themselves rather than masses following the most charismatic, the richest or the maddest leader of the time. This is the point of education for non-violence.

Exercise 1 – The vital questions:

Ask yourself the questions and discuss as a group: "Do I want to live? And in what conditions?" Write down what elements of your life would have to change to match your desires. Feel free to be as idealistic as you like.

Write down a list of the people you care about and what things would need to change in their lives in order for them to stop suffering.

What social changes would make the above possible?

What could you do to bring about those changes?

Exercise 2 – Organisation as a living organism

Most people have negative experiences of organisation(s) therefore "joining" gives them the heebie-jeebies. The system reinforces the notion of "the power of the individual". This, of course, serves the interests of those in control who wish to maintain the status quo. We are going to study differences between organisations that dehumanise and others that make people feel that they are at the service of their own development and freedom.

Use the table below to brainstorm with the group.

What are the characteristics of organisations that make me feel dehumanised?	What are the characteristics of organisations that help me grow and develop?:
Example: Lack of communication Etc.	Example: My opinion is valued Etc.

We are interested in a biological model where the main functions of a living organism; reproduction, nutrition and growth are present in its action in the world. The inanimate world lacks intentions. It changes mechanically. Life, even in its most primitive expressions, already expresses a direction towards growth and away from pain. Complex life is the maximum expression of the capacity for intentional existence. An organisation based on the biological model should be capable of offering such intentional participation for their members rather than making them feel, as they do, like a cog in the machine of the system.

We are creating a network formed by orientators who inspire others to participate and begin new groups, also as orientators, administrative members, who feed the structure with information and support members who take care of the personal development of the network. This specialisation functions by promoting individual creativity and diversity.

Exercise 3 – Models

We have all admired and wished to be like people who have been an inspiration for us or have taken good care of us. The common qualities of these people are that they possess kindness, wisdom and strength. We are going to concentrate on our positive experiences of models in life in order to find, for ourselves, roles that are also a source of inspiration for others.

a) List the people you admired or have played a very positive role in your life. Try to reflect on your childhood, adolescence and adulthood.
b) Describe their qualities.
c) Remember moments in your life when you acted with kindness, wisdom and strength.

Exercise 4 – Good moment and bad moment:

a) Consider a bad moment from your life (not the worst moment, just a bad one) and consider the following aspects of that time: Communication with others; Faith in oneself; Vision of the future

b) Consider a good moment from your life and take a few moments to consider the same aspects: Communication with others; Faith in oneself; Vision of the future.

Conclusions: If bad moments are characterised, more often than not, by feelings that the future is closed, that we are isolated from our environment and unable to communicate and feel powerless to modify any given situation, identify the elements of the present system that keep a vision of a closed future, promote lack of communication and reduce faith in themselves for ordinary people. In which way does the direction of the most powerful global institutions contribute to this negative outlook?

What are the most important qualities to promote in a society fit for human development by grassroots and alternative organisations, with reference to communication, people's faith in themselves and the future?

Feedback and proposal to form a network of educators for non-violence: Review your experiences over the last six workshops and summarise what positive experiences are valuable to communicate to others. How do you think that this course of education for non-violence can be improved or adapted and made available for others? Consider what part you may be able to play in making that happen. Discuss this as a group.

Course 2

Introductory notes

In the first set of workshops we have seen that violence is complex, that there are no easy or simplistic remedies and that all the factors need to be considered. You may have found in the previous series that many people found themselves at a point where there was a need to give a response to a situation that had already created a lot of distress and desire for revenge.

You may have asked yourself "But what can we do?" In this series of workshops we shall delve into tools that will help instructors find responses for those situations; not magical solutions but rather responses based on experience. Some of the responses will be related to organising the social base to look at everything as a whole picture and make proposals in all fields of action. We have chosen the workshops in series 2 as a response to the needs discovered in the first workshops. Although this series is presented as a process, individual or groups of exercises may be chosen to deal with a particular situation.

Common elements, found by the participants of the first series of workshops in the genesis and maintenance of a situation of violence, were:

- Breakdown in communication;
- Experiences, cultural forms and values acquired during our formative years that prepared us for a world different to the one we have to live in;
- Rigidity in one's own point of view and inability to see others'

points of view;

- Lack of awareness of the choices available to oneself and feeling compelled to react in ways that are not coherent;
- Frustration when faced with an oppressive situation and not being able to see a solution;
- Perception that somebody else is "getting away" with bad behaviour;
- Feelings of extreme injustice;
- Not being able to move on because of grief for one's losses.

This second set of workshops in the Education for Non-violence course has the following aims:

- To go deeper into the theme of active non-violence so that the participants can make it more real in their lives and become more efficient in influencing the direction of this globalised world.
- To strengthen the idea that violence is not an appropriate response to deal with violent situations. Not only is it violent and therefore incoherent, it is also counter-productive.
- To prepare the participants to become leaders of a social movement capable of giving the type of responses that so many people are crying out for.
- To focus on the social aspects of violence with an understanding of existential issues.

Some of the workshops are based on a system of conflict resolution that has been specifically designed. There are many forms of conflict resolution that can be employed and some of these workshops will echo such examples as: truth and reconciliation (e.g. South Africa); forgive and forget (e.g. Christianity); trial and punishment (e.g. the International Criminal Court). These forms are generally prescriptive, that is, the protagonists of the conflict receive external indications as to the "right" way. In our phenomenological style of conflict resolution we use a more experiential and existential process by those involved that leads to discovering the non-violent perspective and resolution to the problem.

Our conflict resolution comes from two Humanist principles that say: "You will make your conflicts disappear when you understand them in their ultimate root, not when you want to resolve them" and "When you treat others as you would have them treat you, you liberate yourself".[44]

Each workshop can be taken individually or they can be taken as a suite of workshops.

As we did in the first series of workshops, it is recommended that each workshop is started with relaxation and the Experience of Peace as a way to get into the right mental frame for the work that will be carried out.

Personal

The Formation Landscape

The methodology of Non-Violence

Conflict Resolution

Relational

Global

As in Course 1 we will take into account the complex factors that must be dealt with in the process of developing a non-violent society

---

[44] From *Humanise the Earth*, Chapter XIII, The Principles, by Silo. *Collected Works*, Latitude Press, San Diego, USA, 2002.

Workshop 1: Conflict Resolution

Part 1: Introduction

Brief history of non-violence

To start off this workshop we will see a presentation on the history of non-violence, the individuals, groups and currents of thought, that have strongly influenced the world. In particular we will highlight the way many of the most prominent actors were inspired by the examples of previous protagonists.

The presentation is not exhaustive and many people, less well known in certain parts of the world than in others, have also made important contributions. As we carry out this workshop over time and in different parts of the world we will expand the list to give a broader perspective to the genealogy of non-violence.

Each one of us here is potentially the next branch on the non-violence family tree. See the accompanying appendix (appendix 1) for a more detailed biography of those we have included in this presentation.

Levels of conflicts

We identify three major categories of conflicts; of course there are many different sub-levels that can be categorised.

A) Interpersonal conflicts: These are the types of conflicts that may occur between neighbours, family members, individuals at work, at school, etc. There may be some level of physical violence in these conflicts, for instance in the case of domestic violence.

B) Collective conflicts without bloodshed: These are the types of conflicts that may occur between trade unions and bosses, students and university management, public opposition to government policies, etc. There may be some level of physical violence involved in these kinds of conflicts, e.g. picket line disturbances, police using tear gas and water cannons to break up demonstrations, etc. In general there is no complete breakdown in the structure of society.

C) Collective, physically violent conflicts, including wars, terrorism: The characteristics of these conflicts are that people are actively trying to kill others. There is death and destruction and the basic needs of the society are not being maintained.

The level of conflict requires varying ways of applying the following programme. When these workshops are being used for training purposes, the material that we work with in the exercises will be taken from the participants' own personal experience, usually type A situations. When these workshops are applied directly to a real-life situation where both sides of the conflict are present, we will be dealing with any of the types of conflict above.

In the exercises based on one's own experiences it will be necessary to repeat those exercises so that each person has the opportunity to work on their own conflict situations with a partner taking the role of the other party in the conflict.

A scheme for conflict resolution

From a humanist point of view there is no "right" or "wrong" in the overview of a conflict, but rather an existential situation construed by the intentionality of each individual submerged in the conflict. This does not, of course, deny the presence of injustice. Therefore this particular strategy begins with an analysis of the situation by all those implicated in a very personal way and it moves towards the more social/political/cultural further along the process. This scheme that we are presenting consists of 12 phases.

There are conflicts where parties are keen to solve them, prepared to make some compromises and understand the need for communication. There may be other situations where the conflict is more resistant to intervention, the wounds are deeper and communication is very difficult. In the latter case, it is recommended that a mediator or a team of mediators aid the process. Mediators should be neutral, well-trained in all aspects of education for non-violence and acceptable to both parties.

As we go through this scheme we ask each of the participants to bear in mind a conflict. Either they are in a conflict situation in their own lives or they can choose a conflict that they are interested in and take one of the sides as their own for the purposes of these exercises.

1. Present situation

Analysis of the conflict from the point of view of personal lives and the way they are affected by the conflict, including family and environment in general of those implicated in the conflict, the city, the country, and even the global system if relevant to give a framework to the conflict.

2. Analysis of tensions

(The physical evidence of the action of the conflict upon the body of those who are involved) and climates (diffuse emotional situation that tinges the point of view not only of those involved but also of the onlookers). To clarify these concepts see Appendix 2.

3. History of the conflict

People involved in the conflict write down how it began, how it grew, how it affects their lives and the losses brought about by the conflict as well as the hidden benefits derived from the conflict that may contribute to a resistance to find a resolution. Participants should also become aware of the influence from important external players that may have a vested interest in the continuation of the conflict.

4. Projection of the conflict into the future

Participants describe the future of the conflict and their lives and the lives of their families and friends if there is no resolution to the conflict. Then, describe the benefits of reaching a positive resolution to the conflict.

5. History of the conflict from the point of view of the "enemy"

Participants describe how the problem began and how personal lives were affected trying to put themselves in the place of those on the other side of the conflict.

6. Discussion in groups

Pay special attention to the personal suffering experienced by both sides of the conflict and the likely losses for both sides if there are no solutions in the near future. Brainstorm by the group looking for possible solutions to each conflict

7. Visualisations

One of the difficulties in effecting change in a conflict situation is that the image of the "enemy", the loved ones that were lost, our own self-image damaged by the conflict and the situation in general become "fixed". This means that even if the person wishes to find a solution the mind returns over and over again to the same frozen point of view and the only outcome that it considers to be possible. Visualisations allow images to become more flexible (mobility of images) which increases the possibility to consider a wider range of outcomes to the situation.

8. Communication

Communication is the single most important tool for conflict resolution. In these exercises we consider what makes good and bad communication, how to recognise the assumptions we make while we communicate, and how to pay more attention to intentional rather than mechanical communication.

9. Possible solutions

Aided by both mobility of images and, if necessary, neutral participants; both sides of the conflict attempt to find common ground.

10. Ceremony of well being

In the previous step there is a high likelihood that potentially insurmountable difficulties will arise in finding possible solutions if we are dealing with a serious or violent conflict. The memories of those who have died or suffered in the conflict will accompany the process and this simple non-religious ceremony gives the opportunity to connect deeply with the images and memories and direct the best possible wishes in their direction. This moves away from the more mechanical desire for revenge that comes with the loss of loved ones or the register of disempowerment, so common in long-standing conflicts.

11. Proposals

The parties in conflict separate to write down proposals starting with the ideal ones, studying the consequences, followed by the proposals they feel may be acceptable to the other side. At this point the participants may be ready to make a first approach to consensus (including some compromises) that may lead to a solution.

12. Discussion of the proposals

In the presence of the mediators, where used, both sides explain the proposals they feel may be acceptable to the other side. The role of the mediators would be to stress the way in which the proposals have been toned down, that is, they must emphasise the goodwill with which the groups have reached those proposals.

Written synthesis of the agreements

The participants and/or mediators write down a document with all the points that the groups have managed to agree and put them to the sides for their approval. The points that remain without agreement may be referred to arbitration by neutral individuals or agencies acceptable to both sides.

Although this process can be repeated as many times as necessary with the same group, it may be more interesting to carry out the work in "waves" with different members of both sides of the conflict, for instance special groups, such as children, women, trade unions, the military, etc.

Exercises

The following exercises refer to items 1 to 5 above. In the next workshop we will cover item 6 and the following workshop will cover the remaining items 7 to 12.

Present situation

Fill in the chart below from the point of view of your chosen conflict. Ask yourself how the conflict affects each area of your life and what climates and tensions are produced. See Appendix 2 for a description of tensions and climates.

Area of life	Description	Climates	Tensions
Work			
Home life			
Health			
Friends			
Social Projects			
Others			
Synthesis			

History of the conflict

Write down a short history of the conflict. How it began, how different parties became involved, etc.

Projection into the future:

What will happen in the future if there is no resolution...? How your life and the lives of your loved ones will benefit from a positive resolution of the conflict?

History of the conflict from the point of view of the "enemy"

Repeat the history of the conflict but this time from the point of view of the other party.

Discussion in groups

Pay special attention to the personal suffering experienced by both sides of the conflict and the likely losses for both sides if there are no solutions in the near future. Brainstorm from the group looking for possible solutions for each conflict. It is important that the positive images of a possible solution are written on a large piece of paper as the brainstorm delivers them, to end the workshop with a clear visual image of hope.

Workshop 2 – Conflict Resolution

Part 2: Mobility of images

In any deep rooted conflict both sides have very strong, and in many cases, fixed ideas about what the problem is, who is to blame, what the solution is, etc. We need to make these fixed images more flexible as a way to reach a compromise and in order to achieve reconciliation with what has happened in the past.

In the Psychology of New Humanism a simple technique, called "Guided Experiences" has been developed using visualisations that allow us to take certain images and work with them.

What is a guided experience?

All of our life experiences are carried within our consciousness and continue to affect us in our daily activities. This might be related to the way we deal with other people; it may be expressed in fears and anxiety in our daily lives and in the way that we treat ourselves also. All of our life experiences are somehow stored in our consciousness even if we cannot remember everything that has happened to us.

From a humanist viewpoint, it is interesting to try to reconcile with ourselves about situations that have happened in our past, to change our present situation and to develop a positive image of the future. This will help us find more joy and meaning in life and an increased capacity to deal with present and future conflicts. All of the fears, worries and anxiety we carry around with us in our daily activities eat away at our mental energy. Guided experiences have been developed to help us tackle the negative aspects of our consciousness so that we can rescue our energy and channel it to our important life projects and not waste it all on issues that are not useful for our future.

A guided experience is a short story that is written so that each one of us listening to it is the subject of the story. The stories are written in such a way that they allow us to enter into a situation or a scene, next the story develops some "tension" in one way or another, then some representation of a life problem is presented. There is then an opportunity to tackle whatever tension occurred in the situation in our own way, with our personal images, which hopefully decreases the tension associated with the original difficulty. Finally an exit from the experience occurs in a way that is hopefully not too abrupt and with a positive feeling. The narratives are allegorical, that is, they do not deal with conflict in a literal way.

So in summary, a guided experience is one of the personal work techniques developed by the Psychology of New Humanism, to help us liberate ourselves from suffering caused by our past experiences, our present situation or our image of the future. In doing so we regain more of our energy that we can then use in a more intentional way.

How do we do a guided experience?

The participants relax and visualise the suggested images, allowing themselves to keep in touch with their emotions. The participants see themselves as the protagonists of the suggested story.

During the experience the story may involve some situation from the past, present, future or something connected with the meaning of life. Participants listen, as relaxed as possible.

Before doing the experience, it should be read out loud to see what it is going to deal with. We will then take five minutes to check that everyone understands the story and can make some notes on the issues that are dealt with. This will be useful material when participants are visualising the experience, although many unexpected images may appear.

We will then read the experience. In the reading there will be gaps at certain important points. This gives the listener time to really go into the detail of what the guided experience has suggested. These pauses are indicated in the text by an asterisk (*). The idea is that during the pauses our own personal contents will appear and be examined in the way suggested by the story.

Some people may have very vivid images and see everything clearly, others may not see things clearly, and others may fall asleep completely. All of this is fine. Sometimes it can be that what happens in an experience is an indicator of external factors and resistances that we have, to tackle the problems being suggested by the experience. Either way, after the experience we will spend 10 minutes writing notes about what happened, and then we will have an interchange about it.

As with all personal work that touches on themes that are very personal to us, we all have total freedom to express or not what things we have noted down. It is a recommendation that the work done in a group remains private and we do not discuss the work of fellow participants with other people. It is possible to carry out discussions in groups where the participants feel comfortable about sharing their experience. In this way we can create an environment of trust and hopefully deeper cooperation and understanding of each other that can improve the chances for conciliation and conflict resolution.

Guided experience: Resentment
(See appendix 3 for the reading):

1. Reading of the experience
Discussion in pairs about what feelings of tensions and suffering each one would like to eliminate by doing the experience
2. Visualisation followed by personal notes about resistances and difficulties;

3. Group discussion.

Guided experience: The Journey
(See appendix 4 for the reading):

1. Reading of the experience.

Discussion in pairs about what feelings of solidarity towards the whole of humanity (including "the other side") may be developed by doing the experience. Discuss how to visualise both sides of the conflict, at the end of the experience in "returning to my people". The idea is to move into a space from where we can see the overall situation and not just the side in which one is implicated.

2. Visualisation followed by personal notes about resistances and difficulties;

3. Group discussion.

Synthesis

Discuss the register of readiness to change old resentments and move forward with joy towards a different future. Repeat these experiences a few times before the next session.

Workshop 3 – Conflict Resolution

Part 3: Communication, proposals and solutions

Introduction exercise:

Working in pairs, ask general questions about the other person and their motivation to be at the workshop. Introduce your partner to the group making a synthesis of the information given by that person.

Conflict resolution: Communication

The great paradox of the times is that in the era of mobile phones, international travel and the Internet, that is, the era of communications, so many people feel completely isolated. Science and technology are advancing at an ever-accelerating pace, soon we'll be able to travel to other planets, we can map the genetic structure of everything that exists, and yet individualism and greed do not allow science to help people resolve basic needs like nutrition and clean water.

Communication is not at the service of spreading and sharing knowledge, but at the service of maintaining the power that knowledge confers restricted to an ever decreasing minority, dedicated to unrestrained competition that reaps the benefits with total disregard for the needs of others.

In this workshop we will train ourselves in developing better communication skills which are necessary to overcome situations of violence.

1. Repeat this exercise taken from the first series of workshops: Remember a bad moment from your life (not the worst moment, just a bad one) and consider the following aspects of that time: Communication with others; Faith in oneself; Vision of the future.

2. Remember a good moment from your life and take a few moments to consider the same aspects: Communication with others; Faith in oneself; Vision of the future.

Observe how the "feel good" factor has much more to do with having an open future, closeness to others and having faith in oneself than with possessions.

Communication with our immediate environment is an essential component of "good moments". However, it is often the case that fictional characters, in sit-coms or soap-operas, communicate more strongly to people than our friends and relatives. The media provide one way communication and decrease our capacity to share and discuss with our peers. The opinions of those who have access to the media are by definition more important or given undue value without taking into account the expertise of the person in the subject.

Owing to the pressure of "saying the right thing" we communicate on the basis of what we believe others want to hear and that does not always coincide with what we want to say. In other words, we make assumptions about who we are speaking to and communicate on that basis.

To see this miscommunication, the following silly story shows how easy it is to make assumptions: "A woman falls asleep on a rail track after a party. She is completely dressed in black! There is a train coming at full speed without lights. There is no moon, nor street lights. The train still manages to stop on time! How is it possible?"[45]

---

[45] The assumption here is that it is night time.

Exercises

Individually, remember situations where you made assumptions about other people which turned out to be wrong, study the consequences:

1. In family situations.
2. At work/study.
3. With friends.

Negative things I assume that people believe about me:

1. At work people think I am…
2. My friends think I am…
3. My family thinks I am…

Positive things I assume people believe about me:

1. At work people think I am…
2. My friends think I am…
3. My family thinks I am…

Observe and discuss with the group what attitudes are generated in you according to what you think other people are assuming about you.

Competition v co-operation

1. Describe the type of communication you establish with those you find yourself forced to compete with.

2. Describe the type of communication you establish with other people when you all share a common objective

3. Find your partner from previously and discuss the good experiences of communication you both had in the past. Each participant makes a synthesis to the group of the other person's experience. Utilise all the elements for good communication seen in the workshop.

4. The facilitator writes down the key words and elements seen during the workshop that are considered to be good for communication. This concludes the communication training.

Final thoughts on communication:

As communication is frequently based on an assumption of what the other person thinks, people are more reserved about what their real opinions are and what they do for social change. Communication is essential to make others aware that they are not alone in their desire for a more human world.

Conflict resolution: Proposals and solutions

Possible solutions

If we are working with conflicts where all sides of the conflict are present, carry out the following exercise:

Exercise

Aided by both mobility of images and, if present, neutral assistants, both sides of the conflict attempt to find common ground, that is the things where there is consensus amongst all participants (e.g. Peace Dividend, better future for children, etc).

List the points that remain to be agreed on or resolved

If only one side of the conflict is present then, work in pairs, with one person taking the role of the absent party and carry out the same exercise.

Ceremony of well being

In the previous step there is a high likelihood that potentially insurmountable difficulties will arise in finding possible solutions, in particular if the conflict we are dealing with has already created victims. The memories of those who have died or suffered in the conflict will accompany the process. This simple non-religious ceremony gives the opportunity to connect deeply with the images and memories and direct the best possible wishes in their direction. This moves away from the more mechanical desire for revenge that comes with the loss of loved ones.

Exercise: Ceremony of well being
Reading from Appendix 5

Proposals

The parties in conflict separate to write down proposals starting with the ideal ones, studying the consequences, followed by the proposals they feel may be acceptable to the other side. If there are neutral assistants or mediators they may act as reminders of the possible gains the participants have discussed earlier in the work.

At this point the participants may be ready to make a first approach to compromises that may lead to a solution.

Again, if only one side of the conflict is present then, work in pairs, with one person taking the role of the absent party and carry out the same exercise.

Exercise

- List the ideal proposals
- List the proposals that may be acceptable to the other side:

Discussion of the proposals

In the presence of the mediators, where used, both sides explain the proposals they feel may be acceptable to the other side. The role of the mediators would be to stress the way in which the proposals have been toned down, that is, they must emphasise the good will with which the groups have reached those proposals.

Written synthesis of the agreements

The mediators, or in their absence the parties themselves, write down a document with all the points that the groups have managed to agree, and it is then reviewed for its approval. Other issues that have not been agreed may be examined again after a period of time during which implementation of the agreed points has been achieved. Possibly after several rounds of this process, the points that remain without agreement can be referred to arbitration by neutral individuals or agencies acceptable to both sides.

Again, if only one side of the conflict is present then, work in pairs, with one person taking the role of the absent party and carry out the same exercise. Then elaborate a plan to address the problem with the real-life party in conflict.

In the case of the collective conflicts, although this process can be repeated as many times as necessary with the same group it may be more interesting to carry out the work in "waves" with different members of both sides of the conflict, for instance special groups, such as children, women, trade unions, the military, etc.

Workshop 4 – Landscape of formation[46] – Part 1

Each of us was born into an era in which there were certain types of cars, certain types of buildings, as well as an enormous number of objects corresponding to that particular time and place. There were certain kinds of clothes and objects we made use of almost daily. And this world of tangible objects has of course continued to change with the passage of time. It is obvious how much our world has changed over the intervening years. Many of these objects that formed part of our childhood no longer exist, or have changed beyond recognition. And the amount of new ones is inexhaustible.

We also recognise that the world of intangible objects has changed as well: values, social aspirations, interpersonal relationships, etc. Families function differently, so do friendships, dating, etc. The norms of the time have changed tremendously as well. Both the tangible and intangible objects that constituted our landscape of formation have undergone dramatic transformations.

There were many factors that acted upon us to produce our personal behaviour over the course of time. We also shaped our conduct within the world of our relationships. As we acted in our world we looked at that world in certain ways and we looked at people in certain ways, and we were also being looked at by others, who either encouraged us or rebuked us; the look of institutions, customs, God, morals, etc.

Our landscape of formation, acquired long ago, continues to act through us in our present behaviour as our way of being and moving among people and things. The velocity of change is accelerating; we are in the presence of a rhythm of life that is very different from what it

---

[46] Based on The Landscape of Formation, from *Self Liberation* by Luis Ammann

used to be in earlier times (communications, globalisation, technology...).

So we find ourselves affected by our personal formative landscape and its interaction with the current historical moment in which we happen to live. Violence arises when those who would wish the world to be what they expected in the light of their education find themselves in a completely different space, whether because it is now multi-cultural or because communication happens through a technology they don't understand or because labour relations are completely different because of the globalised neo-liberal work ethic. The compulsion to impose their "old" landscape upon the younger generations or simply to be vociferously critical of them widens the generational gap and the resentment of the newcomers against what they perceive as a resistance to letting go of power. On the other hand the new world exercises violence against the old by increasingly making them feel obsolete and disposable, creating codes, languages and culture that excludes them.

This theme of the formative landscape therefore not only works at an inter-personal level but also throughout society. One of the most widespread phenomena, the migration of whole families, shows how the landscape of formation works in the destruction of communication between parents and children. It is common to see parents attribute the changes they see in their children to the fact that they moved to another country or another culture, not realising that the young are also undergoing similar changes in their country of origin.

To be a reference to others for non-violent resolution of conflicts that arise from this lack of "fitting" between the world we were brought up to live in and the real one, we need to become internally flexible and aware, so that we can help others breach the generational gap which at the economic level expresses itself as Bankers and Neo-liberal gurus (old) versus the anti-globalisation movement (young, with a few encouraging exceptions!). Occasionally older generations look at the young, feeling "We've seen it all before, you'll grow up like us and lose your idealism", not realising that in trading their idealism for cynical "realism" they lost a big and meaningful part of themselves.

Exercise 1 – Tangible objects

a) We know that many objects have changed between the period when we were children and the present. The landscape in general in which our lives have unfolded has undergone great changes.

b) Write a brief summary in which you describe the situation and circumstances in which you lived during your childhood and your adolescence. Reconstruct your formative landscape in broad outline, focusing on the tangible objects of that time. (Remember the fashions, cars, appliances, music, books, TV programmes, etc.) Do not worry if you cannot remember too much, in the discussion with others you will probably be reminded of more things.

c) Group discussion: the landscapes of formation, trying to identify the changes that have taken place from that earlier time until today.

Exercise 2 – Intangible objects

We define the intangible factors like the values, social aspirations, relationships, etc. that surrounded us as we were growing up; the norms of the time, the personal ideals, the status quo, the fashion and music. We could call it, in general, the "sensibility" of the time.

a) Write a brief summary in which you describe the situation and the circumstances in which you lived during your childhood and adolescence. Focus on the intangible factors. Remember the accepted values, what was good and what was bad, what was happiness, who were the heroes, values at home, school, what about friendships, work? What were the social themes? Try and capture that "sensibility".

b) Group discussion: identify the changes that have taken place since then.

Exercise 3 – Looks

The factors that have acted in us to produce our personal behaviour over the course of time are numerous, and form a system of codes upon which we base our current responses and adjustments to our environment. We can notice that in facing our formative environment we behaved in certain characteristic ways. With established values, we either fought against them, accepted them, or retreated within ourselves. We shaped our conduct within the world of our relationships. This means that there were continuous readjustments, for as we acted in our formative world, we looked at that world in certain ways, and we looked at people in certain ways as well. At the same time, we were being looked at by others (either encouraging us or rebuking us). There was also the look of the institutions, the law, the customs and conventions of the times. Some may have felt a more complex look that examined us in our external behaviour and in our deeper intentions as well, the religious look.

In conclusion, both our own looks and the looks of others led to readjustments in our conduct. And out of all this we formed a certain behaviour, a certain way of being, and of seeing.

In our present lives each of us has many different codified forms of behaviour that were moulded in our formative stage. And since then, the world has changed enormously...

a) Write a brief summary describing the situation in which you lived during your childhood and your adolescence. Reconstruct your landscape of formation, mainly focusing on how you looked at others and were looked at by others (family, school, friends, work, sexual partners, neighbourhood, etc.). Ask yourself questions like: what type of person where you supposed to be? What type of life were you supposed to have? (from others' and your own point of view). Try and recall how you judged and felt judged by the world and how you reacted to it. With what situations did you clash? Do not bother with whether it was good or bad, simply describe.

b) Group discussion: your personal way of looking (at yourself and others). Describe the most important changes that have taken place.

Workshop 5 – Landscape of formation – Part 2

Exercise 4 – Compulsions

Our typical behaviour in the present is made up of numerous forms of conduct. We can understand our conduct as the "tactics" we use to unfold our lives in the world. While many of those tactics have been adequate thus far, we can recognise that other tactics are clearly ineffective, and others even generate conflict. Here it is a good idea to discuss this briefly.

Why do I continue applying tactics that I can recognise are ineffective or counterproductive? Why do I feel powerless against those forms of conduct, which seem to operate automatically? To refer to those internal forces that compel us to act in spite of ourselves, or inhibit us from actions that we wish to accomplish, we will use the term compulsion, which is borrowed from classical psychology.

The importance of this workshop is that compulsions give us a register of "lack of freedom" and they also make us act in a way that reduces other people's freedom, which generally results in some form of violence whether it be psychological, economic, etc.

a) Try to discover using the table below that behaviour which you feel is clearly "dragged" from your formative years (when it developed as a response to a specific situation) and which is not only no longer useful but sometimes even harmful to your life today. We shall scan different ambits of our lives to detect where the compulsions lie and try to recall in what moments of our lives they appeared and were useful as a response to a conflict situation.

Ambit	List behaviours you register as compulsive	To which situations in your formation landscape does this respond to?
Family		
School/ Work		
Partner		
Friends		
Other		

b) Then, discuss amongst the group what you have discovered.

If possible, this week try to "catch" yourself, or register when you realise that you are responding compulsively to a situation. Be aware of the "dragging" and apply more intentional decisions.

Exercise 5 – Living mechanically or intentionally

Ask yourself, if my life goes on mechanically in the same direction in an environment that maintains the same values and priorities, where am I going to be in 2, 5 and 10 years' time?

Think about personal life, relationships with friends and family and the world in general.

c) 2 years
d) 5 years
e) 10 years

Exercise 6 – Image of the future – An intentional life

Many people get stuck in their past suffering, not realising that an open future has the power to change the point of view from where they see their own history. An intentional life that actively constructs the future may still drag elements from the landscape of formation, but in the process a new way of being in the world can arise as one learns to give new responses. Some elements from the landscape of formation may be positively useful for the future but they will have been intentionally selected.

The aim of these workshops has been to help everyone develop an image of a world without violence. Images move the body, thoughts, emotions and society; without images there is no movement. We need to give precision to the image of the future we want because there is no construction without a clear image.

We also need images for the steps we are going to take in our construction; images that fit with the type of life we want to live. There is no point planning to spend one's life developing projects in tropical countries if we can't stand hot weather and mosquitoes!

Exercise

A table is a piece of wood to which an image has been applied.[47]

A meaningful life is a mechanical and haphazard sea of events to which an intentional image gives direction.

---

[47] Based on an idea from *La Mirada del Sentido (The Look of Meaning)* by Dario Ergas, Editorial Catalonia, Chile, 2006

A non-violent world is THIS world with a positive image working to change it.

a) What is your intentional image for your own life?
b) What is your intentional image to work on the world?

Workshop 6 – Social change

The tools of non-violent direct action

A non-violent campaign can consist of a combination of different techniques and events. For instance, Martin Luther King, like Gandhi, used a step-wise approach. The King Center lists six steps:

- Step One. Information gathering
- Step Two. Education
- Step Three. Personal commitment
- Step Four. Negotiations
- Step Five. Direct action
- Step Six. Reconciliation

Exercise

Brainstorm in a group about the tools of non-violent action, on the basis of the participants' knowledge from examples in history and in the present day. For each heading we will consider how it works. The headings that you might consider are:

Tool	How it works	Examples
Information to the population, slogans, advertising, posters, leaflets, etc.		
Creative entertainment; street theatre, comedy, concerts, etc.		
Publicity stunts.		
Putting together networks of people, forums,		

Tool	How it works	Examples
System channels; complaints, letters to MPs, courts, petitions, etc		
Demonstrations, vigils and strikes		
Civil disobedience, hunger strikes		

The proposal of New Humanism

How are we going to become protagonists of non-violent change, leaders of our own communities, guides to give, not orders, but reference on how to overcome the personal and social resistances to the creation of a non-violent world?

Exercise

In this exercise the aim is to find a conflict that you would like to work on and imagine the steps that are necessary in order to give a coherent response to that conflict. Such elements are necessary as communicating to others, inviting others to join you in this project, overcoming difficulties that you face along the way, learning to respond from the point of view of non-violence, etc.

a) Choose a conflict or an injustice close to your heart.
b) Building a team to influence this conflict: Who, How, Where and When?
c) Introductory meeting; write down the points you would explain to your future team members.
d) Likely resistances you will encounter in yourself and in others.
e) Leaping over difficulties as a response to the violence of the system.
f) Clear images.
g) See how frustration is part of the process of producing change (if everything we undertake is successful, it is because change would have happened anyway).
h) Sense of humour.
i) Enthusiasm without expectation.

j)   Meditate about the following Principle of Valid Action: "If you pursue an end you enchain yourself to suffering, if everything you do is an end in itself, you liberate yourself."[48]

The Internal Guide

The internal guide is an image we can all configure, capable of aiding our work in the world by giving us strength, confidence and direction. It can also help us become guides in order to give reference to others.

(The following extract is taken from the book *Humanise the Earth* by Silo)

"Whom do you so admire that you would like to have been that person?

Let me ask you in a more gentle fashion: Whom do you consider so exemplary that you wish you could find some of that person's virtues in yourself?

Perhaps there have been moments when in sorrow or confusion you have appealed to the memory of someone who, whether existing or not, came to your aid as a comforting image?

I am speaking of those particular models that we could call internal "guides", which at times coincide with real people.

Those models which you have wanted to follow from the time you were very young, have changed only in the most external layers of your daily awareness.

I have seen how children talk and play with their imaginary companions and guides. I have seen people of all ages connect with these guides in prayers offered in sincere devotion. The more strongly these guides were called, the further away they responded from and the better the signal they sent. Because of this I knew that the most profound guides are the most powerful. But only a great need can awaken them from their millennia of lethargy.

---

[48] From *Humanise the Earth*, Chapter XIII, The Principles, *Collected Works* by Silo, Latitude Press 2002

Such a model "possesses" three important attributes: strength, wisdom, and kindness.

If you want to know yourself better, observe the characteristics of the men and women you admire. Notice how the qualities you most value in them are also at work in the configuration of your own internal guides. Consider that even though your initial references may have disappeared with the passage of time, they have left "traces" within you that continue to motivate you toward the external landscape.

And if you want to understand how diverse cultures interact with each other, in addition to studying their modes of producing objects, study as well the methods by which they transmit their models.

It is important, then, to direct your attention to the best qualities in others, because you will project into the world those qualities you have managed to configure in yourself.

Exercise

We can review now those models we looked at in the last workshop of the previous series. Who were our examples of kindness, wisdom and strength in our childhood, adolescence and adult life?

In small groups, discuss what are the elements; kindness, wisdom and strength? Try to connect with the registers taking examples from your own experience.

Begin to configure an image or a sensation of someone who could have these qualities to derive inspiration, protection and strength from.

Closing

We hope you all find these workshops helpful in your work, home or projects. We recommend all those who wish to become instructors in the use of these techniques to continue training oneself as we train others in the use of these materials to gain more depth and understanding of the problems of violence. It is recommended also to continue working in network rather than in isolation as we all need support when confronting these issues.

Appendix 1 – Biographical notes of non-violent protagonists and currents of thought

These are some historical figures and currents of thought that appear in the family tree of the non-violent movement. To study their ideas and actions is to come into contact with the process of choosing non violence as a methodology for action. Some of the characters may not have existed in the form that history or tradition tells us, but whatever their reality, they are important as part of the chain of inspiration and models. Some may not have been always committed to non violence and their ethical and methodological struggle contributes to our own discussion about this important choice.

Amenhotep IV (Akhenaton), Ancient Egypt

In the XIV century BC this Pharaoh led a dramatic revolution, establishing a monotheistic religion and political changes based on peace and social justice.

Zarathustra, Persia

About 600 BC Zarathustra (said to be born from a virgin) began to preach that there was only one true God and saviour, Ahura Mazda (Lord of Wisdom). This gave birth to Zorastrianism as a religion. His teachings were: "Think well, do good, speak the truth" as well as an ethic of personal responsibility: "There is only one way to fight evil, by increasing kindness, and only one way to fight against darkness, by expanding the light. In the same way, only by broadening love and not fighting and opposing one another we can eliminate hatred and enmity."

Jainism: Ahimsa

Jainism was born in India about the same period as Buddhism. It was established by Mahavira (c. 599-527 BC) in about 500 BC. Mahavira, like Buddha, belonged to the warrior caste. Mahavira was called "Jina" meaning the "big winner", and from this name was derived the name of the religion.

In many senses Jainism is similar to Buddhism. Both developed as dissidence from the Brahmanic philosophy that was dominant during that period in north-east India. Both share a belief in reincarnation which eventually leads to liberation. Jainism is different to Buddhism in its ascetic beliefs. Both these religions emphasise non-violence, but non-violence is the main core in Jainism.

Gautama Buddha, India

He was born a Prince, and his father attempted to keep him in the Palace, away from all suffering and given to unlimited pleasure. In his youth he walked in the world where he was shocked to see so much sorrow in the form of old age, illness and death. He attempted to reach spiritual development through the known ascetic ways of the time, but in failing to do so he developed the "middle path" and communicated it to his disciples.

He propounded the philosophy of non-violence, universal love and peace 2,500 years ago. Emperor Asoka Maurya from India gave this pacifist philosophy official recognition in the 3rd century BC and sent Buddhist missionaries to the Far East and central Asia. For this initiative in spreading the message of peace and non-violence, he is remembered not only by Indians but by pacifists all around the globe.

King Asoka, India

His edicts, based on Ahimsa, are mainly concerned with the reforms he instituted and the moral principles he recommended in his attempt to create a just and humane society. He was born in India in 304 BC. Eight years after his coronation, Asoka's armies attacked and conquered Kalinga. The loss of life caused by battle, reprisals, deportations and the turmoil that always exists in the aftermath of war so horrified Asoka that it brought about a complete change in his personality. After the war Asoka dedicated the rest of his life trying to apply Buddhist principles to the administration of his vast empire. He had a crucial part to play in helping Buddhism to spread both throughout India and abroad. Asoka died in 232 BC in the thirty-eighth year of his reign.

Plato 427- 347 BC, Greece

In both the *Republic* and the *Laws*, Plato asserts not only that factionalism and civil war are the greatest dangers to the city, but also that peace obtained by the victory of one part and the destruction of its rivals is not to be preferred to social peace obtained through the friendship and cooperation of all the city's parts. Peace for Plato is not a status quo notion, related to the interest of the privileged group, but a value that most people usually desire. He does not stand for war and the victory of one class, but for peace in social diversity.

Jesus Christ, Judaea
Here are some of the non-violent teachings attributed to him in the writings of the Apostles:

"Put your sword in its place, for all who take the sword will perish by the sword" (Matthew 26:52).

"You have learnt how it was said: 'Eye for eye and tooth for tooth.' But I say to you, Offer the wicked man no resistance. If anyone strikes you on the right cheek, turn the other also; if a man takes you to law and would have your tunic, let him have your cloak as well. And if anyone orders you to go one mile, go two miles with him." Mt. 5.38-41.

"If there is one of you who has not sinned, let him be the first to throw a stone at her." John 8.7

Judaism: The Talmud
"For the sake of peace one may lie, but peace itself should never be a lie."

"Whoever destroys a single life is as guilty as though he had destroyed the entire world; and whoever rescues a single life earns as much merit as though he had rescued the entire world." (This is also in the Koran!)

Bahai Faith
"I charge you all that each one of you concentrate all the thoughts of your heart on love and unity. When a thought of war comes, oppose it by a stronger thought of peace. A thought of hatred must be destroyed by a more powerful thought of love. Thoughts of war bring destruction to all harmony, well-being, restfulness and content. Thoughts of love are constructive of brotherhood, peace, friendship, and happiness." - Abdu'l-Baha

Islam and Sufism

Ibn Arabi's doctrine is that the entire universe is God's manifestation. This leads to demolition of barriers between people of one religion and the other. Thus peace, friendship and love have been at the centre of this school of Sufism. Mansur Al-Hallaj (martyred in 922) exposed the psychospiritual doctrine of "two natures". Sufis resist the notion that religious authority should be based on titles and offices. Rather, Sufi teachers gain acceptance and support by their insights and capacity for transmission of enlightenment to their students. The history of Sufism is filled with examples of interfaith co-operation.

Laura Cereta, 1469-1499, Italy

Renaissance Feminist who stressed the emotions in a genre (criticism) long assumed to be the domain of the rational faculties only. She attempted to reconstruct and redefine the concept of gender, proposing mutual support of women by women and the idea of a community of women. She saw housework as a barrier to women's literary aspirations and held that "all human beings, women included, are born with the right to an education". She raised the mainstreaming of women's writing into genres and venues that were once for men only and searched for ways to give women access to public life.

Bartolomé de las Casas, 1484-1566, Spain

Fray Bartolomé de las Casas dedicated his life to the defence of indigenous peoples and is today seen as one of the precursors of the theory and practice of Human Rights. A Spanish colonist, a priest, founder of a Utopian community and first Bishop of Chiapas in Mexico, he was a scholar, historian and 16th century human rights advocate. He has been called the Father of anti-imperialism and anti-racism.

George Fox, 1624 –1691, England. Founder of the Quakers

Living in a time of great social upheaval, he rebelled against the religious and political consensus by proposing an unusual and uncompromising approach to the Christian faith. It was as early as the XVI century that Quakers began their fight against slavery, and thus began the abolitionist movement.

On Non-Violence: "We utterly deny all outward wars and strife and fightings with outward weapons, for any end or under any pretence whatsoever, and this is our testimony to the whole world": Quaker statement to King Charles II, 1660. "A good end cannot sanctify evil means; nor must we ever do evil, that good may come of it": William Penn, 1693.

Tom Paine, England, 1737-1809.

Poverty, Paine suggested, is unacceptable and something that should and could be eliminated. He fought for American independence. His book *The Rights of Man* was published in the UK in 1792. It was banned for its antiestablishment stance, but became a best seller. He opposed slavery and was amongst the earliest proponents of social security, universal free public education and a guaranteed minimum wage.

Mary Wollstonecroft, 1759-1797, England

She described the process by which parents brought their daughters up to be docile and domesticated. She maintained that if girls were encouraged from an early age to develop their minds, it would be seen that they were rational creatures and there was no reason whatsoever for them not to be given the same opportunities as boys with regard to education and training. Women could enter the professions and have careers just the same as men (*A Vindication of the Rights of Woman* was published during the French Revolution). She died in childbirth (her daughter Mary Shelley wrote *Frankenstein*).

Immanuel Kant, 1724-1804, Prussia.

In 1795 Kant published an essay entitled "Toward Perpetual Peace: A Philosophical Sketch." In his view the Treaty of Basel between Prussia and France was only "the suspension of hostilities, not a peace". In the essay, Kant argues that it is humankind's immediate duty to solve the problem of violence and enter into the cosmopolitan ideal of a universal community of all peoples governed by the rule of law. Kant believed that peace could be gradually extended. The first step was for states to become Republican. As a second step, all Republican states would join a federation. One day, this federation would embrace all states of the earth. He is considered to be the inspiration for the creation of the League of Nations as the way to end all wars.

Henry David Thoreau, 1817-62, US

US essayist, poet, and practical philosopher, renowned for having lived the doctrines of Transcendentalism (which was amongst other things concerned with the end of slavery) as recorded in his masterwork, *Walden* (1854), and for having been a vigorous advocate of civil liberties, as evidenced in the essay "Civil Disobedience" (1849). "One has a moral obligation to refuse to cooperate with an unjust social system."

Leon Tolstoy, 1828 –1910, Russia

He was a Russian novelist, reformer, pacifist and moral thinker, notable for his ideas on non-violent resistance. He was born into the aristocracy but renounced its privileges. Tolstoy's Christian beliefs were based on the Sermon on the Mount, and particularly on the comment about turning the other cheek, which he saw as a justification of pacifism. These beliefs came out of a severe depression with suicidal feelings. He believed that a Christian should look inside their own heart to find inner happiness rather than looking outward toward the church or state. His belief in non-violence when facing oppression is another distinct attribute of his philosophy. By directly influencing Mohandas Gandhi with this idea Tolstoy has had a huge influence on the non-violent resistance movement to this day. He believed that the aristocracy was a burden on the poor, and that the only solution to how we live together is through anarchy. He also opposed private property and the institution of marriage and valued the ideals of chastity and sexual abstinence.

In one of his letters, Tolstoy noted that Thoreau had written about Civil Disobedience fifty years previously. He claims to have been influenced by the Quakers and the anti-slavery movement in the United States.

Mohandas K. Gandhi, 1869-1948, India

Gandhi went to England to study law in 1889, and graduated from the Inner Temple of London. While he was in England, a number of vegetarian friends who formed his support group persuaded Gandhi to study Indian religions and literature.

When he returned to India, however, he could not find a job; so he accepted an offer to go to South Africa. He was hired to serve as a lawyer to a rich Indian merchant who had settled there. While travelling in South Africa to his place of employment, Gandhi was badly mistreated by the white officials of the railway company because of his skin colour. As a result of this incident, Gandhi began to think about the treatment of minorities and what could be done to improve the situation. In those days, racial segregation, later called apartheid, was the law and policy of the government of South Africa. So after Gandhi settled his employer's legal matters, he began to organise the Indian community to demand their civil rights.

During his 20 years in South Africa, Gandhi developed his principles of non-violent resistance. He led this struggle in non-violent confrontations with the government. The rules of non-violent resistance that he laid down are:

- No hitting back (no retaliation),
- Endure personal pain and suffering, even death,
- Express love and forgiveness toward the oppressor, and
- Harbour no intent to harm or humiliate the oppressor, but rather a desire to settle (reconcile) differences.

After gaining many civil rights reforms, Gandhi left South Africa and returned to India in 1914. At first he travelled widely in the country to see for himself the conditions in which the poor lived, and to learn from them the ways in which he could help.

Then he became leader of the Indian National Congress in 1920 and began to protest against the British government's rule over India. He successfully mediated in a labour dispute in the textile industry in the city of Ahmedabad. When the district of Bardoli refused to pay what they considered unfair taxes, Gandhi encouraged other districts to do the same in support, believing that this would overthrow the British government. However, when some of his supporters rioted and killed 22 policemen in Chauri-Chaura, Gandhi called off the rebellion. He felt personally responsible for the killings, and he did not want to kill the British to achieve peace and justice for his people. He believed that killing to get what you want was wrong, and he chose to fail, rather than achieve independence for India. He continued to stand by his principles of non-violence, and earned the title of Mahatma - "The Great Soul."

During the second World War, the Muslim League broke from Gandhi and demanded that India be divided into two countries - one mostly Muslim and one mostly Hindu. Since every city, town and village had mixed populations of many religions and sects, Gandhi did not agree with their position. He felt that this division would lead to war, and in 1947, when the British divided the country into India and Pakistan, his prediction came true. During this time of civil war, Gandhi resided in the state of Bengal, in Eastern India. He brought peace to that part of the country. He then went to Delhi and accomplished the same thing there, after which he planned to move to the newly created country of Pakistan and plead for peace. But on 30 January 1948, his peaceful mission ended. He was assassinated by a fanatic he had helped free from British rule.

The Suffragettes, UK and USA

In Britain and the United States they worked for decades to win equality in voting rights, first through calm persuasion and, when that failed, through civil disobedience, a tactic that protesters would adopt later. They broke street lamps, cut telephone lines and slashed museum paintings. One suffragist threw herself under the king's horse during a race and was killed.

In March 1913, 5,000 women staged a suffrage pageant in Washington, withstanding a mob's attacks until cavalry troops intervened. "Nothing less than riots," was an associated press correspondent's description.

Eight months later in London, a protest at parliament became "black Friday," which a historian described as "a battle between the police and not the unemployed, the homeless or the destitute - but middle- and upper-class women of all ages." Not all agreed with the escalation or the Pankhurst style of leadership and a number of members left the group in 1907 with Despard, Edith How Martyn, Teresa Hillington-Greig, Octavia Lewin, and Caroline Hodgeson to form another militant, but this time non-violent, organisation: the Women 's Freedom League which engaged in acts of civil disobedience.

Aldo Capitini, Italy

He was, during Mussolini's reign, very active in covert, anti-fascism propaganda among the youth of central Italy. He wrote a book where he stressed the infinite potentialities inherent in any layman, since a great experience of liberation may start from an interior process, although oppressed by a negative society; a characteristic statement of this period is: "God is not truth, God is to choose". Although he did not belong to any political party, his life became an example among the Italian anti-fascists, He observed that "the fundamental question is not the knowledge of the method but to have the will, to be open to the spirit of non-violence".

In 1962 he launched a peace march (at the time of the Cuban Missile Crisis) from Perugia to Assisi (28 km). For the first time the march collected together all eminent friends of peace, although coming from very different ideologies (philosophers as N. Bobbio and A. Calogero were his close friends). This event started an Italian tradition: the peace march was repeated several times (twice in 1999) as the most important national peace action.

Albert Einstein, Germany, USA

Einstein believed in non-violence and opposed World War I. As he put it, "a moral attitude to life, love of justice and knowledge, and a desire for personal independence influenced me." Thus, he supported Jews and their desire for a homeland in Palestine, not as a political state, but as a place where Jews could develop their culture and share the land with their neighbours.

Martin Luther King, USA

Martin Luther King, Jr. came from a hard-working, honest and well-educated middle-class family. He studied the writings of Mahatma Gandhi during his student days, and realised that Gandhi's methods of non-violent resistance were the correct tools to use to gain civil rights for poor minorities. To those who accused him of causing trouble, King replied that the downtrodden and mistreated people can only get justice and peace by agitating non-violently until their grievances were redressed.

The Montgomery bus boycott of 1955-1956 gave the Reverend King his first chance to practice non-violent resistance to unjust laws. Rosa

Parks, a black seamstress, refused to give up her seat in the bus to a white passenger, which was required by the law in the South at that time. For this she was arrested and summoned to court. The black citizens of Montgomery, Alabama decided to boycott the buses for one day. This boycott proved to be so successful that they continued it. They refused to ride the buses at all until they were given what they considered to be civil rights under the law. All they asked for was courteous treatment from the bus drivers, and an end to segregated seating in the buses.

Dr King was named the leader of this boycott. During the 382-day ordeal, he succeeded in getting his people to walk, ride mules or bikes, and to car-pool, but never to ride the bus to work, school or play. During this time, Dr King was harassed, imprisoned, and humiliated. His home was even bombed, but he never retaliated physically. He taught his followers to use peace, not violence, to win their battles. The highest court in the land, the Supreme Court, finally heard the case, and decided that the cause was just. The buses of Montgomery were finally integrated.

Martin Luther King was awarded the Nobel Prize for peace in 1964, but was murdered in 1968.

Aung San Suu Kyi, Myanmar (formerly Burma)

The sources of her inspiration were Mahatma Gandhi, about whom she had learned when her mother was the ambassador to India, and her father, Aung San, the leader in Burma's struggle for liberation. She was only two when her father was assassinated, but she had made his life a centre of her studies. From Gandhi she drew her commitment to non-violence, from her father the understanding that leadership was a duty and that one can only lead in humility and with the confidence and respect of the people to be led. Both were examples for her of independence and modesty, and Aung San represented what was called "a profound simplicity" (Nobel Peace Prize speech). At the Nobel Prize ceremony for Aung San Suu Kyi in December 1991, she was still being held in detention by the military dictatorship in Myanmar and could only be represented by her two sons, her husband and her picture facing the audience.

The National League for Democracy was formed, with Suu Kyi as general secretary. It promoted a policy of non-violence and civil disobedience. Defying a ban, Suu Kyi made a speech-making tour throughout the country to large audiences. Suu Kyi continued to campaign despite harassment, arrests and killings by soldiers. She was prohibited from standing for election.

There was a famous incident in the Irawaddy delta when Suu Kyi courageously walked towards soldiers' rifles aiming at her. She was placed under house arrest, without charge or trial. Despite her detention her party won the elections with 82% of parliamentary seats. The military junta refused to recognise the results.

She was granted the 1990 Rafto human rights prize as well as the 1991 Nobel peace prize. Suu Kyi remains in detention, having rejected an offer to free her if she would leave Burma and withdraw from politics.

Bertrand Russell, 1872-1970, UK

Russell was an influential British mathematician, philosopher, and logician; an example of a non-religious peace campaigner. He was dismissed from Trinity College and imprisoned for five months as a result of anti-war protests. His appointment at City College New York was revoked following public protests. He was dismissed from the Barnes Foundation in Pennsylvania and organised the first Pugwash Conference. He became the founding President of the Campaign for Nuclear Disarmament and imprisoned aged 89 for one week in connection with anti-nuclear protests.

Kwame Nkrumah, Ghana 1909-1972

Inspired by Gandhi's teachings Nkrumah adopted the philosophy of Positive Action on the principle of non-violence. Nkrumah rose to prominence in the 1950's when he won independence for the former Gold Coast (now Ghana). In 1957 he made her the first nation in sub-Saharan Africa country to win independence from European colonial rule. Nkrumah used the independence of Ghana as a platform to lead the fight for the total emancipation of Africa from colonial rule, and also to campaign for a political union of the newly independent states and the integration of their economies. Although his rule has been criticised as authoritarian and undemocratic he was aware that his socialist project had many enemies abroad, and he survived five assassination attempts. He is still considered one of the great leaders of the Pan African Movement.

Betty Williams and Mairead Corrigan, Northern Ireland

The two women led marches in which Protestants and Catholics walked together in demonstrations for peace and against violence. Awarded the Nobel Peace Prize in 1976 The Ceremony's speech stated that "Williams and Corrigan have shown us what ordinary people can do to promote peace." They had the courage to take the first step. "They did so in the name of humanity and love of their neighbour; someone had to start forgiving. ... Love of one's neighbour is one of the foundation stones of the humanism on which our western civilisation is built." It is vitally important that it "should shine forth when hatred and revenge threaten to dominate." Theirs was "a courageous unselfish act that proved an inspiration to thousands, that lit a light in the darkness...". They founded the Community of Peace People to continue working for the end of violence in Ireland.

Patrice Lumumba, Congo

Independence speech: "...We are going to put an end to suppression of free thought and see to it that all our citizens enjoy to the full the fundamental liberties foreseen in the Declaration of the Rights of Man.

"We are going to do away with all discrimination of every variety and assure for each and all the position to which human dignity, work, and dedication entitles him.

"We are going to rule not by the peace of guns and bayonets but by a peace of the heart and the will...."

The Mandela Conundrum. South Africa

Nelson Mandela's initial campaign against apartheid was based on non-violence. Then he judged that sabotage and even the arms struggle had their place in the fight against one of the most violent systems the world has known. He received the Nobel Peace Prize (Nobel apparently created the award to make up for inventing dynamite). Much of the campaign that led to the end of apartheid was in fact based on non-violence: international pressure, civil disobedience and Mandela's own refusal to leave prison (by not renouncing violence) which further increased the international pressure. Should he take his place in this tree of non-violent leaders? This debate may help us clarify many issues.

Shirin Ebadi, Iran

"As a lawyer, judge, lecturer, writer and activist, she has spoken out clearly and strongly in her country, Iran, and far beyond its borders. She has stood up as a sound professional, a courageous person, and has never heeded the threats to her own safety.

Her principal arena is the struggle for basic human rights, and no society deserves to be labelled civilised unless the rights of women and children are respected. In an era of violence, she has consistently supported non-violence. It is fundamental to her view that the supreme political power in a community must be built on democratic elections. She favours enlightenment and dialogue as the best path to changing attitudes and resolving conflict." (Nobel Peace Prize speech, 2003)

Mikhail Sergeyevich Gorbachev, Russia

Gorbachev was the leader and president of the USSR from 1985–91. He attempted to revive the faltering Soviet economy through economic reforms (*perestroika*) and liberalise society and politics through *glasnost* (openness) and competition in elections, and to halt the arms race abroad through arms reduction agreements with the USA. He pulled Soviet troops out of Afghanistan and allowed the Soviet-bloc states in central Europe greater autonomy, a move which soon led to the break-up of the USSR and the end of the Cold War. He was awarded the Nobel Prize for Peace in 1990 for promoting greater openness in the USSR and helping to end the Cold War. He helped launch with other Peace Prize winners the "Decade of Peace and Non Violence for the children of the world" programme for the first 10 years of the new millennium, to be dedicated to Education for Non Violence, now run by UNESCO.

Rigoberta Menchú, Guatemala

It was announced in October 1992 that the Nobel Peace prize would go to Rigoberta Menchú, a Mayan Indian of Guatemala, "in recognition of her work for social justice and ethno-cultural reconciliation based on respect for the rights of indigenous peoples." She received the prize in recognition for her political and social work rather than turning to violence. She became an active member of the Committee for Campesino Unity and then helped found the Revolutionary Christians. Menchú explained that "we understood revolutionary in the real meaning of the word 'transformation.' If I had chosen the armed struggle, I would be in the mountains now." Although she has admitted her book contains some events later proven to be not true, the Nobel committee accepted it as a true representation of the lives of Guatemalan Indians, if not her real biography.

Mario Rodriguez Cobos, pen-name Silo, Argentina

Silo is a thinker and writer who launched a non-violence movement as a response to the growing violence during the military dictatorships in South America. Throughout the sixties his thinking developed to the point where the first public exposition of his work was made in 1969 in a location called Punta de Vacas in the Andes mountain range with a speech called "The Healing of Suffering". This non violent movement has developed since then and has been translated into expressions in the political, social and cultural fields through the formation in many countries of the Humanist Party, the Community for Human Development and the Centre of Cultures, each of which bases their activities on the principles of non-violence and anti-discrimination. Today, the philosophy of this Movement is known by the name New or Universalist Humanism and can be distilled down to two primary guidelines: 1. Solidarity: Treating others the way we would like to be treated and 2. Coherence: Thinking, feeling and acting in the same direction.

Other projects in Education, Health and Development continue to grow in more than 100 countries in most continents. Although Silo has withdrawn from the Humanist Movement he continues to write and to carry his profoundly spiritual Message of Non Violence and social/personal change to all corners of the Earth.

Appendix 2 – Climates and Tensions

These definitions are taken from the Glossary of *Self-liberation* by L.A. Ammann[49].

CLIMATE: A diffuse emotional background or mood; any new object a person perceives when he is in a climatic state is tainted with the characteristics of this background or mood. A climate may be temporary and situational, or it may be permanently fixed in the psyche. If it is permanent and fixed, it will perturb the whole structure by impeding the mobility of the consciousness towards more positive and favourable climates, and by impeding the mobility of responses towards the correct centres. A fixed climate can persist through the different levels of consciousness and thus take away the operational freedom of the consciousness.

CLIMATES, Characteristics of: (a) Climates escape voluntary control; (b) a climate may persist in a subject even long after the situation that generated it has ended. We call this a non-situational climate. Such climates drag old contents and situations with them through time and through the different levels of consciousness; (c) climates are translated and registered in a diffuse, overall way because they come from coenaesthetic impulses which are not localized in any one point of the body; (d) sometimes the mechanism of translation of impulses will generate images which correspond to the climate, and in this case there will be a strong correlation between the climate and the image or theme; (e) other climates are not accompanied by visual images and such climates are registered or experienced as being without images. In reality, however, every climate is always associated with a coenaesthetic image that is placed in a diffuse and general way within the space of representation. These coenaesthetic images mobilise perturbed activities in the centres of response, especially in the instinctive (vegetative and sexual) centres, through other images which arise from the initial climate and trigger activity in the centres.

---

[49] Latitude Press, San Diego, USA. First English version: Samuel Wiser, 1981. Revised Spanish version, Editorial Altamira, Buenos Aires, 2004

CLIMATES, Origin of: Climates may originate in (a) the internal senses; (b) actions of the memory which mobilise internal registers; or (c) actions of the consciousness, especially the operation of the imagination. In some cases, a climate arises when impulses from internal coenaesthetic senses are associated with situations characteristic of external perception or from the memory, or at other times the chain of events begins when impulses from the external senses mobilise internal coenaesthetic registers; these events are in turn recorded in the memory. Climates may also arise when one associates impulses from the external senses, internal senses, or memory with images generated in the imagination. One can notice in these three pathways, where climates originate, that the enchainment of senses memory consciousness is inseparable, non linear, and structural.

TENSIONS: This refers to more or less deep contractions of the muscular systems. Because such tensions are not always directly linked to the activities of the psyche, muscular relaxation will not necessarily result in mental relaxation. From a psychological point of view, psychological or mental tensions are related to excessive expectations in which the psyche is led in a search, in which it is waiting for something, with a possessive kind of background. In contrast, mental relaxation occurs when there is psychological non-possession or letting go, that is, giving actions accompanied by the register of release. We are more concerned with being able to pinpoint the registers of tension in the body than we are with looking for the "causes" of tension. We are also concerned with being able to dissociate the unnecessary surrounding tensions which often accompany tension in a given part of the body. We distinguish external tensions of a temporary (situational) nature from those of a permanent nature, and internal tensions of a deep muscular kind from internal tensions characterised by a general visceral irritation. The internal kinds of tension are accompanied by an important emotional component; they are emotionally tainted by what we call climates. Internal tensions may or may not be accompanied by external muscular tensions. Internal tensions can originate when data from the memory bring up a climate, which then causes the register of internal tension corresponding to the climate to arise.

Appendix 3 – Resentment

Taken from the book *The Guided Experiences – Tales for Heart and Mind* by Silo[50]

It is night, and I'm in an old city crisscrossed by canals that pass beneath timeworn bridges. Leaning on a railing, I gaze at the slow movement of the murky liquid mass below. Through the fog I can make out a group of people on another bridge, and I can faintly hear musical instruments that accompany voices sadly out of tune. Faraway bells toll to me in haunting waves of sorrow.

Now the group has gone and the bells have fallen silent. Down a narrow diagonal street, coloured neon lights emit their sickly glow.

I move on, once again entering the fog. After wandering aimlessly down side streets and over bridges, I come out into the open space of an old square paved with tiles; the square seems empty, and the tiled surface draws me toward one end that is submerged in still water.

Ahead a boat that looks like a hearse awaits me. But to reach it, I must first pass between two long lines of women dressed in black tunics and holding torches overhead. As I pass they say in chorus:

> *Oh Death! Whose unlimited domain*
> *Reaches the living wherever they may be,*
> *On you depends the span allotted to our life.*
> *Your endless sleep annihilates the multitudes,*
> *For no one escapes your powerful presence.*
> *You alone have the judgment that absolves,*
> *And no art can prevail upon your fury,*
> *Nor plea revoke your design.*

I step into the boat, aided by the boatman, who remains standing behind me. Settling into the spacious seat, I notice that the craft rises slightly until we're just above the water. Then we begin to move, suspended above an open and immobile sea that is like an endless mirror reflecting the moon.

We arrive at the island, and in the dim light I can see a long road bordered by cypress trees. The boat rests on the water, rocking gently, and I step out while the boatman remains behind, impassive.

---

[50] Latitude Press, San Diego, USA 1993

I walk down the road between the trees, which sigh in the wind. I feel that I'm being observed, and I stop, sensing something or someone hidden up ahead. From behind a tree a shadowy figure beckons me with slow gestures. I begin to approach, and just as I reach it, a grave whisper like the sigh of death brushes against my face.

"Help me!" the shadow moans, "I know you have come to free me from this confusing prison. Only you can do this - help me!"

The shadowy figure tells me it is someone toward whom I bear a deep resentment. (*)

As though reading my thoughts, the voice adds, "It does not matter whether the person to whom you are bound by this most profound resentment is dead or alive, for the domain of dark memory respects no borders.

"Nor does it matter," the shadow continues, "whether the hatred and desire for revenge have been knotted in your heart since childhood, or began only yesterday. Here time is immobile. This is why we are always lurking in the shadows, only to emerge again at any opportunity, transformed into your various fears. And these fears are our revenge for the poison we must continually taste."

Just as I ask what I should do, a ray of moonlight faintly illuminates the figure's cloaked head. Then the spectre allows me to see it clearly, and I recognize the features of the person who has wounded me the most deeply. (*)

I tell the spectre all about my resentment, expressing things I've never told anyone - I speak as frankly as I can. (*)

The apparition asks me to consider the problem once again, and to communicate everything that is important, even if my words are insulting. The shadow insists that I not fail to express any bitterness I feel, lest it remain imprisoned forever. So I go ahead and follow these instructions. (*)

The spectre shows me a strong chain that binds it to a cypress tree. Without hesitating, I break the chain with a single sharp jerk. The cloak collapses and lies spread out on the ground as the shadow vanishes into thin air and the voice recedes toward the heights, repeating these familiar words: "I must be gone, for the firefly's fading glow shows that dawn is near. Farewell, farewell. Remember me!"

Realising that daybreak will soon arrive, I turn to go back to the boat, but first I pick up the cloak, which is lying at my feet. Draping it over my shoulders, I hurriedly retrace my steps. On my way back to the sea, several furtive shadows ask me if I'll return someday to free other resentments.

Near the shore I see a group of women dressed in white tunics and holding torches overhead. When I reach the boat, I hand the cloak to the boatman. He in turn passes it to the women, and one of them sets it afire. The cloak flares up and is quickly consumed by the flames, without leaving a trace. At this moment I feel a tremendous relief, as though I've sincerely forgiven an enormous wrong. (*)

I step into the boat, which now looks like a modern speedboat. As we push off from the shore, not yet starting the motor, I hear the chorus of women say:

> *You have the power to awaken us from our stupor,*
> *Uniting heart with head,*
> *Freeing our minds from emptiness,*
> *Removing darkness and forgetfulness from inner sight.*
> *Come, beneficial power: True memory*
> *That straightens life into its rightful meaning.*

The motor comes to life just as the sun appears above the ocean horizon. The boat accelerates, and I look at the young driver, his strong clear face smiling toward the sea. We approach the city swiftly, bouncing lightly on the smooth swells. The sun's golden rays gild the magnificent domes of the city, while bright flocks of doves circle overhead.

Appendix 4 – The Journey

Taken from the book *The Guided Experiences – Tales for Heart and Mind*, by Silo

I'm climbing along a mountain path, and stop briefly to look behind me. In the distance I see the thin line of a river and what could be a grove of trees. Farther off, the reddish desert disappears into the haze of the late afternoon.

I walk a few more steps, and the path narrows until it disappears. I know that I still have the last and most difficult stretch ahead of me before I reach the plateau on top. The snow on the ground scarcely hinders my steps, and I continue my ascent.

I come to a rock wall. Studying it carefully, I discover a large crevice that I think I can climb. I begin to climb it, wedging my hiking boots into the footholds. Pressing my back against one side, I lever myself up with one elbow and my other arm. Slowly I inch higher.

Now the crevice has narrowed. I look up and I look down. I've reached an impasse—it's impossible to move in either direction.

I shift my position, flattening myself against the slippery rock face. Planting both feet firmly, I slowly stretch one arm upward. I can feel my moist breath reflecting from the smooth rock. I keep groping with my fingers, not knowing whether I'll find some small handhold. Gingerly I stretch out my other arm. Suddenly I feel myself swaying, and my head falls slowly away from the rock. My whole body follows, until I'm on the verge of falling backwards - but at the last second, I find a tiny crack and grasp it tightly with my fingers. Recovering my balance I continue the ascent, making the final assault on the top without difficulty.

At last I reach the plateau. I stand up, and an endless prairie stretches before me. Taking a few steps forward I turn around. Toward the abyss it is already night. Toward the plain the last rays of the sun escape in varied hues. As I compare these two spaces, suddenly I hear a piercing sound. Looking up, I see a luminous disk hovering high overhead. Circling around, it begins to descend.

The disk lands close by. Moved by some inner call, I approach it without hesitation. As I enter the luminous object, it feels as if I'm passing through a curtain of warm air. I find myself inside a transparent bubble that's flattened on its base, and immediately my body feels lighter.

As though propelled by a giant slingshot, we shoot straight upward into the sky. I think we're heading toward the star Beta Hydris, or perhaps the galaxy NGC 3621.

Fleetingly I see the late afternoon light on the prairie below. We climb at great speed as the sky turns black and the Earth slips away. I can feel our velocity steadily increasing and the clear white light of the stars changes colour until all the stars have disappeared in total darkness.

Directly ahead I see a single point of golden light, which steadily grows larger. As we approach, I see it is a vast ring that continues into a very long transparent tube. We enter the tube, and after a while come to a sudden stop, landing in an open area. Passing through the curtain of warm air, I leave the bubble.

I find myself between transparent walls, which shimmer in musical variations of colour as I pass through them. I walk onward until I come to a flat area. In the centre I see a large object, alive with movement, and impossible to capture with my eye as it flows endlessly into itself; regardless of which direction I look on its surface, my gaze always ends up immersed, drawn deep into the object's interior. Feeling dizzy, I look away.

Now I encounter a figure, apparently human, whose face I cannot see. This being extends a hand toward me, in which I see a radiant sphere. I begin to approach, and in an act of complete acceptance, I take the sphere and place it on my forehead. (*)

In total silence I feel something new coming to life within me. A growing force bathes my body in successive waves as a profound joy fills my being. (*)

Somehow I know that even without words this figure is speaking to me, saying, "Return to the world with your forehead and your hands luminous." (*)

And so I accept my destiny, returning to the bubble and through the vast ring to the stars, and the prairie, and the rock wall below. (*)

Finally I am back on the mountain path, a humble pilgrim returning to my people. (*)

Filled with light, I return to the hours, to the daily routine, to the pain of humanity, and to its simple joys.

I, who give with my hands what I can, who receive both insults and the warmest of greetings, sing to the heart, which from the darkest abyss is reborn in the light of Meaning.

Appendix 5 - Ceremony of Well Being[51]

This ceremony is carried out at the request of a group of people.

The Participants are seated. The Officiant and Assistant are standing.

Assistant: We are gathered here to direct our thoughts to those dear to us. Some of them are having difficulties in their emotional lives, some in their relationships with others, and some with their health. To them we direct our thoughts and our best wishes.

Officiant: We have faith that our call for well being will reach them. Let us think of those dear to us; let us feel the presence of those dear to us, let us experience contact with those dear to us.

Assistant: Let us take some time to meditate on the difficulties that they are facing…

A few minutes go by allowing the participants to meditate.

Officiant: Now we would like these people to feel our best hopes for them. A wave of relief and well being will reach them…

Assistant: Let us take a short time to locate in our minds the situation of well being that we wish for our loved ones...

A few minutes are given so that the participants can concentrate their minds on this.

Officiant: We close this ceremony by giving the opportunity, to those who so wish, to feel the presence of those loved ones who, although not present in our time or in our space, are connected to us in this experience of love, peace, and warm joy…

A short time is given for this.

Officiant: This has been good for others, comforting for ourselves, and an inspiration for our lives… Greetings to everyone who is immersed in this current of well being, which has been strengthened by the best wishes of all those present…

---

[51] From Silo's Message: www.silo.net

INDEX

www.ingramcontent.com/pod-product-compliance
Lightning Source LLC
Chambersburg PA
CBHW020659270326
41928CB00005B/199